OXFORD HISPANIC STUDIES

General Editor

PAUL JULIAN SMITH

Cervantes, the Novel, and the New World

DIANA DE ARMAS WILSON

OXFORD
UNIVERSITY PRESS

#45350314

*This book has been printed digitally and produced in a standard specification
in order to ensure its continuing availability*

OXFORD

UNIVERSITY PRESS

Great Clarendon Street, Oxford OX2 6DP

Oxford University Press is a department of the University of Oxford.
It furthers the University's objective of excellence in research, scholarship,
and education by publishing worldwide in

Oxford New York

Auckland Bangkok Buenos Aires Cape Town Chennai
Dar es Salaam Delhi Hong Kong Istanbul Karachi Kolkata
Kuala Lumpur Madrid Melbourne Mexico City Mumbai Nairobi
São Paulo Shanghai Taipei Tokyo Toronto

Oxford is a registered trade mark of Oxford University Press
in the UK and in certain other countries

Published in the United States
by Oxford University Press Inc., New York

© Diana de Armas Wilson

ISBN 0-19-816005-4

A mi fénix Amalia,
y a mis hijas Antonia, Andrea, Fiona, y Miranda

Oxford Hispanic Studies

General Editor: Paul Julian Smith

THE last twenty years have seen a revolution in the humanities. On the one hand, there has been a massive influence on literary studies of other disciplines: philosophy, psychoanalysis, and anthropology. On the other, there has been a displacement of the boundaries of literary studies, an opening out on to other forms of expression: cinema, popular culture, and historical documentation.

The *Oxford Hispanic Studies* series reflects the fact that Hispanic studies are particularly well placed to take advantage of this revolution. Unlike those working in French or English studies, Hispanists have little reason to genuflect to a canon of European culture which has tended to exclude them. Historically, moreover, Hispanic societies tend to exhibit plurality and difference: thus Medieval Spain was the product of the three cultures of Jew, Moslem, and Christian; modern Spain is a federation of discrete autonomous regions; and Spanish America is a continent in which cultural identity must always be brought into question, can never be taken for granted.

The incursion of new models of critical theory into Spanish-speaking countries has been uneven. And while cultural studies in other language areas have moved through post-structuralism (Lacan, Derrida, Foucault) to create new disciplines focusing on gender, ethnicity, and homosexuality, it is only recently that Hispanists have contributed to the latest fields of enquiry. Now, however, there is an upsurge of exciting new work in both Europe and the Americas. *Oxford Hispanic Studies* provides a medium for writing engaged in and taking account of these developments. It serves both as a vehicle and a stimulus for innovative and challenging work in an important and rapidly changing field. The series aims to facilitate both the development of new approaches in Hispanic studies and the awareness of Hispanic studies in other subject areas. It embraces discussions of literary and non-literary cultural forms, and focuses on the publication of illuminating original research and theory.

Acknowledgements

I thank María Antonia Garcés for her uncompromising intellectual support during all stages of this project. Our constant exchanges about Cervantes—both in and out of captivity—have been invaluable to this book. I am also deeply indebted to Anne J. Cruz, whose wide learning enhanced this project, and whose picaresque puns lightened many of its darker moments. Rachel Jacoff helped me weigh the importance of León Hebreo to Cervantes, who celebrated him, and to Inca Garcilaso de la Vega, who translated him. I thank her for assisting my first tottering steps into Americana, and for her encouragement during many crucial negotiations, academic and otherwise. I also owe a singular debt to Andrea Wilson Nightingale—accomplished Platonist, Guggenheim Fellow, and *hija querida*—who gave various sections of this book generous and incisive commentary.

Individual chapters also benefited from the critical and scholarly strengths of Daniel Eisenberg, Barbara Fuchs, Javier Herrero, Michael McGaha, Elias Rivers, and Henry Sullivan. Richard L. Kagan generously critiqued my Prescottian forays. I thank Paul Julian Smith, General Editor of this Oxford Hispanic Series, for lending a supportive ear to my project one drizzly summer afternoon in London.

Joseph Foote, editor *par excellence*, rehabilitated an essay that served as the germ of this book, and I remain grateful for his attention to those unruly beginnings. David Thatcher Gies, ebullient Hispanist and wise friend, encouraged me to continue this project at a time when it nearly foundered.

Edward T. Aylward, Georgina Dopico Black, Marina S. Brownlee, Luis Ernesto Cárcamo, Juan Pablo Dabove, Carroll B. Johnson, Jorge Olivares, Betty Sasaki, Barbara Simerka, Christopher Weimer, and Nicolás Wey-Gómez read embryonic versions of various chapters. James D. Fernández gave some valuable generic directions to a partial manuscript. Yvonne Jehenson and Peter Dunn generously shared with me their prospectus of a major study on Utopianism in Cervantes.

Robert ter Horst sent me helpful chapters from his forth-coming *Fortunes of the Novel.* I am deeply grateful to all these readers and writers. Memorable exchanges with John J. Allen, Andrew Bush, Anthony Cascardi, Edward Dudley, Edward Friedman, Patrick Henry, Joseph R. Jones, Adrienne Martín, James A. Parr, Anson Piper, Burton Raffel, and the late Ruth El Saffar have vastly enriched my thinking about Cervantes.

For their dedication and generosity in and around Cervantes studies, I wish to thank a trio of my graduate students: Lisbeth Chapin, Erin Garrett, and Cynthia Kuhn. For some elegant insights about the novelistic genre, I am warmly indebted to my former students Dilek Kececi, currently an English professor in Turkey, and José Rodríguez García, currently an English professor in Spain.

Special recognition is due to Daniel Wilson for his wizardry with reluctant computers, and to Birgitte Bønning Espitia for her superb library research skills. I thank Perry Weissman, who updated my manuscript with newsmedia reports on Cervantes, and Edward Piper, who helped it to criss-cross the Atlantic in timely fashion.

The idea for this book first emerged during an NEH Fellow-ship, the last of three grants from that foundation that I grate-fully acknowledge. I also thank Walter S. Rosenberry III, whose generous funding to the University of Denver covered the indexing of this book; Gregg Kvistad, Dean at the University, who facilitated this grant; and Eric Gould, Chair of the English Department, who supported me during an insupportable phase.

Editors Sophie Goldsworthy and Matthew Hollis showed my manuscript great care and kindness, and copyeditor Rowena Anketell saved it from countless infelicities.

Let me mark the great debt I owe my husband, Douglas Brownlow Wilson, for emotional support during the decade that my thoughts were occupied with cannibals and kings.

This book is dedicated to four beloved daughters and one granddaughter. All five women—one of them just beginning to read—have taught me that there is a life beyond books.

Various chapters in this book contain pages that have appeared in earlier publications: 'Where Does the Novel Rise?

Cultural Hybrids and Cervantine Heresies', in *Cervantes and His Postmodern Constituencies*, ed. Anne J. Cruz and Carroll B. Johnson (New York: Garland, 1999), 43–67; ' "De gracia estraña": Cervantes, Ercilla y el Nuevo Mundo', in *En un lugar de La Mancha: Estudios cervantinos en honor de Manuel Durán*, ed. Georgina Dopico Black and Roberto González Echevarría (Salamanca: Ediciones Almar, 1999), 37–55; ' "Ocean Chivalry": Issues of Alterity in *Don Quixote*', in *Colby Quarterly*, ed. Betty Sasaki and Jorge Olivares, 32, 4 (December 1996): 221–35; 'The Matter of America: Cervantes Romances Inca Garcilaso de la Vega', in *Cultural Authority in Early Modern Spain*, ed. Marina S. Brownlee and Hans Ulrich Gumbrecht (Baltimore: Johns Hopkins University Press, 1995), 234–59; and 'Cervantes on Cannibals', *Revista de estudios hispánicos*, 22, 3 (October 1988): 1–25. I thank the editors for permission to incorporate sections of the above essays into this book.

Contents

Note to the Reader

ALL Spanish citations from *Don Quixote* are taken from Rico's edition (1998) and will be parenthetically documented by part and chapter number only, so as to orient readers to their preferred edition of the text. Unless otherwise noted English translations are my own. Sometimes I have consulted Raffel's translation of *Don Quijote*.

All Spanish citations from the *Persiles* are taken from Avalle-Arce's edition (1969) and will be parenthetically documented in my text by page numbers. All English translations are my own. I have occasionally consulted the excellent scholarly apparatus in Romero Muñoz's new edition of the *Persiles*.

Introduction:
Novel Genres, Novel Worlds

IN a mythy-minded parable, Jorge Luis Borges portrays Cervantes as an ageing soldier 'fed up with his Spanish homeland' ('harto de su tierra de España'). Before being wholly defeated by reality, equated in Borges's parable with Golden Age Spain, Cervantes seeks comfort in the world of chivalric fictions—'in Ariosto's vast geographies' ('en las vastas geografías de Ariosto') (1960: 38). Without denying the call of oriental deserts and lunar valleys for both Cervantes and his mad knight, I would extend these chivalric geographies westward to the Indies—to a world where chivalry rode again, perhaps for the last time. From the early *Galatea* (1585) to the posthumous *Persiles* (1617), the relatively new and similarly vast geographies of the occidental Indies haunt Cervantes's writings. Sometimes the site of these hauntings is small—a word, a phrase, a paragraph. The Cuban novelist Alejo Carpentier describes a grain of rice, displayed in the museum of a provincial South American city, on which several paragraphs of *Don Quixote* are copied (1979: 66). The present book argues the inverse of this minimalist fiction: that *Don Quixote* itself contains many grains of rice on which the New World is inscribed, and that the *Persiles* contains even more.

Some vivid instances of these transatlantic scriptures come to us courtesy of Sancho Panza, as when he assures the Duke that he is no more interested in whipping himself in order to disenchant Dulcinea than he is in becoming a 'cacique'—'an American Indian chief' (2. 35)—or when he tells Tosilos, the former lackey of the Dukes now 'enchanted' into a postman, that he'll be glad to drink and eat with him despite 'all the enchanters in the Indies' ('de cuantos encantadores hay en las Indias', 2. 66). Perhaps the most outlandish of these American allusions appears in Sancho's linkage of Dulcinea to a Mexican horseman (2. 10), a passage overlooked in Erich Auerbach's classic treatment of this episode in *Mimesis*. When the enchanted Dulcinea is bucked off her 'palfrey', she quickly scrambles to

her feet, steps back a few paces, and then takes a running leap
right over the saddle-hump to drop on the donkey's back.
Seeing Don Quixote's supreme feminine fiction mannishly
sitting astride her donkey, Sancho recycles her yet again, this
time into a riding instructor. She could teach 'the most skilled
Cordoban or Mexican rider', he exclaims in admiration, 'a thing
or two about getting up on a horse' ('a subir a la jineta al
más diestro cordobés o mejicano', 2. 10). Influenced by Don
Quixote's obsessive chivalric discourse—his contagious dreams
of a martial aristocracy in a post-feudal world—Sancho's fertile
wit leaps across the Atlantic, from Spain to New Spain. Although
less flamboyant than Sir Philip Sidney's literary portrait of his
riding instructor in the court of Vienna,[1] Sancho's image of
Dulcinea as a potential equestrian teacher in Mexico presents
readers with *más mundo*. Sancho is the first though hardly
the last to yoke Dulcinea to the occidental Indies: a recent
essay ecstatically concludes that Dulcinea *is*, in fact, America
('Dulcinea es América').[2]

Sometimes Cervantes conflates oriental and occidental geographies, recalling Columbus, who famously considered Cuba
to be a part of Asia. In the Dedication to Part 2 of *Don Quixote*,
Cervantes fictionalizes the arrival of a letter from 'the great
emperor of China' ('el grande emperador de la China'), who
begs him in Chinese ('en lengua chinesca') to send him a copy
of *Don Quixote*, Part 1. That the Chinese emperor wishes to learn
more about Castilian letters—even offering to found a college
with Cervantes himself as its Rector—functions as a blatant parody of Columbus's fantasy that the 'Grand Khan'—a generic
Asian *Serenissimo principe*—might wish to learn more about the
Spanish Crown. Various entries in Columbus's *Diario* mention a
Mongol presence in or near the city of 'Cathay'.[3] Although these

---

[1] For this portrait of John Pietro Pugliano, see the Exordium of Sidney's nearly
contemporary *Defence of Poetry*, possibly composed in 1579 but not published until
1595.

[2] Correa-Díaz 1998: 113. But see also Muñiz-Huberman's *Dulcinea encantada* (1992),
which posits a Dulcinea at once Mexican and universal. See also Durán, who equates
Columbus's hallucinations—his strange conversion of Caribbean 'manatees or sea
cows' ('manatíes o vacas marinas') into enchanted sirens—with the enchanted
Dulcinea (1996).

[3] Both of these diplomatic exchanges—Columbus's triply drafted Letter of
Credence and Cervantes's fictional letter from the Chinese emperor to himself—
revive the 13th-cent. correspondence between Europe and the Mongols (Pelliot

great expectations look back to a Grand Khan, they also look forward to the protagonist of Cervantes's *Jealous Extremaduran* (*El celoso extremeño*), Felipe de Carrizales, a latter-day Columbus who sails off to the Indies in quest of gold and self-aggrandizement. In an essay that fruitfully aligns Carrizales with Columbus, the British Hispanist B. W. Ife glances at 'two sets of issues, neither of which has really been properly examined in the context of the other: the birth of America in the European consciousness, and the birth of the novel in Spain' (1994: 66). This book aims to examine these two issues—not always 'properly' and never as expansively as they merit—keeping each in the other's light and narrowing the second to the rise of the specifically Cervantine novel.

Far more than criticism has acknowledged, Cervantes's novels come into being in the age of, and under the sign of, imperial Spain. In the chapters that follow, I discuss how the cross-cultural contacts that Columbus inaugurated in the Indies—exploration, conquest, and colonization—resonate throughout Cervantes's two long novels, *Don Quixote* (1605, 1615) and *Persiles and Sigismunda* (1617). The aim of all this historicizing, however, is a more *spatial* understanding of his achievement. I believe that Cervantes's novels were stimulated by the geographical excitement of a new world. The rise of the early modern novel came on the heels of the incorporation of the Indies—the *Indias occidentales*—into European maps and legal documents. In the context of cartographic writing in early modern France, for example, Tom Conley suggests that 'even Cervantes's tales of a knight errant's misinformed adventures' were 'born of a new cartographic impulse' (1996: 2). Don Quixote himself shows a keen awareness of this new impulse during the adventure of the enchanted boat (2. 29), when he sails down the river Ebro, fully expecting to emerge into the broad Atlantic. During that short riverine voyage—saved from becoming a maritime tragedy by some alert millworkers—Don Quixote lectures Sancho about astrolabes and equatorial lines, polar circles, zodiacs, poles, ecliptics,

1922–3: 4–28). See the entries in Columbus's *Diario* showing his determination to reach *tierra firme* and the city of Quinsay ('quisay') in order to deliver the letters of the Crown to the Grand Khan (21 Oct.: 108–9); his voyage west along the Cuban coast in quest of the Grand Khan (29 Oct.: 118–23); and his belief that the Grand Khan was in, or close to, the city of 'Cathay' (30 Oct.: 122–5). I thank Nicolás Wey-Gómez for his assistance with Columbian matters.

solstices, equinoxes, geographical bearings, and various other entities known to contemporary mariners and cartographers, these last engaged across Cervantes's lifetime in mapping all of Philip II's kingdoms (2. 29). The cartographic impulse surfaces again, this time on dry land, when Don Quixote rides into a web of green nets that festoon a simulated Arcadia. Even if the pastoral community's little web of nets were to stretch around the whole span of the earth ('la redondez de la tierra'), he assures an admiring pseudo-shepherdess, 'I would seek for new worlds to avoid breaking them' ('buscara yo nuevos mundos por do pasar sin romperlas') (2. 58).

An impulse similar to Don Quixote's to seek for new worlds —to light out for unknown territories in a formula later adopted by the American novel—had led imperial Spain to conquer, Christianize, and Castilianize the New World in a series of widely debated imperial moves. Because Cervantes's novels absorb and reply to these moves, they offer readers some new and richly heteroglot slants on the conquest and colonization of the Indies, an enterprise that severely challenged Europe's repertoire of thinking about civilization and barbary. To the multiple targets of satire proffered for *Don Quixote*, then—romance fictions, bad readers, the ideals of knighthood, utopian evasionism, the desire to live the past—I would draw attention to the 1950s claim, by the Peruvian scholar Raúl Porras Barrenechea, that *Don Quixote* is 'a benevolent satire of the conquistador of *ínsulas* or Indies' ('una sátira benévola del conquistador de ínsulas o de Indias') · (1955: 238).

A few words on satire, benevolent or malevolent, may not be amiss here. Numerous distinguished critics have argued that *Don Quixote* is a satire, though the precise object of its ridicule varies widely. Categorizing Cervantes's novel as 'a mennipean *satura* in the best homiletic tradition of Horace', James A. Parr usefully reminds us that satires are not self-referential but point instead at some possible target in the real world, outside the text (1988: pp. xv–xvi). Anthony Close—who regards *Don Quixote* as 'a satire which uses the techniques of burlesque'—lists a cluster of 'fanciful' targets that critics have proferred for it: the Spanish aristocracy, Spanish militarism, the Spanish honour code, Charles V, Philip II, or the Duke of Lerma (1977: 1, 12). Don Quixote himself would have frowned on these last three figures as objects of satire, given his claim, in a vigorous defence of satire, that it is legitimate to compose an assault on vices if not on individuals (2. 16). In their avoidance of *ad hominem* attacks, Cervantes's writings tilt toward the 'friendly ethos' of satire (Close 1993).

The issue of satire in its interaction with parody, a notably Cervantine interaction, deserves much more than the passing glance we can give it here. Parody has been classically defined as dealing with strictly literary norms: it is precisely through the metalinguistic uses of the preformed language of chivalry that we recognize *Don Quixote* as a parodic text. But satire is commonly transmitted through the medium of parody. Indeed, the terminological confusion between parody and satire stands as a sign of their cooperation (Rose 1979: 47). In his 1615 'Prologue to the Reader' of *Don Quixote*, Part 2, Cervantes pointedly thanks Alonso Fernández de Avellaneda, the pseudo-author of a continuation of *Don Quixote*, for saying that his novels were more satirical than exemplary ('más satíricas que ejemplares'). Although Cervantes would inflict upon the figure of Clodio—who virtually personifies satire in the *Persiles*—the 'deserved punishment' ('castigo merecido') of a deadly arrow through the tongue, clearly not all of his satirists were to be regarded as 'evilspeaking' ('maldiciente', 203).

Although the present study targets for discussion the New World conquistadores and their chroniclers, these are not meant to trump other objects of satire. I am well aware—and almost four centuries of criticism have made it abundantly clear—that Cervantes's novels point at multiple targets of satire and assault a great number of 'vices' in the real world of the sixteenth century. Indeed, both *Don Quixote* and the *Persiles* provide an encyclopaedic context for the experiences of their heroes, presenting their respective errancies, whether out of La Mancha or Ultima Thule, in terms of an astonishing range of classical and biblical, as well as geographical, discoveries and encounters. Like Shakespeare's Coriolanus—whose own selfhood has been labelled 'quixotic' (González 1992: p. xvi)—Cervantes's novelistic heroes journey from home confident that 'there is a world elsewhere' (3. 3. 135). That 'elsewhere' is what I try to characterize in this book. The beneficiary of a number of discourses —including genre, gender, colonial, and post-colonial studies —this book also participates in the kinds of critique currently associated with cultural studies, although not without reservations about the alleged presentism of that discipline or its tendency to turn primary texts into commodities. The aim of this study, written in a framework of geography more than grievance, is not to reduce Cervantes's novels to instruments in a quixotic attack against Spanish atrocities in the New World. My interest in hybridity, heterogeneity, and interstitial spaces—concepts whose understanding may help to reduce future atrocities—is largely indebted to Cervantes, that early modern fabricator of the 'basin-helmet' ('baciyelmo').

In the chapters that follow, I engage a few humanist guides —all more resourceful than Don Quixote's guide to the Cave of Montesinos—to enlighten some of the many conflicting and parallel narratives of imperial Spain. But my arguments also turn, selectively and cautiously, to various post-colonial readings that articulate some of the structures and legacies of colonialism. The field of post-colonialism is currently much beleaguered, as Ania Loomba explains in her illuminating *Colonialism/ Postcolonialism* (1998), and the interdisciplinary nature of post-colonial theory makes it heterogeneous, diffuse, and confusing. Sometimes it defines 'imperialism' as capitalist colonialism, the Leninist definition, ignoring both imperial Russia and imperial Spain. Given the multiple sprawling histories of colonialism, any attempt to theorize it goes beyond the limits of this book. It is enough, for my purposes, to adopt Peter Hulme's broad definition of colonial discourse as any kind of discursive production related to, and produced in and by, colonial situations (1986: 2).

While these situations are legion, critical descriptions of the historical experience of empire in the early modern novel are rare. Although Edward Said notes that the novel and imperialism 'are unthinkable without each other'—that it is impossible 'to read one without in some way dealing with the other'—his classic study of these two entities excludes any discussion of the Spanish empire (1993: pp. 71, xxii). Said's ideas of the imperial enterprise, in any case, go hand in hand with the discursive formation he theorized in *Orientalism,* with its catalogue of Western stereotypes that justified French and English colonialism (1978). Responding, in part, to Said's influential study, Walter Mignolo reminds us that the geo-historical category of occidentalism has been discussed in Latin America since Edmundo O'Gorman's 1958 publication of *The Invention of America*:

Before Orientalism developed as a massive discursive formation during the eighteenth and nineteenth centuries, a similar imaginary construction flourished with the inclusion of Indias Occidentales in the map and the subsequent invention of America. Spain and the rest of Europe began to look West to build an extension of their own destiny by enacting the ambiguity between Indias Orientales and Indias Occidentales. (1995: 323–5)

Mignolo justly notes that occidentalism has seldom been addressed by traditional European Renaissance scholars, whose field of enquiry was largely Italy and who, in any case, tended to downplay Spanish contributions 'to the European (mainly Italian) Renaissance' (1995: 324). Along the same lines, Said claims that his study of orientalism was partly motivated by the way in which fields such as English or Comparative Literatures—linked as they were to the emergence of imperial geography—disdained the study of African, Asian, or Latin American texts (1993: 44).

Sensitive to disdain, colonial and post-colonial studies are also anxious about similitudes. Although these studies often stress the dangers of homogenizing the imperial practices of different nations, this is scarcely a mandate to ignore their commonalities. In a remark that, despite its litotes, endorses comparative explorations of British and Spanish colonization, Sir John Elliott claims that 'the collective predicament' of his own generation in the aftermath of the World War II was 'not entirely dissimilar' to 'the collective predicament of the last great imperial generation of Spaniards after the triumphs of the sixteenth century' (1989: p. ix). Cervantes had lived through both those triumphs and their decline. Because Spanish and English imperialisms display various formations in common, including though not confined to their respective post-imperial predicaments, I occasionally turn to post-colonial readings of British colonial historiography as an optic for Cervantes's fictions. While under no assumption that the legacies of the British empire provide the best theoretical models to describe colonial experiences, I see these legacies as illuminating many transcultural literary affiliations, for example, Salman Rushdie's explicit embrace of Cervantes as one of his literary 'parents' (1991: 21). The frame tale for *The Moor's Last Sigh*, a speculative fiction about British and Islamic imperial expansionism in India, takes place in a remote Spanish village called 'Benengeli'. And that is only one of Rushdie's many homages to Cervantes.

To bring Cervantes's novels to the occidental front is to
engage them in other ongoing debates, including attempts
to compare and contrast the major imperial enterprises in
America—the Spanish enterprise of conquest and settlement
and the British enterprise of commerce and exploitation. The
dangers of lumpen homogenization, of flattening histories and
blurring differences, always inform these debates. In a study of
different ceremonies of possession in the New World, Patricia
Seed rehearses what various European imperial projects shared
and did not share:

> French, Spanish, Portuguese, Dutch, and English ceremonies and sym-
> bolic means for initiating colonial authority are frequently lumped
> together, as if there were a single common European political picture
> of colonial rule. What Europeans shared was a common technolo-
> gical and ecological platform—trans-Atlantic ships bearing crossbows,
> cannon, harquebuses, horses, siege warfare, and disease. But they did
> not share a common understanding of even the political objectives of
> military action. (1995: 3)

Over and above technology and ecology, however, Europeans
shared a Virgilian platform, a common fount of Roman imperial
imagery, as the British historian Anthony Pagden argues in his
comparative history of imperial strategies. Pagden's (1995) study,
as it turns out, sheds much light on the culture of barbarians
who inaugurate Cervantes's *Persiles*, characters specifically groom-
ing themselves to become, in the arresting words of Pagden's
book title, 'lords of all the world'.

Don Quixote, too, shares these imperial longings. They regularly erupt and are regularly excused by the charge of lunacy.
At the very beginnings of his narrative, he imagines himself
'already crowned through the valour of his arm, at the very least,
of the empire of Trebizond' ('ya coronado por el valor de su
brazo, por lo menos, del imperio de Trapisonda', 1. 1). Not long
after this happy hallucination, he poses a rhetorical question
whose triumphalist weight is manifest: 'what greater contentment
or pleasure can there be in the world than winning a battle and
triumphing over one's enemy?' ('¿qué mayor contento puede
haber en el mundo o qué gusto puede igualarse al de vencer
una batalla y al de triunfar de su enemigo?', 1. 18). Although
Don Quixote's chosen vocation is laudable—to rescue damsels,
succour widows and orphans, and give aid to the needy—it is

not altogether disinterested. Or as he himself puts it, a knight errant is always 'on the verge of becoming the most powerful lord on earth' ('en potencia propincua de ser el mayor señor del mundo', 2. 39). The text of *Don Quixote* manages to do what Don Quixote never does in the text—ironize, de-idealize, and even reappraise Spain's imperialist history. Regarding Don Quixote as the symbol of 'a nation that had come to envision its very existence as a vocation', one critic sums up the fourfold aim of that vocation: 'to liberate Spain from the infidels, to vanquish Islam in all of Europe, to eradicate Northern heresies, to conquer and convert the New World' (Dupré 1993: 126). Although the history of Cervantine criticism shows the futility of reading any one meaning into Don Quixote's significance,[4] the idea of a brilliant, prodigal, and courageous lunatic as a symbol of Spain's grandiose vocation demands, and is already receiving, a closer look. Through some of Don Quixote's chivalric antics, whether philanthrophic or delusional, Cervantes comically satirizes many of the imperial policies that, across the sixteenth century, had relentlessly destabilized Spain's foundations.

Although the traditional discourses of imperialism are often fractured, as we shall see, in Cervantes's two novels, signs of these fractures also appear at strategic points in his other writings. Readers may wonder, for example, why the gypsy heroine of *La gitanilla*—thoroughly occupied with singing her *villancicos* and testing her aristocratic suitor—should need to register her disapproval of Spain's imperial wars against the Protestant Princes: 'I'm not happy with these comings and goings to Flanders' ('no estoy bien con estas idas y venidas a Flandes') (1975*a*: i. 55). A more oblique and more devastating critique of imperialism occurs in *The Colloquy of the Dogs* (*El coloquio de los perros*). The imperial dream of unifying language and territory —famously launched by Antonio de Nebrija's 1492 description of language as the handmaiden of empire—is terminally debunked in Cervantes's novella when the schoolboys hock or sell their '*Antonios*'—their copies of Nebrija's century-old but still popular textbook of grammar (*Arte de Gramática*)—to feed

---

[4] See e.g. Cruz and Johnson's recent collection of essays, *Cervantes and His Postmodern Constituencies* (1998). See also Allen's 2-vol. study of the changing representations of *Don Quixote* (1969 and 1979).

the dog Berganza (1982: iii. 265). Seen from either a canine or a colonial perspective, the boys have their priorities straight.

Such fictional critiques of empire reflect the serious decline of Spain as a national power, a fact acknowledged by many Spaniards even as Cervantes was writing his novels. Indeed, the term *declinación* was already being used by 1600 in the wake of the nation's various famines, plagues, and bankruptcies.[5] Gone were all the frenzies of patriotic fervour that Spain had experienced just prior to the military disaster of the Armada in 1588. 'Never in seven hundred years of continuous war', Luis Valle de la Cerda lamented in 1600, 'nor in one hundred years of continuous peace, has Spain as a whole been as ruined and as poor as it is now' (Elliott 1977: 53). For readers who believe that culture is always embedded in the contingencies of history, this lament is not inert historical knowledge. Nor is it unconnected with Spain's colonial situation in America and the discourses it provided Cervantes.

The rise of the Cervantine novel had multiple ties to the New World colonial adventure, some of whose discourses were codified into genres, subgenres, or mixed genres—in our retrospective sense of kinds—that Cervantes would incorporate into his writings. In the belief that his novels need to be read against the wide spectrum of colonial situations integrated into them, I have framed many of the arguments of this book in terms of colonial discourse and structured the book through genres codifying this discourse. Postmodern critics who regard genre studies as an 'anachronistic pastime' might chafe at the sixteenth-century fascination with them that is thematized in, and illustrated by, *Don Quixote*.[6] Scholars who still recognize distinctions between genres, even fraying genres, are also aware of the robust combativeness that academicians often bring to their classifications. That every era possesses its own system of genres, each with its own distinctive geopolitics, is by now a commonplace. My use of generic categories neither stresses their fixity nor sees them as mutually exclusive. The idea that classifying genres is a two-way street—that '*genre does not belong to texts alone, but to the*

---

[5] Martín González de Cellorigo's use of the term *declinación* is cited by Elliott (1989: 264).

[6] See Todorov's testy response to Maurice Blanchot's privileging of the '*here and now*'—to the 'egocentric illusion' that literature 'no longer recognizes the distinction between genres and seeks to destroy their limits' (1990: 13–16).

interaction between texts and a classifier' (Morson 1981: p. viii)—should appeal greatly to anyone who has seen this very interaction played out in Cervantes's texts.

More familiar to his contemporaries than the novel form he was creating were many of the narrative forms that Cervantes ransacked for its construction: epic and Ovidian poetry, Menippean satire, the ancient Graeco-Latin novel, the Italian novella, ballads, proverbs, the pastoral novel, topographical legends, criminal and/or picaresque autobiography, and stage plays—including allegorical masques and closet dramas. Sections of Cervantes's novels also assimilate contemporary critical treatises, whose debates are re-enacted in *Don Quixote*, Part 1 (1. 6, 1. 32, 1. 47 ff.), as well as in some critically self-conscious moments in the *Persiles*. Although the Cervantine novel incorporates into itself many genres, this book focuses only on those kinds of writing precipitated by, or affiliated with, Spain's conquest and colonization of the New World.

New genres are made not only from genres already at hand, to anticipate the Bakhtinian argument, but also out of 'real-world' experiences that lead to new forms of thought. Four genres internalized by Cervantes's novels have pointed alliances with Spain's New World colonies: the Books of Chivalry, the utopias, the colonial war epic, and ethnohistory. Although their nomenclature remains in dispute—what I call the Books of Chivalry, for example, others call 'romances'—their presence in early modern Europe does not. Retrospectively understood as genres, if not always or easily legitimized as such, these four kinds of literature were notably instrumental in the construction of the Cervantine novel. They provided writers, in a handily codified form, a wide spectrum of colonialist discourse, from triumphalist to Lascasian. Despite their widely dispersed locations of origin—Spain, England, Chile, Peru—these genres all converged in, and vastly enriched, the Cervantine novel. As always with Cervantes, our task is to learn how to read not only between the lines, as Cide Hamete encourages us, but also between and even among the genres. We must take into account, in short, the interaction of these New World genres both with older kinds and with each other.

Although an unsystematic and unruly model for the rise of the novel, Mikhail Bakhtin's *Dialogic Imagination*—a collection of translated essays dating back to the 1930s and addressing the

history of narrative genres—provides an indispensable entry
into any generic approach to the Cervantine novel. Bypassing
Bakhtin's Chronotope and Carnival theories, my arguments
exploit some of the ideas developed in 'From the Prehistory
of Novelistic Discourse' and 'Discourse in the Novel'. Bakhtin's
formulation that 'discourse in the novel is structured on an unin-
terrupted mutual interaction with the discourse of life' (1981:
383) informs many passages of this book. The 'discourse of life'
it addresses emerges from both sixteenth-century Spain and
its New World colonies to be codified into genres. As a study
of his 'prosaics' discloses, Bakhtin viewed genres not as a strictly
literary phenomenon but in multiple ways: as forms of thought,
as ways of seeing, as modes of representing the world through
concrete examples, as vehicles of historicity, as residues of
past behaviour, as form-shaping ideologies, as specific types of
a culture's great repository of 'speech genres', and as 'congealed
events' or 'crystallizations' of earlier discursive interactions
(Morson and Emerson 1990: 276–92). Bakhtin was also given
to defining genres, through a curiously epic personification, as
the 'great heroes' of literature, with 'trends' and 'schools' star-
ring as merely its 'second- or third-rank protagonists' (1981: 8).
In the belief that genres contained and shaped social experience for individuals, he remained antithetical to the Formalist
model, devoid as it was of any real sense of history. He also
regarded the dialogic aspect of discourse as 'beyond the ken
of linguistics' (1981: 273). Although Bakhtin repeatedly claimed
that Cervantes wrote 'the classic and purest model of the novel
as genre' (1981: 324), he never cites *Don Quixote*, never documents the modes of representing the world that made the
Cervantine novel into such a generic model. These modes were
linked not only to 'Ariosto's vast geographies'—Borges's phrase
for Don Quixote's imaginary homelands—but also to America's
equally vast and only slightly less unreal geographies.

The opening chapter of this book, titled 'The Americanist
Cervantes', surveys the role of the New World, from 1492 to
1616, in both Cervantes's writing projects and his personal
history. Cervantes's novels respond to the events precipitated
by Spain's ultramarine enterprise in startling ways. As cultural
forms, these novels are engaged in a dialogue with a great
ensemble of lived and fictional practices that we now call

Spanish colonialism. This chapter reviews some of the promising twentieth-century research on Cervantes's reading—what he had access to, what he was indebted to—in the huge textual family of the Chronicles of the Indies (*crónicas de Indias*), classified as a 'mass of texts' covering Spain's exploration, conquest, and colonization of the Americas (Mignolo 1981: 359). The Chronicles have intricate connections both with the Books of Chivalry and with the Cervantine novels that exposed or replaced their seductive discourses. After pledging allegiance to a characteristically American concept of intertextuality that acknowledges the author as an embodied agent, I close this chapter with a biographical sketch of Cervantes's life—including his various frustrated attempts to emigrate to what he himself called the 'refuge and haven for all the desperate men of Spain'.

By way of a comparative context for the achievement of Cervantes, Chapter 2, 'The Novel about the Novel', surveys his status in both Continental and Anglo-American criticism. This chapter documents how the Wattian rise of the novel—a critical construct responsible for marginalizing Cervantes while canonizing Defoe—has been fiercely contested by scholars of the ancient novel, whose complaints are both legitimate and timely. In addition to questioning the usefulness of the term 'romance'—a critical move that is sure to complicate Anglo-American discussions of the 'romances of chivalry' ('*libros de caballerías*')—these scholars of antiquity are enriching our notions of Cervantes's Graeco-Latin subtexts, concealed or avowed. Margaret Anne Doody's recent rehabilitation of Heliodorus (1996: 89–105), for example, is fundamental to any fresh reading of the *Persiles*, advertised by Cervantes in the Prologue to his *Exemplary Novels* (1613) as a 'book that dares to compete with Heliodorus' ('libro que se atreve a competir con Heliodoro') (1982: i. 65). Having discussed that competition elsewhere (1991: 3–23), here I turn to a book that dares to compete with Cervantes: *Robinson Crusoe*.

Chapter 3, titled 'The Novel as "Moletta"', examines Samuel Taylor Coleridge's intriguing idea that Cervantes's *Persiles* provided the 'germ' of *Robinson Crusoe*. This idea, which itself served as the germ of this chapter, does not automatically remit novelistic firsthood back to Cervantes. Aiming for coevolutionary histories of the novel as alternatives to evolutionary ones, I try to focus less on historical 'origins' than on geographical entities, specifically places and people in the New World that challenged old forms of thought. To that end, I examine Defoe's continued interest in the Spanish Indies for both his colonial propaganda and his novelizing. After a scrutiny of Robinson Crusoe's 'broken Spanish', I examine the shards of Columbus and Las Casas in his speeches. In closing, I compare the writings of Cervantes and Defoe on the topic of eating 'humane Bodies'. More weighty than Defoe's debt to Cervantes, I suggest here, is the debt of both writers to the Caribbean cannibals.

Chapter 4, 'Some Versions of Hybridity: *cacao* and *Potosí*', speculates on why the novel rises with special vigour in locations of culture that tolerate, and sometimes even flaunt, hybridity. After a glance at the recent post-colonial debates on hybridity, transculturation, and heterogeneity, I argue that patterns of hybridity are the inescapable cultural condition of Cervantes's prosaics. Over sixty years ago (1934–5), Bakhtin claimed that ancient novelistic discourse was a consciously structured hybrid, developing in the peripheries of the Hellenistic world and constituting itself as a genre out of a new polyglot consciousness (1981: 50). Shards of this Mediterranean consciousness enter Cervantes through his Graeco-Latin models, who may be regarded as hybrids themselves: the African-born Apuleius— a Platonist who composed Greek fictions in Latin—and the Hellenized Phoenician Heliodorus. But Cervantes also inherits this polyglot consciousness from contemporaneous sources, from both the 'Babel' of Algiers and the 'bar-bar' of the Indies.[7] Still episodic in *Don Quixote*, which represents some half-dozen languages, polyglossia is a dominant feature of the *Persiles*, whose multinational cast of characters negotiates in some dozen languages. Their utterances weaken the conviction that a language is the specific property of any one nation. This chapter scrutinizes Cervantes's use of two New World signifiers for wealth —*cacao* (invoked by his fictional gypsies) and *Potosí* (invoked across his canon). This use of American loan words—from Caribbean (Taíno) or Mexican (Nahuatl) or Andean (Aymara) languages—may be described by a process Bakhtin calls *hybridization*: the mixing of at least two linguistic consciousnesses 'within a single concrete utterance' (1981: 429). Since Bakhtin, and partly because of him, classicists have continued to ponder the

---

[7] See Hegyi's instructive essay on Algerian polyglots (1999).

ideological forces motivating novelistic hybrids. Like the ancient novel, which arose within an expanding multilingual empire, the Cervantine novel also rises through a fascination with the 'other', an analytic category occupied not only by Spain's recognized minorities—gypsies, Basques, *conversos, moriscos*—but also by its colonial subjects, the New World *indios*.

Chapter 5—titled 'Scorpion Oil' from the sixteenth-century humanist notion of the Books of Chivalry as toxic reading—addresses a literary genre not necessarily precipitated by but deeply implicated in Spain's enterprises of conquest and colonization. Evidence of this implication surfaces in Bernal Díaz del Castillo's well-known response to the conquistadores' initial sighting of today's Mexico City: 'we said that it seemed like an enchanted vision from the book of Amadís' ('decíamos que parecía a las cosas de encantamiento que cuentan en el libro de Amadís') (1980: 159). Many critics have described the conquest of America as 'a chivalric enterprise' (Mañach 1950: 153–4) or romanticized it as 'ocean chivalry' (Prescott 1873: i. 217). Some critics have linked these New World chivalric exploits to Don Quixote by describing the conquistadores, through a rhetorically preposterous construction, as 'quixotic'. Together with the books themselves—banned but irrepressible—the discourses of this popular genre crossed over to the New World with the conquistadores and, during the reign of Philip II, penetrated the great bureaucratic and military apparatus required for the maintenance of empire. Often referred to by Spanish officials as a *máquina* (Bakewell 1995: 314), this apparatus interlocks with what the Prologue to Part 1 of *Don Quixote* calls the 'ill-founded machine' ('máquina mal fundada') of the Books of Chivalry. This chapter speculates on the transatlantic impact of these massively popular books. One and the same genre gave to the conquistadores their delirious dreams of El Dorado, to Spanish cartographers such exotic toponyms as 'California' and 'Patagonia', to the Chroniclers of the Indies a 'lying' genre against which to compare their own 'true histories', to Cervantes an exhausted genre he could revive and parody, and to Don Quixote an endearing case of bibliomania.

In Chapter 6, subtitled 'Utopography', I examine Cervantes's 'generic contact' (to use Bakhtin's phrase) with the utopias. First launched by Thomas More's *Utopia*, this generic tradition is inaugurated with a voyage to the New World, an American connection that bears stressing. Indeed, More's Iberian protagonist, the Portuguese mariner Raphael Hythlodaeus, claims to have sailed with Amerigo Vespucci on all four voyages to South America. On the historical front, *Don Quixote* is classified as a 'counter-utopia' by José Antonio Maravall, who claims that Cervantes intended his book to satirize the false utopianism of Spain's lower nobility. On the literary front, *Don Quixote* is regarded as an 'anti-utopia' by Gary Saul Morson—who claims that the novel parodies and discredits the utopian genre as a whole (1981: 115). My focus in this chapter is on a special kind of anti-utopia or 'dystopia' fashioned by Cervantes: the island of Barataria in *Don Quixote*. Sancho's real problems begin when he gets what he wants—Barataria, a sham *ínsula* from the Books of Chivalry to govern. As well as generic parody here, I see social satire of the territorial gifts often promised, and sometimes delivered, by many of the conquistadores to their 'vassals'—Columbus's 'gift' of the island of 'La Bella Saonese' to Michele da Cuneo, for example (Cuneo 1984: 256).

Chapter 7, 'Jewels in the Crown: The Colonial War Epic', addresses America's first epic, Alonso de Ercilla's *La Araucana* (1569–89), a long narrative poem about Spain's conquest of Chile that Cervantes periodically quarries for his writings. Ercilla is celebrated for his 'strange grace' ('gracia estraña') in Cervantes's 1585 *Galatea* (1968: ii. 191), a text that includes a gallery of sixteen poets either born or settled in the New World. Passages in *Don Quixote* and the *Persiles*, as well as other Cervantine fictions, also serve as inky monuments to Ercilla. As a special homage to Ercilla, Cervantes places his epic in Don Quixote's library and then allows the priest to save it from the bonfire because it ranks among 'the richest jewels of Spain's poetry' ('las más ricas prendas de poesía que tiene España') (1. 6). Why is this literary 'jewel' so rich? Does it function as a problematic 'jewel in the crown' of a vast empire? What makes Cervantes call *La Araucana* both 'rich' and 'strange'? Such questions motivate the argument of this chapter, whose main purpose is to explore Cervantes's transactions—lexical, structural, and thematic—with Ercilla's American epic, a poem widely known as the 'Chilean *Aeneid*'.

The argument of Chapter 8—'Remembrance of Things Lost: Ethnohistory'—returns to Cervantes's posthumously published *Persiles*, the novel that most strenuously references America and on which Cervantes wagered his posthumous literary fame. The novel's opening 'Barbaric Isle' narrative—what one editor calls its 'long repellent beginning' ('largo comienzo repelente')[8] —invites readers into a world of slavery and cannibalism. This chapter examines the role of Inca Garcilaso—the so-called 'Herodotus of the Incas'—in this atrocious world. Although I shall be nodding to the Inca's work as a translator, historiographer, and autobiographer, my chief focus is on his work as an ethnohistorian. The oft-remarked presence in Cervantes of the *Royal Commentaries* of the Incas (*Comentarios reales*, 1609) needs to be investigated with more rigour. This chapter both documents and augments the role of Inca Garcilaso as Cervantes's main precursor in 'barbaric' scriptures. The central question posed at the threshold of Cervantes's last novel—a question that emerged in many virulent sixteenth-century peninsular debates —is 'What constitutes a barbarian?' Cervantes's text enacts an unambiguous answer: 'any person harbouring aspirations of universal empire'. Such a response would seem to incriminate many of Cervantes's own countrymen, not only conquistadores like Cortés, with his vision of a universal monarchy, but also those Spaniards who subscribed to the 'Messianic imperialism' originating with Charles V in the 1520s—'a complex dream of Spanish hegemony' ('un sueño complejo de hegemonía español') (Bataillon 1950: 226) that would still be operative in Philip II's court in the 1580s.

The Conclusion of this book, subtitled 'Transila and La Malinche', reflects on 'Women in Translation', both linguistic and libidinal. Here I sketch out some correspondences between the fictional Transila, the 'kidnapped translator' in the *Persiles*, and the 'real world' Doña Marina, also known as La Malinche or La Lengua.[9] Transila differs sharply from the memorable company of translators featured in *Don Quixote*—the *morisco* translator in the Toledo market place (1. 9), Agi Morato in his Algerian garden (1. 41), and the Italian translator in the Barcelona printing press (2. 62)—in that she braids together the sexual and colonial subject. Paul Julian Smith suggested, over a decade ago, that any alternative readings of either language

---

[8] See the Espasa-Calpe edn. of *Los trabajos* (Buenos Aires, 1952) for its anonymous editor's warning about these beginnings.

[9] On the phenomena of 'kidnapped translators' and 'cultural go-betweens', see Greenblatt (1991: 86–151).

or psychology in Cervantes would involve 'redefinitions of both the place of women in the oeuvre and the historical conditions of representation itself' (1988: 180). To read Cervantes's lingual metaphors for Transila is to redefine—for the female translator in and out of his oeuvre—the sexualized conditions of her representation in the early modern period. 'Translating' herself from a primitive society that practices ritual defloration to a barbaric society that practices ritual cannibalism, Transila signifies the colonization of both language and sexuality.

But Cervantes's kidnapped translator also moves us to enquire why his novels are themselves presented as translations: *Don Quixote* from the Arabic (1. 9), and the *Persiles*—which defensively identifies itself as a 'traducción' (159)—from an unidentified language. An activity that concerns much more than readability, translation involves movements between perceptions, places, cultures, and even empires—these last invoked in the formula *translatio imperii*, the transferral of Rome's imperial tradition to nascent European empires. In the most prescient moments of novelizing, translation involves movements between Europe and America. As the main mechanism of transcultural European communication during the humanist recovery of antiquity, translations—whether of Homer, Virgil, or Heliodorus—contributed significantly to the rise of the Cervantine novel. But geographically as well as chronologically distant materials must be factored into this rise. For the recovery of time would give way—precisely during the age of Cervantes—to the expansion of space.

1

The Americanist Cervantes

ALLUSIONS to the Indies are only part of the story of the rise of the Cervantine novel. This great discursive achievement—which I see as transnational, cross-cultural, and interlingual—was intricately linked to the pivotal events of 1492: the defeat of the Muslims in Granada, the expulsion of the Jews of Sefarad (the Christian nomenclature for Spain), and the arrival of Columbus in the New World. Harold Bloom is not alone in his view of Cervantes as 'subtly haunted' by the 'terrible year' of 1492, 'which did much harm to Jews and Moors, as well as to Spain's well-being as an economy and a society' (1994: 128). The Shakespearean scholar Paul Cantor, for example, cites a Pakistani novel in which a sixteenth-century Spanish Muslim character observes that 'the men who set fire to books, torture their opponents and burn heretics at the stake will not be able to build a house with stable foundations'. 'As odd as it may sound', Cantor continues, 'I believe that, read carefully, *Don Quixote* presents the same view of Catholic policy in Spain' (1997: 338 n.). Cantor's reading does not sound at all odd. The foundations of Spain's 'house' were unstable across the sixteenth century, and Cervantes's mad hero—whose own books are set on fire in a comically inquisitorial chapter (1. 6)—is one of the inmates of that house.

The year 1492 haunts Cervantes's novels for multiple other reasons as well, many of them subtle, most of them unremarked. Less subtle about that year, perhaps, are the critical readings that ritually trot out Cervantes and Columbus together for comparison as naive and imperceptive discoverers. The tired myth of Cervantes as an unconscious achiever or 'untutored wit [*ingenio lego*]' taps into a phenomenon as old as Plato, that great artists seem to inform their works with more than they themselves consciously recognize. Although it has been persuasively shown that this interpretation of Cervantes as an unconscious or untutored creator 'is destroyed from within' (Spadaccini and Talens 1993: 146–7), the myth seems to remain perennially hardy. Carlos Fuentes summons it when he recalls the 'common saying in Spain that Cervantes and Columbus resemble each other in that both died without clearly perceiving the importance of their discoveries' (1976: 11). Stephen Gilman renders a less topical version of the same myth of imperception: 'Like Columbus, without knowing exactly what it was, Cervantes had set foot on a new continent later to be called the novel' (1989: 184).

But Cervantes had also set foot—if only in his mind's eye— on the new continent of America. As this chapter will elaborate, he tried several times to emigrate to the New World. Refused a passage to the Indies, he began to write instead, sometimes referencing, often allegorizing, Iberian colonial expansion. The publication of his first book, the modishly pastoral *La Galatea* (1585), coincided with what Fernand Braudel sees as a new 'physics of Spanish policy': 'In the 1580s the might of Spain turned towards the Atlantic. It was out there, whether conscious or not of the dangers involved, that the empire of Philip II had to concentrate its forces and fight for its threatened existence. A powerful swing of the pendulum carried it towards its transatlantic destiny' (1972: i. 19). Cervantes evidently wanted to share in that same destiny. It is scarcely accidental that his great novels appeared at the close of Spain's age of discovery and exploration. These novels arose, much as the ancient novel arose in the Mediterranean, from a multilingual imperial culture, from the massive relocation of languages and cultures taking place as Cervantes wrote.[1] As cultural forms, his novels are engaged in a dialogue with a great ensemble of lived and fictional practices that we now call Spanish colonialism. If we are willing to entertain the theatrical claim of one of Cervantes's most recent biographers, Fernando Arrabal, these practices began in 1547—precisely the year of Cervantes's birth (1996: 152).

---

[1] I consciously echo here the name of a transnational and transdisciplinary workshop that took place at Duke University on 6–10 May 1997.

1. NEW WORLD 'VASSALS'

Colonial discourse—that is, the huge welter of contradictory discourses precipitated by Spain's New World enterprise— informed both Cervantes's personal history and his project of 'novelizing'. Emerging from an imperial matrix, his novels are bearers of major cultural events, including, for one, 'the discovery of the Indies', an occurrence that Charles V's official historiographer, López de Gómara, famously assessed in 1552 —when Cervantes was 5 years old—as 'the greatest event since the creation of the world, excepting the incarnation and death of its Creator' ('La mayor cosa después de la creación del mundo, sacando la encarnación y muerte del que lo crío, es el descubrimiento de Indias') (1858: 156). The 'shock' of this discovery was followed by what Anthony Grafton thumbnails as a crucial cultural revolution: 'Between 1550 and 1650 Western thinkers ceased to believe that they could find all important truths in ancient books' (1992: 1). Cervantes can be said to thematize this revolution in his Prologue to *Don Quixote*, Part 1. Variously called a 'masterpiece of prestidigitation' (Rivers 1976: 301) and 'the bitchiest piece that Cervantes ever wrote' (Close 1993: 40), this Prologue issues a comically rude challenge to the truths found in those ancient 'maxims from Aristotle, Plato, and the whole herd of philosophers' ('sentencias de Aristóteles, de Platón y de toda la caterva de filósofos'). Although mediated through the conventions of ancient Greek novels and early modern Books of Chivalry—this last a genre, as the Prologue itself puts it, 'of which Aristotle never dreamed' ('de quien nunca se acordó Aristóteles')—Cervantes's novels respond to the discourse of real-world events, both at home and in Spain's ultramarine empire.

As the pioneering imperial power in America, Spain was also the site of countless debates about the legalities of that power, with theologians and politicians alike pronouncing on the validity of each and every imperial move in the New World. Unless he were deaf to current events, Cervantes would have been aware of the impact and aftermath of the theological and political debates that took place during his childhood, most notably the Great Debate at Valladolid (1550–1) between Las Casas and Sepúlveda, a protracted dispute on the application of Aristotle's theory of 'natural slavery' to the New World peoples.

The aftermath of that debate continued across Cervantes's lifetime. Because the judges at Valladolid could reach no collective decision, the Council of the Indies struggled for years afterwards, as Lewis Hanke explains in his classic study *Aristotle and the American Indians*, 'to get them to give their opinions in writing' (1970: 75). At least one political theorist connects the 'striking flourishing of natural law theories in international relations' with Cervantes's writings (Higuera 1995: 4). Given that these events and their 'afterlife' were occurring in the colonies across the whole of Cervantes's lifetime, it is difficult *not* to speculate on the relations between the Spanish debates about, say, 'just wars'—a topic about which Don Quixote has much to say—and the rise of the Cervantine novel.

Cervantes may be alluding to these debates when Don Quixote and Sancho encounter, on the road out of Toboso, a cartful of players in costume (2. 11). Identifying themselves as the troupe of Angulo el Malo—a real-life contemporary of Cervantes whom Berganza mentions in *The Colloquy of the Dogs*—the actors explain that they are en route to a repeat performance, in a nearby village, of an *auto sacramental* or morality play entitled *Las Cortes de la Muerte* (*The Parliament of Death*). The authorship of this *auto* remains contested, in a kind of 'reader, you decide' situation. Some scholars nominate Lope de Vega and some Luis Hurtado de Toledo (1523–90), who claims to have finished a piece begun by Micael de Carvajal, a writer who had been to the Indies.[2] The distinction of this last *auto* by Carvajal and Hurtado, published in Toledo in 1557, is that New World peoples appear on the Spanish stage for the first time in history. A scene represents them as coming to court with their *cacique* to complain of the injuries received at the hands of the Spaniards. Valentín de Pedro persuasively argues that the complaints of the *indios* take up the subject position of Bartolomé de las Casas, whose fiery pamphlets of some five years earlier had defended the Indians

---

[2] Valentín de Pedro attributes the *auto* to Caravajal [*sic*] and Hurtado (1954: 47). Diego Clemencín first noted the possibility that Cervantes was alluding to the Carvajal and Hurtado *Cortes* (1993: 1571). Ángel Valbuena Prat considered the Carvajal and Hurtado *auto* as the one remembered in *Don Quixote* (1964: i. 773). Saínz de Robles claimed that this auto, 'without a doubt' [*sin duda*] is the one to which Cervantes refers (1953: ii. 208). Scholars who tilt toward the Lope de Vega *auto*—although with no degree of certainty—are Rodríguez Marín (1947–9: iv. 243 n.), Allen (1977: 104 n.), Murillo (Cervantes 1978: 116 n.), and Rico (Cervantes 1998: i. 714 n.).

with 'quixotic impetus and tenacity' ('con impetú y tenacidad quijotescos') (1954: 54). If indeed Cervantes is referring to this 1557 *auto*, he does so deviously. The costumed actors that Don Quixote encounters in the cart—a demon, an angel, Death, Cupid, a Queen, a crowned Emperor, and an armed soldier —include no Indians. We are left with a tantalizing allusion, nothing more, to a morality play in which *indios* lament their lost liberty.

There is less reticence in Cervantes's representation of blacks, whom he portrays through the conventionally exploitative rhetoric of the sixteenth-century slave trader. Readers are often shocked at Sancho Panza's expressed eagerness to become a slave trader, to convert into 'silver and gold' the black vassals from Dorotea's fantasy kingdom of Micomicón ('por negros que sean, los he de volver blancos o amarillos', 1. 29). The kingdom of Micomicón, as Sancho reminds his master, is in Ethiopia ('Etiopía')—the general Spanish term for all of black Africa. Two chapters later, Sancho recommends for Don Quixote's dowry an African kingdom by the sea ('hacia la marina'), so that if life there is not pleasant, he could always pack his black vassals on a boat ('embarcar [sus] negros vasallos') and make that earlier mentioned profit (1. 31). Although the number of black slaves residing on the Iberian peninsula toward the end of the sixteenth century has been estimated at 37,500 (Cortés López 1990: 39–48), the greatest profits to be made from 'black vassals' at the time of Sancho's fictional speech were in the transatlantic slave trade. Spain had begun slave-trading on a large scale in 1518, when the Crown issued a royal decree licensing the importation of African slaves to the New World—4,000 to the Antilles, of which half were targeted for Hispaniola. Renewed in 1523 and 1528, these royal decrees began a trend that, encouraged by an incipient sugar oligarchy, resulted in a tragic dynamic: by the second half of the sixteenth century, when Sancho is dreaming of his profits, the demographic presence of blacks in the Antilles, as Antonio Benítez-Rojo chillingly documents, 'was substantially greater than that of the white colonists' (1992: 41–4). Cervantes has been justly numbered as one of the few Golden Age writers 'who pays attention to the mentality of the slave-trader' ('que presta atención a la mentalidad del negrero') (Fra-Molinero 1994: 25). He allows Sancho to enact a mentality that, although deplored by later ages, was largely sanctioned by early modern European cultures, in and out of Spain. As is well known, Cervantes himself never owned slaves; during his captivity in Algiers he *was* a slave—as the title of Arrabal's creative biography reminds us: *Un esclavo llamado Cervantes.* Sancho's sadly orthodox remarks about slave-trading, however, show that old Christian Spanish peasants were alert to, and could even dream of profiting from, the same seigneurial aspirations entertained by those enterprising conquistadores and colonists—largely royal functionaries, as Benítez-Rojo documents (1992: 42–3)—who owned the great sugar mills in Hispaniola and Mexico.

2. CHRONICLES OF THE INDIES

Although Cervantes did not need to turn to books for the discourse of the slave-trader, there is no doubt that he was familiar with some of the Chronicles of the Indies, texts now under intense investigation within colonial studies. We know, for instance, that he read Fray Agustín Dávila Padilla's 1596 history of the Dominican missionary order in Mexico in order to write *The Fortunate Pimp* (*El rufián dichoso*). Beyond its haunting references to an 'huracán'—an American word for the European *tempest*—and to the fraught transatlantic voyages to 'Bermuda', Cervantes's text personifies Florida as the 'killer of a thousand bodies' ('de mil cuerpos homicida') (1991*b*: i. 415). This little-known *comedia* fictionalizes a historical figure, Fray Cristóbal de la Cruz, who served as the provincial head of the Dominican order in Mexico before his death in 1565. The protagonist, a man without rank or wealth, begins life in Seville as a delinquent, a cross between a *pícaro* and a pander. He ends up as an American saint, however, having rescued a sinful and unrepentant noblewoman by procuring her salvation through his own painful, and to many postmodern readers unpalatable, thirteen-year case of leprosy. Although the French Hispanist Jean Canavaggio classifies Dávila Padilla's history as hagiography ('*L'hagiographie*') instead of Americana, he has no doubts that 'Cervantes consulted it, and abundantly' ('Cervantès l'ait consulté, et abondamment') (1977: 46).

Research continues on Cervantes's reading—what he had access to, what he drew on, what he was indebted to—in the huge textual family known as the Chronicles of the Indies (*crónicas de Indias*). It has become a distended family in our generation, including not only chronicles but also letters, diaries, official reports, notarial records, eyewitness accounts, royal proclamations, memoranda, questionnaires, theological debates, papal bulls, legal depositions, inventories, charters, essays, epics, and even certain *comedias* in the 'American canon'. Texts such as these last, of a pronounced 'literary' character, are being increasingly adopted, because of their documental status, into the family of New World Chronicles. Walter Mignolo has described this family as 'a mass of texts' ('una masa de textos') from the sixteenth and seventeenth centuries whose central topic is the nature of the Indies, its pre-Columbian cultures, and its conquest by Spain (1981: 359). In a later and indispensable essay, Mignolo subdivides this 'mass' into three discursive types—letters, reports, and chronicles ('cartas, relaciones, y crónicas')—that run a chronological spectrum from Columbus's *Diario* (1492–3) to J. B. Muñoz's history of the New World (1793). To these three types, Mignolo adds a fourth category of writings whose discursive ambiguity, their cross between history and poetry, makes them difficult to classify (1982: 58, 98–102). Ercilla's *La Araucana*—well known to Cervantes and discussed in Chapter 7, below,—belongs to this ambiguous category.

The classification of the Chronicles of the Indies has been endlessly problematic. The *relación* is a case in point, perhaps best known to readers from Cortés's *Cartas de relación*, letters addressed to Charles V which describe, and legitimate, the conquest of Mexico. But countless other *relaciones* from the Indies—brief printed texts that recorded contemporary events—informed Europe about, for example, the conquest of Peru (1534) or the earthquake in 'Guatimala' (1541) (Agulló y Cobo 1966: 9, 12). To distinguish a *relación* from a *history*, Mignolo describes it as a response to an official request that would be codified, after 1574, into a questionnaire; to align a *chronicle* to a *history*, on the other hand, demands much more documentation (1982: 71, 75–98). Inconsistencies of classification still plague the Chronicles of the Indies. Antonio Benítez-Rojo refers to all these writings as a *protocol*—'that vast and inconsistent protocol covering America's exploration, conquest, and colonization which we call the chronicles' (1992: 88).

That protocol includes over a dozen major texts published before and during Cervantes's lifetime and therefore available to him as a reader, some in multiple editions and continuations: Américo Vespucci's *Lettera* and his *Mundus Novus* (*c.* 1505); Peter Martyr's *De Orbe Novo* (1511, 1516, and 1530); Hernán Cortés's *Letters from Mexico* (1522, 1523, and 1525); Francisco de Jerez's *True Account of the Conquest of Peru* (1534); Fernández de Oviedo's *General and Natural History of the Indies* (Part 1, 1535); López de Gómara's *General History of the Indies* (1552); Cieza de León's *Chronicle of Peru (Part One)* (1553); Bartolomé de las Casas's *Very Brief Account of the Destruction of the Indies* (1553); Agustín de Zárate's *History of the Discovery and Conquest of Peru* (1555); Diego Fernández, el Palatino's *First and Second Part of the History of Peru* (1571); José de Acosta's *Natural and Moral History of the Indies* (1590); Antonio de Herrera's *General History of the Deeds of the Castilians in the Indies* (1601–15); and, finally, Inca Garcilaso de la Vega's *La Florida* (1605) and his *Royal Commentaries of the Incas*, Part 1 (1609).[3]

After going through various editions, some of the above texts were banned by royal decree, making it necessary for interested Spaniards to read around the bans. In 1527, for example, the Crown forbade any further Spanish printings of the letters of Cortés, having found his 'mythologizing of the conquest', as Anthony Pagden puts it, 'an obvious political embarrassment'; and in 1553, the Crown placed a similar ban on López de Gómara's works (1986: pp. lviii–lix). Trevor J. Dadson's

---

[3] For publication details on Vespucci's *Mundus novus* (1505), see Ch. 6 ('Utopography'), below. For publication details on Las Casas's *Brevísima relación* (1552), see Ch. 3 ('The Novel as "Moletta" '), below. For the following list of other titles, in the original, of published Americana available to Cervantes, I have consulted the periodic charts of historiographers of the Indies cited by Mignolo (1982: 103–10), as well as the study of books on the New World in peninsular libraries inventoried by Dadson (1998: 71–92): Pedro Mártir de Anglería, *Décadas de Orbe Novo* (1530); Hernán Cortés, *Cartas de relación* (1522, 1523, and 1525); Francisco de Jerez, *Verdadera relación de la conquista del Perú* (1534); Gonzalo Fernández de Oviedo, *Historia General y Natural de las Indias* (1535 and 1547); Francisco López de Gómara, *Historia de las Indias y conquista de México* (1552–54); Pedro Cieza de León, *Parte primera de la Crónica del Perú* (1553); Agustín de Zárate, *Historia del descubrimiento y conquista del Perú* (1555); Diego Fernández, el Palatino, *Primera y segunda parte de la historia del Perú* (1571); José de Acosta, *Historia natural y moral de las Indias* (1590); Antonio de Herrera, *Historia general de los hechos de los castellanos en las islas y tierra firme del mar océano* (1601–1615); Inca Garcilaso de la Vega, *La Florida* (1605) and *Primera parte de los Comentarios reales que tratan del origen de los Incas* (1609).

scrupulous inventories of some ninety peninsular libraries—
including those of royals and nobles, ecclesiastics and artists,
humanists and bureaucrats, printers, one merchant, and eight
women—show that the most popular of all the aforementioned
works on the Indies during the sixteenth and seventeenth centuries were Oviedo's *General History of the Indies* (*Historia general
de las Indias*), especially in its best-known Salamanca edition of
1547, and López de Gómara's *History of the Indies* (*Historia de
las Indias*), almost a 'bestseller': whatever cultured Spaniards
of the Golden Age would have known about the New World,
Dadson concludes, they are likely to have learned it from these
two books (1998: 80–1).

There is no question that many Spaniards, cultured or otherwise, were indifferent to events in the New World. At least one
Golden Age scholar thinks that Cervantes was one of these, that
the Indies have 'very little importance' ('bien poca importancia')
in his writings, and that his references to America are generally accompanied 'with a grimace of annoyance' ('con un
mohín de disgusto') (Avalle-Arce 1982: ii. 175 n.)—a gesture
that, to my thinking, belies the idea of indifference. Another
scholar wonders about the scantiness of American allusions
in Cervantes: 'Why there are so few references to the New
World in Cervantes' novels is likely to remain an enigma', he
writes, concluding that America 'as a locus of narrative' was 'off
limits' (Hutchinson 1992: 162–3). Paucity, like irony, is in the
eye of the beholder, but the notion of America as 'off limits'
to Cervantes should trigger some generative questions. A
few decades ago we would have cited Sir J. H. Elliott on the
'historiographical divorce' between European and American
writings to account for the relative scarcity of New World references in European writings of the period (1970: 7). Elliott
himself now allows, however, that he may have 'overemphasized
the degree of indifference shown by early modern Europeans
to the new discoveries' (1995: 395). Our understanding of
the impact of the New World on Spanish peninsular culture
is increasing rapidly, as local and regional governments release
new primary sources, and as scholars continue to search out
inventories of private libraries with an eye to New World holdings. Thanks to critics willing to cross 'the high seas, jungles,
and deserts of colonial literary production' (Adorno 1988*a*: 170),
Spanish colonial traditions of historiography are becoming

increasingly available. This means, among other things, that more studies will connect Cervantes's writings with the colonial processes of which they were manifestly a part. Although these processes still remain stubbornly resistant to our understanding, we have begun to scrutinize—far more responsibly than the priest and barber's scrutiny of Don Quixote's library—the received history that Cervantes so acutely ironized. As new data on early modern America is unearthed, readers may feel less obliged to praise Cervantes as he praises his own Arab historian—not for what he writes but for what he has refrained from writing ('no por lo que escribe, sino por lo que ha dejado de escribir', 2. 44).

3. FROM INVENTORY TO INTERPRETATION

Although Cervantes's repeated references to America—to Mexico and Peru, parrots and alligators, tobacco and cacao, cannibals and Caribs—have been dutifully catalogued, the American connection has been seriously underestimated and, until recently, undertheorized in Cervantine studies. A search of the 2,119 pre-1975 entries on Cervantes at the British Library brings up such generalized transatlantic titles as *Cervantes en Colombia, Cervantes en Cuba, Don Quijote en América,* or *Don Quijote en Yanquilandia (Yankeeland)*.[4] A closer look at some of these works discloses, in many cases, a wildly creative or defensively nationalistic streak and, in one case, an uncanny resemblance to Pierre Menard's modernist enterprises. A Colombian writer of children's literature, for example, dates his book from an unnamed city in the ancient Inca empire ('del antiguo Tahuantinsuyo') (Polar 1927: 9). A Venezuelan novelist aims to upgrade his nation's fallen *criollo* culture by dreaming up an additional 'fourth sally' ('*o sea la cuarta salida*') for Don Quixote (Febres Cordero 1930). A Cuban writer attaches to his text a '*Reproduction in verse of Don Eugenio de Arriaza*' ('*Reproducción en verso de Don Eugenio de Arriaza*') (Pérez Beato 1929). Although these writings are more creative than scholarly, they attest to the frequent deployment of Cervantes by Latin Americans, an interest dating back

---

[4] The works cited here are, respectively, by Caballero Calderón (1948); Pérez Beato (1929); Febres Cordero (1930), and Polar (1927).

to 1607, when a lively Peruvian report about *fiestas* celebrated at the 'court of Paussa' ('*la corte de Paussa*')—published as a documentary appendix by Francisco Rodrígez Marín in 1911—demonstrated the early popularity of Don Quixote in America (1911: 97–118).

For a transatlantic study of commendable specificity, we may turn to a 1915 essay titled 'Cervantes americanista'—my source for the title of the present chapter—in which the Chilean scholar José Toribio Medina produced an inventory of Cervantes's references to the New World: 'what he said about the men and things of America' ('lo que dijo de los hombres y cosas de América') (1958: 507). Another important inventory surfaced in 1947, in an essay that catalogued, among other Americana, the various references to the Bolivian silver mine of *Potosí* across the Cervantine canon (Campos 1947: 375–8), a topic to be addressed in Chapter 4, below. As this essay rightly noted, signs of the presence of the New World increase in strength and number across Cervantes's *obra*, peaking in the *Persiles* (Campos 1947: 389).

More historicized connections between Cervantes and the New World, however, began surfacing in the second half of the twentieth century. In the 1960s, Don Quixote was linked to an American explorer related to Cervantes's wife, a linkage to be addressed in the biographical section closing this chapter. In the 1970s, a catalogue of American historiography available to Cervantes since 1503 was furnished for readers of the *Persiles* (Cro 1975: 7 n. 3). In the 1980s, *Don Quixote* was linked, on the grounds of its 'chivalric textuality', to 'the first conquistadors and seekers of new worlds' (Testa 1986: 63–71). By 1992, the year of the Columbian Quincentenary, at least one writer considered the writing of *Don Quixote* as impossible 'without the Discovery' ('sin el Descubrimiento') (Acosta 1993: 15). In 1994, a study of Bernal Díaz del Castillo's 'relación de fechos'—sent from Guatemala to Spain in 1575—was examined as a precedent to Cervantes's narratological experiments in *Don Quixote* (Mayer 1994: 93–118). Another 1994 study entangled Don Quixote with both Columbus and Feliciano de Silva, whose paradoxical phrase—'the reason of unreason' ('la razón de la sinrazón')—cost the hero his sanity (Aladro Font 1994). An essay from 1996 explored the concept of 'true history', memorably employed in Bernal Díaz del Castillo's posthumously titled *Historia verdadera*

de la conquista de la Nueva España (1632) but used in a great
variety of earlier texts and, as a central metaphor, in *Don Quixote*
(Gaylord 1996: 213–35). A 1997 article titled 'Caribbean
Knights' discussed Don Quixote as an 'exiled creator of new
realities, new histories, new homes' (Reiss 1997: 308). And
in 1998 a long essay appeared in *Anales cervantinos* with yet
another Caribbeanized title—'The Indiano / Caribbean Quixote'
('El Quijote Indiano / Caribeño')—at once a homage to the
Colombian writer Pedro Gómez Valderrama and a penetrating
enquiry into the relations between the Books of Chivalry and
the Chronicles of the Indies (Correa-Díaz 1998).

   Let me close this survey by calling attention to a New World
reading of one of Cervantes's novellas, a notably ideological
reading that may shed light on some of the Americana in his
novels. Attempting 'to come to terms with' the multiple American allusions in *The Jealous Extremaduran* (*El celoso extremeño*),
James D. Fernández interprets the fortified house of the aged
protagonist Carrizales 'as an ínsula inhabited by a racially
diverse group of natives' and zealously ruled over by an 'indiano
governor' (1994: 974). Juxtaposing New World figures with
strategies of domination, this essay explores Cervantes's intervention in one of the central debates of modernity: 'how to
create subjects—docile bodies—in the colonies and at home'
(1994: 972, 976). Our New World readings of Cervantes, in short,
are beginning to move well beyond what Fernández himself,
looking back at 100 years of Cervantine scholarship, rightly calls
mere 'inventories' of Americana (1994: 969–70). In this book
—which focuses on various genres of discourse implicated in the
social and political institutions of Spain's empire in the Indies
—I aim to move from inventory to interpretation. The first step
in this move is to determine a method of thinking in broad terms
of influence that will maintain the idea of Cervantes's agency,
crucial here for my historical enquiry, while considering his
intertextuality with the Chronicles of the Indies.

4. IMITATION, INFLUENCE, AND INTERTEXTUALITY

The relations between Cervantes and the Chronicles may be
approached through a trio of methodological avenues—imitation,
influence, and intertextuality—each with many side streets and

some dead ends. Various mergers of the three approaches, with an accompanying purge of their respective weaknesses, have been in process since the late 1980s, when Barbara Johnson noted that the 'intertextual house has many mansions' (1987: 133). The notion that imitation and influence were limited or flawed tools, an idea that began to gain currency in the late 1960s, has led not to their impeachment but to various revisions of intertextuality that are returning it, ironically, to the old sites of imitation and influence. These sites have undergone considerable remodelling, however. The post-colonial advent of such practices as 'colonial mimesis' or 'cultural mimesis' has vastly complicated Sir Philip Sidney's classically Aristotelian definition of mimesis as an 'art of imitation'—'a representing, counterfeiting, or figuring forth' (1966: 25). Although Thomas M. Greene magisterially enlightened the art of *imitatio* for Renaissance poetry in the early 1980s, he admitted to a neglect 'most notably' of Hispanic literature in his study (1982: 2). This neglect was partly repaired by Anne J. Cruz's study of Petrarchism in Golden Age poets, which lucidly explains *imitatio* as a nostalgia for lost classical culture, a desire to close the historical gap between 'the classical world and Christianity' ('el mundo clásico y la cristianidad') (1988: 1–3). The taxonomies of imitation could shed light on Cervantes's prosaic uses of prestigious classical models like Virgil, or even of less prestigious ones like Heliodorus or Apuleius. The sophisticated allusiveness to *The Ethiopica* or *The Golden Ass* in Cervantes's novels, for example, may be handily enlightened by humanist imitation strategies based on anachronism, strategies that presuppose, between Renaissance text and ancient subtext, a vast temporal gulf in language, culture, and sensibility. That gulf is negotiated not only by Cervantes but by many of his precursors among the chroniclers, for example, Alonso de Ercilla, whose intense imitation of Virgil in *La Araucana* justifies its well-known classification as the 'Chilean *Aeneid*'. Some scholars are returning to imitation by having broadened the notion of intertextuality. Under the rubric of 'imperial mimesis', for example, Barbara Fuchs theorizes a wider kind of intertextuality, one that may be paired with instances of literary mimesis—citation, allusion, and ventriloquism (forthcoming).

When the temporal gulf between text and subtext is a mere generation or less, however—as in Cervantes's relations to Ercilla or Inca Garcilaso—the relations between them are best approached through theories of literary influence, or intertextuality, or a broader theory that dissolves the boundaries between the two.[5] To opt for influence in its older and narrower forms is to reach for a criticism that is author-centred, evaluative, concerned with notions of originality, committed to hierarchy, and sometimes focused on Oedipal struggles. Harold Bloom's theory of Oedipal warfare—the father–son reformulation of textual influence that posits an all-male paradigm of Western literary history—was part of this traditional package (1973). Although many of the hallmarks of influence began to seem shopworn and tendentious during the late 1970s, when intertextuality became all the rage, one of them has survived and even prospered in the recycled versions of influence emerging across the 1990s: the authority of the author. Conceiving of the author as an agent intentionally and purposefully engaging other literary works need not, it would appear, inhibit the role of the reader in making meaning. Author-centredness becomes dismaying, however, when it grounds influence theory in questions of canonicity— a grounding that has sometimes led to the pernicious institutionalization of one national literature over another (a topic discussed in Chapter 2, below).

Some critics are returning to influence by prying open intertextuality, a term originally coined by Julia Kristeva in keeping with the Saussurean model of language. Unlike influence, the earlier notions of intertextuality were reader-centred, synchronic, and open to a variety of ideological networks and systems of discourse. Although Kristeva has expressed her intellectual debt to Bakhtin's concept of dialogism, her notion of intertextuality, in which Derrida and Lacan function as largely unacknowledged intertexts, includes dimensions of psychoanalysis not present in Bakhtin's prosaics. By drawing from both Kristevan intertextuality and Bakhtinian dialogism, some critics are returning to theories of influence to ask how authors construct *themselves*.[6] A cross between influence and

---

[5] Many of the arguments in this section are indebted to Clayton and Rothstein's collection *Influence and Intertextuality in Literary History* (1991).

[6] See Clayton and Rothstein on Kristeva (1991: 18–21). For a psychoanalytic reading of Cervantes's more subhuman worlds, see Garcés's 'Berganza and the Abject' (1993: 292–314).

intertextuality that comes directly out of Cervantine studies offers a promising new avenue. Nicholas Round has suggested a broad notion of intertextuality based on cognitive linguistics that posits a continuum of influence, from outright conscious 'appropriation' of previous linguistic expressions to 'influence by availability' (1994: 10–11). This continuum suggests that some of the distinction between influence and intertextuality may be based on degrees of authorial awareness, a quality difficult to measure. Somewhere in Round's hospitable continuum we might interpolate what imitation studies calls 'a borderline teaser' (Greene 1982: 50).

My own arguments in the chapters that follow—which discuss Cervantes's relations with such New World chroniclers as Ercilla and Inca Garcilaso—assume intertextuality as an enlargement, not a replacement, of influence. The present study retains Cervantes as agent even while analysing the impact of many discursive and non-discursive formations on his writings—from royal decrees and theological debates to the profession of soldiering or the craft of cartography. The intertextual practices in this book—based on a revised concept of intertextuality that includes the notion of agency and that participates in a historical project—are as American as its central topic. My methods align themselves, in other words, with 'a characteristically American redefinition of intertextuality, not a naïve misunderstanding of French theory' (Clayton and Rothstein 1991: 29). This redefinition opens itself both to authors and to their lives. As telescoped in the following section, Cervantes's impoverished and vagabond life led him to speculate on, as well as to fictionalize, the New World, which he represents as both a refuge and a disappointment for Spain's 'desperate' populations.

5. 'PATIENCE IN ADVERSITY'

The mapping of American territories, the return of wealthy *indianos* from the Indies to the Peninsula, the dispatch of formal reports (*Relaciones geográficas*) of different American territories to the Council of the Indies—these were but a few of the elements that helped trigger an emigration rush during Cervantes's lifetime. That rush is indirectly alluded to in the

Persiles, by the sacristan of a church in a *morisco* village, who
laments that Spanish Moors multiply so rapidly that even 'the
Indies cannot contain them' ('no los entresacan las Indias',
359)—an ironic remark, given that *moriscos* were forbidden to
emigrate to America. The opening passage of Cervantes's *Jealous
Extremaduran* (*El celoso extremeño*) catalogues various types of
emigrants to the Indies, a world grimly portrayed as the

refuge and haven for all the desperate men of Spain, the sanctuary
of the bankrupt, the safeguard of murderers, an asylum for those
gamblers whom professional cardplayers call *ciertos,* the promised
land for ladies of easy virtue, a lure and disillusionment for many, and
a satisying solution for few.

refugio y amparo de los desesperados de España, iglesia de los alzados,
salvoconducto de los homicidas, pala y cubierta de los jugadores a
quien llaman *ciertos* los peritos en el arte, añagaza general de mujeres
libres, engaño común de muchos y remedio particular de pocos
(1982: ii. 175–6).[7]

The idea of America as a 'refuge' is reiterated in Cervantes's
novela of *The English Spanishwoman* (*La española inglesa*), where
the parents of the protagonist determine, at a low point in their
fortunes, to emigrate to the Indies—'the common refuge of impoverished nobility' ('común refugio de los pobres generosos')
(1982: ii. 65). The historian Fernand Braudel offers a longer
and—given his somewhat imaginative entry of runaway husbands
—perhaps even more novelistic catalogue than Cervantes of the
'hungry crowd of emigrants to America' who streamed into
Seville: 'impoverished gentlemen hoping to restore their
family fortunes, soldiers seeking adventure, young men of no
property hoping to make good, and along with them the dregs
of Spanish society, branded thieves, bandits, tramps all hoping
to find some lucrative activity overseas, debtors fleeing pressing
creditors and husbands fleeing nagging wives' (1972: ii. 740).

At several points in his life Cervantes was one of these
aspiring emigrants. Born during the last decade of the reign
of Charles V—lord of an empire, as Ariosto claimed, on which

---

[7] Because of the high quality of its general and particular introductions to
Cervantes's *Exemplary novels* (*Novelas ejemplares*), I recommend the 4-vol. Ife ed., with
its facing page Spanish and English versions. I generally cite from Avalle-Arce's Spanish
edn. (1982) of this text because of its scholarly apparatus. All English translations
are my own.

the sun never set—Cervantes could in no way prosper from the great military and bureaucratic apparatus required to maintain that empire. Apart from Spain's New World dominions, Charles V presided over three different European cultures and communities: his Burgundian inheritance of the Low Countries, his Habsburg inheritance of the Austrian lands, and his Castilian-Aragonese inheritance of Iberia, which brought him Aragon's territories in Italy. Some fifty years after the king's death Cervantes would write, in the Prologue to his *Exemplary Novels*, of that 'lightning-bolt of war, Charles V, of happy memory' ('hijo del rayo de la guerra, Carlo Quinto, de felice memoria') (1982: i. 2). Spain's warrior king and his expansionist empire managed to inflate Cervantes's rhetoric if not his fortunes.

As the fourth child of Leonor de Cortinas and Rodrigo de Cervantes, an impecunious hidalgo and luckless barber-surgeon, Cervantes was introduced early to economic hardship. He experienced the shame of a father sentenced, at least once, to debtor's prison. Thanks, in part, to his father's legacy, Cervantes would spend much of his life at the margins of respectable society, often in the company of vagrants and delinquents. Although born in a famous university town, Alcalá de Henares (whose Arabic name Alfonso VI retained when he reconquered it from the Moors), Cervantes was never to enjoy the university education that he depicts, often satirically, in his writings. After a season in Cardinal Acquaviva's retinue in Italy, he enlisted as a harquebusier in the military, a career he sums up in the Prologue to his *Exemplary Novels* (*Novelas ejemplares*), where he writes about himself in the third person: 'He was a soldier for many years, and five and a half of them a captive, where he learned to have patience in adversity' ('Fue soldado muchos años, y cinco y medio cautivo, donde aprendió a tener paciencia en las adversidades') (1992: i. 2). In the same text Cervantes mentions the blunderbuss wound he suffered during the naval battle of Lepanto, on 7 October 1571, while fighting from the galley *Marquesa*, under Diego de Urbina's captainship—a wound that cost him the use of his left hand. En route home several years later, after various other engagements in the Mediterranean, Cervantes was captured by Turkish pirates. He spent five and a half years as a prisoner of war in an Algerian dungeon (*baño*)—an experience that at many points coincides with that of Ruy Pérez de Viedma, hero of *The Captive's*

Tale in Part 1 of *Don Quixote.* Returning to Spain in 1580, as a
maimed veteran whose ransom had further ravaged the family
finances, Cervantes quickly discovered that his postwar career
prospects were bleak.

The same year as his liberation from captivity, Philip II
annexed Portugal, a move that would have some notable literary
repercussions. Philip's annexation is addressed in the closing
cantos of Ercilla's *La Araucana* (1589), a critical subtext, as
Chapter 7, below, argues, of both *Don Quixote* and the
Persiles. On the Anglo-Hispanic literary front, the annexation
of Portugal would contribute the political background for
Thomas Kyd's influential Elizabethan play, *The Spanish Tragedy*
(1592). With all of its possessions in Africa, Brazil, and the East
Indies, Portugal brought new territories and new problems
to an enormous and unwieldy empire. Philip's dominions now
encircled the globe, stretching from Europe to America to
the Philippines, which had been conquered in the 1560s, and
from there back to Europe via Spain's newly acquired possessions in Macao, Malacca, India, Mozambique, and Angola.
Despite this global reach—or, more likely, because of it—Spain's
glory was already in eclipse, its empire beginning to fragment.
The desperate actions of the *indiano* protagonist of *The Jealous
Extremaduran* (*El celoso extremeño*), as William Clamurro argues,
may be read 'as a figure for the ultimate profligate, if putatively
"prudent" and serious endeavors of a monarchy trying to hold
on to the rebellious fragments of an impossible empire' (1997:
165). The wages of that 'impossible empire' was, among other
things, inflation. A huge tide of silver from the American
mines poured into Europe, some of it trickling, as Chapter 4,
below, discusses, into Cervantes's writings. By the end of the
century, bullion, largely silver, accounted for more than 95 per
cent of all exports to Europe from the American colonies.
No sooner was it deposited in King Philip's coffers, however,
than it was drained away to pay Spain's creditors. This flow
of bullion from the colonies, on which the royal finances
had become utterly dependent, produced a wildly inflationary
economy in the metropolis, with Castile bearing the heaviest
burden of the Crown's constant fiscal and military demands.
The Cervantes family confronted this punitive inflation and,
given the ransoms they had to cobble together, much more.
Cervantes has been rightly portrayed as 'the wise and partially

disenchanted citizen of a vast empire, an empire that embraced half the world, but that could not pay its soldiers and its bureaucrats' (Durán 1974: 98).

During the lean years of the early 1580s, Cervantes seems to have joined the ranks of those 'desperate men of Spain' he would depict, some thirty years later, in *The Jealous Extremaduran* (*El celoso extremeño*). Only two years home from his Algerian captivity, he begins to consider the idea of emigrating to the New World. We have a letter in Cervantes's own hand, dated 17 February 1582, addressed to Antonio de Eraso—a member of the Council of the Indies in Lisbon who appears to have backed his application for a post in the New World. Cervantes's letter laments that His Majesty is, in fact, *not* going to fill it (Canavaggio 1990: 102). This letter would not be unearthed until the mid-twentieth century in the castle at Simancas, a state archive created by Charles V as a kind of a paper fortress for the countless documents generated by an increasingly sprawling empire. When nothing came of Cervantes's application, he applied himself to completing *La Galatea*, his first publication (1585).

Although his marriage in 1584 to Catalina de Salazar would tie him to the family circle of the Quesadas, well known for their American connections, Cervantes was still not tapped for any post in the Indies. On the strength of these family ties, Germán Arciniegas has linked the character of Don Quixote (in his saner persona as Alonso Quesada) to Gonzalo Jiménez de Quesada—explorer of El Dorado, founder of the New Kingdom of Granada, and governor of Cartagena (1965: 11–16). In a later study, Arciniegas suggests that Don Quixote is, indeed, 'The Son of Don Quesada' ('El hijo de don Quesada'), the historical *adelantado* who died c.1579 in America. Don Quesada's niece and heir María de Oruña—the wife of Antonio de Berrío, a historical figure discussed in Chapter 6, below— may have crossed paths with Cervantes, her future kinsman, during 1580–3, when he was actively seeking employment and she was claiming her inheritance at the Spanish court. Although highly speculative, Arciniegas's imaginative historicizing gestures to the possible American roots of one of the three possible surnames of the fictional figure who would become Don Quixote: 'Quijada', 'Quesada', or 'Quijana' (1. 1). Evidently nothing came of Cervantes's Quesada connections, and he was obliged to accept work, at home in Spain, as a commissary. Hired to requisition provisions targeted for Philip's would-be Invincible Armada, he was to wander from one Andalusian village to another, trying to wring out of grudging villagers their assigned quotas of wheat, olive oil, and fodder.

The shabby job of foraging for the King comes to a temporary halt in 1588, with the inglorious defeat of the Armada. Andalusia is able to rid itself, at least for a while, of its plague of royal commissioners. Cervantes, still resolving his affairs at Écija, begins to think once more about the possibility of America. On 21 May 1590, he tries again to emigrate. In a petition to the Council of the Indies, he begs to be considered for 'a post in the Indies' ('un oficio en las yndias'), one of the three or four then vacant: the comptrollership of the New Kingdom of Granada (Colombia), the governorship of the province of Soconusco in Guatemala, the post of auditor of the galleys at Cartagena, or that of magistrate of the city of La Paz. This second and final petition is rejected on 6 June 1590, when some functionary from the Council of Indies curtly denies Cervantes his emigration papers. Dr Núñez Morquecho scribbles on the petition the laconic response, 'let him look around here for some favour that may be granted him' ('[que] busque por acá en qué se le haga merced').[8]

It was clear that all colonial prospects were now closed to Cervantes. He would remain in Spain, working as an itinerant tax collector in Andalusia: always on the road, haggling with municipal bureaucrats, justifying himself to auditors, enduring a series of dispiriting tangles with the Treasury, earning a few excommunications and at least two arrests. A brief gaol sentence in 1592, in Castro del Río, was followed by a stint of several months (1597–8), in the Royal Prison of Seville, on charges of peculation. The innocent victim of a bankrupt financier to whom he had entrusted his state funds, Cervantes endured a sobering confinement in Seville's Royal Prison (scarcely unique among Spain's treasury agents of the period) because of a shortfall in his tax moneys. As the Prologue to Part 1 of *Don Quixote* teasingly suggests, the idea for the novel, although scarcely the manuscript, was engendered ('engendrado') during his incarceration.

---

[8] For the whole text of Cervantes's 1590 application, see Torres Lanzas (1981: 11–13). See also Toribio Medina (1958: 535–6) and Canavaggio (1990: 157).

In the interpolated *Captive's Tale* (1. 39–41) and through the fictional Captain Ruy Pérez de Viedma, Cervantes re-enacted many of his own personal experiences in Algiers. But he also projected his frustrated transatlantic desires on the two younger Viedma brothers, one thriving in Peru, the other headed for a post on the High Court of Mexico. Despite some earlier textual confusion over *which* of the Captive's two younger brothers headed for the New World—the second, who at the story's out-set pledges himself to travel to the Indies and there put to good use his father's inheritance (1. 39), or the third, who is later described as a wealthy man already settled in Peru (1. 42)—when the Captive finally reconnects with his middle brother, His Honour Juan Pérez de Viedma is en route to serve as a judge in the Indies (1. 42). Apart from drawing on many of his own experiences in Barbary for the *Captive's Tale*, then, Cervantes also gives his fictional persona two younger brothers who emigrate to the Indies, recipients of all the wealth and honours denied both to him and to the Captive (1. 39–42).

6. PASSAGE TO THE INDIES

Cervantes's French biographer Jean Canavaggio—who exalts Cervantes as 'the father of the modern novel'—claims that the 'renown' of Don Quixote would have suffered had he come 'into the world under the skies of Colombia or Guatemala' (1990: 313, 156). That may be so. But although Don Quixote did not come into the world under American skies, his renown there was almost immediate and has never flagged. In a metafictional vignette taking place at Cervantes's deathbed in 1616, the Uruguayan writer Eduardo Galeano imagines Don Quixote and Sancho as fulfilling the frustrated desires of their creator:

'What'll we do without him, sir?' . . .

'We'll go where he wanted to go but couldn't.'

'Where's that, sir?'

'To set right whatever is crooked on the shores of Cartagena, in the ravines of La Paz and the woods of Soconusco.' (1985: 186)

Although Cervantes was denied a passage to the Indies—to all those places 'where he wanted to go but couldn't'—Don Quixote and Sancho went in his place.

Apart from the unknown number of copies of *Don Quixote* that crossed the Atlantic in the personal baggage of travellers —many of them lost at sea with their owners in the frequent maritime disasters of the era—seventy-two copies of Juan de la Cuesta's first edition of *Don Quixote* made it to the Spanish colonies within a year of publication. These copies of Cervantes's newly published novel were part of a larger consignment of books shipped from Seville in 1605 by a bookdealer, Juan de Sarria, to his son in the Indies, who met the books on the tropical coastal town of Puertobelo and escorted them to Lima, in arduous stages, by 5 June 1606. The story of this bookish voyage—told in rich detail by Irving A. Leonard under the rubric 'Don Quixote Invades the Spanish Indies'—remains one of the most gripping accounts of Cervantes's 'conquest' of America. This account is authenticated by a receipt of delivery, discovered by Leonard himself, that had for centuries languished in the National Archive of Peru. With an appropriately Cervantine accent—as if the books were human beings—Leonard recounts the journey of these copies of *Don Quixote* on a pack train of mules across the Isthmus of Panama via the terrifying Gorgona trail, where the least slip of his mule's foot could plunge the rider and his books into a frighteningly deep gorge; their complicated transport down the Pacific Coast from Old Panama to Lima; the repacking of nine copies of this princeps edition for a harrowing two-month trip up the cold *punas* of the Andes, skirting terrifying precipices and craggy ravines, to finally end up in Cuzco (1992: 270–89). Rolena Adorno justly regards the tracing of this single consignment of books as Leonard's 'greatest contribution' in the annals of book-trade transactions (1992: p. xviii). It documents that *Don Quixote* was being read in the Hispanic Indies within a year of its publication. That reading has been continuous and extensive, as Julio Ortega's 1992 *La Cervantiada* documents.

Unlike Cervantes, his contemporary and literary rival Mateo Alemán, a probable *converso*, was able to secure a passage to the Indies through moves that have exercised scholars for ages.[9] When Alemán finally arrived in the New World, in San Juan de

---

[9] On Alemán's probable 'purchase' of his emigration papers from Pedro de Ledesma, Philip III's secretary to the Royal Council of the Indies, see Márquez Villanueva (1995: 249). On Alemán as a *converso*, see also Márquez Villanueva (1995: 266 n.).

Ulúa on 19 August 1608, agents of the Holy Office confiscated from his baggage a copy of the 1605 Juan de la Cuesta edition of *Don Quixote*. These agents were vainly enforcing legislation against the introduction of 'profane' reading materials into the Indies—legislation initiated by royal decrees of the 1530s and 1540s that often went ignored. By 1608, Part 1 of *Don Quixote* was already a success in the American colonies. Cervantes's last novel, the posthumous *Persiles*, managed the transatlantic crossing a few years after his death in 1616 and went on to enjoy 'considerable popularity in the Indies in the seventeenth century' (Leonard 1992: 111).

But enjoyment of Cervantes was not confined to the Spanish colonies, at least not for long. Thanks to Thomas Shelton's English translations of Don Quixote—Part 1 appearing in 1612, Part 2 in 1620—by the 1630s Cervantes's mad hero would also be tilting at windmills in the New England colonies. Thomas Morton, for example, would compare the attack on him by Miles Standish and other Puritan 'worthies' as 'like Don Quixote against the Windmill'. Cotton Mather would also appropriate those windmills, using them to vilify Roger Williams, whom he portrayed as a violent Don Quixote. Williams was not only 'the first rebel against the divine-church order in the wilderness', as Mather put it, but also a man with such a furious 'windmill' whirling in his head that 'a whole country in America' was likely 'to be set on fire'.[10] But these early colonial, and intensely Puritan, uses of Don Quixote are another story, perhaps one reserved for Americanist scholars. The chapter that follows addresses some later, more widespread, and far more evaluative Anglo-American responses to Cervantes's novels.

[10] Both Thomas Morton's and Cotton Mather's invocations of Don Quixote are cited in *The Heath Anthology of American Literature* (1990: i. 186–7 and 232).

2

The Novel about the Novel

HISPANISTS are generally gratified to hear any inaugural claims for Cervantes: that he wrote 'the first great novel of world literature', as Lukács claimed (1971: 103); or 'the classic and purest model of the novel as genre', as Bakhtin noted (1981: 324); or even 'the first European novel', as Kundera labelled what he had earlier called Cervantes's 'psychoanalysis of politics' (1981: 237 and 234). Walter Benjamin joined this continental chorus by characterizing *Don Quixote*, in one of his darker 'illuminations', as 'the earliest perfect specimen of the novel' (1969: 96). As is well known, Benjamin did not welcome this new generic specimen. In 'The Storyteller', he explicitly laments that the decline of the oral tradition of storytelling gave rise to the novel, with its 'essential dependence on the book' as a product of the isolated, solitary, and uncounselled novelist: 'Even the first great book of the genre, *Don Quixote*, teaches how the spiritual greatness, the boldness, the helpfulness of one of the noblest of men, Don Quixote, are completely devoid of counsel and do not contain the slightest scintilla of wisdom' (1969: 87–8). Whatever *Don Quixote* teaches, Benjamin—and not only Benjamin —still sees it as the first of its kind.

All of these prioritizing remarks, together with a cluster of more genealogical claims—as, for example, Carlos Fuentes's image of Cervantes as the 'Founding Father' of Latin American fiction (1976: 9, 48), or Fredric Jameson's view of *Don Quixote* as 'the totemic ancestor of the novel' (1981: 152)—have become increasingly problematic, and not only for that sex which is not seminal. Models of heredity, genetics, or evolution pose a problem because, as Nicholas Round reminds us, texts are 'produced, not reproduced' (1994: 9). The notion of Cervantes's novelistic imitators as a series of 'whelps' or 'fantastical puppies' ('cachorros')—terms used by Jacques Lezra for Sterne, Fielding, and others—holds, for some readers, great metaphorical appeal:

in this canine model, 'Don Quixote quickly becomes Lovelace, Dulcinea Pamela, and the "cachorros" any of a brood of subsequent, Dickensian children' (1997: 240, 144–5). Whatever mammalian metaphors are chosen for it, however, the biological model remains a seductive fiction. As Homer Obed Brown writes in the context of the eighteenth-century English novel, the linear history of the novel taught to our generation, 'with its genealogies, lines of descent and influence, family resemblances, is itself a fictional narrative—a kind of novel about the novel' (1995–6: 300).[1]

1. STEPFATHERS AND SONS

This 'novel' about literary filiation—which pictures first-borns in, or founding fathers of, whole novelistic dynasties—is, in any case, called into question by Cervantes. Readers are always astonished at the disturbed 'father–son' relationship that virtually opens *Don Quixote*, with a prologuist who distances himself from his 'son'—from the 'ugly and graceless child' ('hijo feo y sin gracia alguna') we are about to read—by identifying himself only its 'stepfather' ('padrastro'). For all the tracing of forebears or genealogies so often foisted on it, Cervantes's text conspicuously refuses to honour its maker as a paterfamilias. He is to be acknowledged, instead, as a 'stepfather' to the book— as a more distanced authority who can see all its faults even as he introduces it to the public. No one who has read beyond chapter 9 of Part 1, where Cide Hamete's lost Arabic manuscript is discovered in the Toledo market place, could justly call *Don Quixote* an authoritarian text, a text that controls and limits meaning. Indeed, the multiple authors in this text—a stepfather, a marketgoer, an Arab historian, a hired translator, a criminal autobiographer, and some dozen interpolated storytellers— encourage readers to question rigid models of paternity, primogeniture, and birth order for Cervantes's writing. The text's own refusal of the paternal relationship, however, scarcely

---

[1] I am indebted to Homer Brown's essay 'The Institution of the English Novel: Defoe's Contribution' for the title of this chapter (Brown 1995–6). See also Brown's longer study *Institutions of the English Novel from Defoe to Scott* (Brown 1997).

justifies the move of many Anglo-American critics to ignore, sidestep, or occult Cervantes's monumental and quite visible impact on the eighteenth-century British novel.

A recent exception to this tendency is Ronald Paulson, whose study of *Don Quixote in England* (1998) offers readers an impressive survey, via 'the aesthetics of laughter', of the influence of Cervantes's novel upon eighteenth century English literature. Another English scholar who defends Spanish influence—and who loudly rejects the eighteenth century as an originary moment for the novel—is Margaret Anne Doody. In a provocatively titled book, *The True Story of the Novel*, she has this 'true story' to tell about the Spanish novel:

A certain chauvinism leads English-speaking critics to treat the Novel as if it were somehow essentially English, and as if the English were pioneers of novel-writing—ignoring, for instance, the very visible Spanish novels of the sixteenth and early seventeenth centuries. A consideration of Spanish phenomena alone would lead to an admission that Catholicism and a pre-modern economic setting could also give rise to the Novel. (Doody 1996: 1–2)

Beyond such a belated admission, any serious consideration of these Spanish phenomena might also lead to some curiosity, which the present study may help to abate, about why the novel arose in Catholic Spain. That the English were scarcely 'pioneers of novel-writing' may come as no surprise to Hispanists, at least to those who have serenely ignored all claims for novelistic primacy on the part of Anglo-American criticism. Classicists, however, specifically those scholars of ancient prose fictions who claim that the novel is already present in antiquity, have recently challenged what they regard as a 'land grab' on the part of English literature. Indeed, the caustic responses of various classicists, to be surveyed in what follows, suggest that the novel never did 'rise' at all, but rather that it was 'raised' by scholars who wished to nationalize, rationalize, or even monopolize the genre. But it is also possible, if more laborious, to 'raise' the novel in order to *trans*nationalize it. The time has come to stop thinking of the novel as a national commodity. Instead, we might think about it as a wildly mixed genre given to vigorous rises —whether with Heliodorus or Cervantes or Defoe—from the hybrid soil of multilingual empires and, in the case of the last two writers, from specifically American soil. My own 'novel' about the modern novel, as what follows will show, locates its rise in both Spain and England but looks to the New World for many of its imaginary cartographies.

2. 'I AM THE FIRST TO HAVE NOVELIZED . . .'

Before moving into this transatlantic narrative, we should re-member that the candidate pool for 'first novel' is an impressive one, often tied to literary nationalisms or to academic disciplines. Disparities of attribution abound, with different constituencies putting forward their own candidates as if they were self-evident: Antoine de la Sale's *Jehan de Saintré*, Chaucer's *Troilus and Criseyde*, Dante's *Vita Nuova*, Boccaccio's *Fiammetta*, the anonymous *Lazarillo de Tormes*, and Madame de Lafayette's *Princess of Cleves*, among others, have all been nominated for the distinction of first European novel. Disparities exist not only among but also within critics: consider, for example, the distinguished Hispanist Stephen Gilman who, in a self-cancelling argument, calls *Don Quixote* 'the world's first novel' soon after calling it an 'antigeneric fictional experiment' that Fielding would transform into a novel (1989: 79, 45).

Cervantes has rarely been granted the status of pioneer in most American English departments, partly because of the Anglo-American habit, inaugurated by Ian Watt, of describing the rise of the novel through the rise of Protestantism and the English middle class. What Robinson Crusoe's father had praised as 'the middle State . . . between the Mean and the Great' was calculated, in Watt's view, to produce not only virtues and pleasures but also a new genre.[2] For about a century after the publication of *Robinson Crusoe*, Cervantes is repeatedly acknow-ledged in Anglo-American circles: his professional sequestration would seem to be a post-Romantic phenomenon. In 1815, for example, Samuel Taylor Coleridge could still remark to an English audience, in a lecture refreshingly devoid of patriotic inflections, that Cervantes was the 'inventor of novels for the Spaniards' (1936: 110). Coleridge may have taken literally

---

[2] *Robinson Crusoe* (1994*a*: 5). All citations from *Robinson Crusoe* are taken from the Shinagel edition. Italics and other oddities in my citations of *Crusoe* are taken from this edition, whose 'Note on the Text' explains that the 'singularities of Defoe's prose . . . have essentially been retained' (1994*a*: 222).

Cervantes's claim, in the Prologue to his *Exemplary Novels* (*Novelas ejemplares*), for a *Hispanic* firsthood in the art of fiction: 'I am the first to have novelized in Castilian' ('yo soy el primero que he novelado en lengua castellana') (1982: i. 64). Coleridge's judgements about the novel were short-lived, however. The Romantic notion that Spaniards, too, could have novels seems to have eroded across the nineteenth century, the high age of British empire. By the 1870s a book review published in the *Spectator* (22 April 1871), tellingly titled 'Novelists as Painters of Morals', acknowledged, if only to dismiss, the earlier Spanish role in 'narrative fiction'. 'England has hardly received the honour she deserves as the birthplace of the modern novel', the reviewer began: 'Except the incomparable *Don Quixote*, what had Europe produced in the way of narrative fiction before the appearance of *Robinson Crusoe* in 1719?' The review went on to claim the novel for the English, specifically giving the 'honour' of its invention to Richardson (*Spectator* 1871: 484–5). That small manifesto in the *Spectator* heralded a series of increasingly parochial, and often anti-historical, claims for the novel on the part of twentieth-century Anglo-American critics. These claims consigned Cervantes, and not only Cervantes, to a liminal space in English letters. When Virginia Woolf invoked the history of the rise and fall of the novel, for example, she questioned, in a witty fit of anti-historicism, the readerly benefits of possessing any such knowledge: 'if we had by heart the history of the origin, rise, growth, decline, and fall of the English novel from its conception (say) in Egypt to its decease in the wilds (perhaps) of Paraguay, should we suck an ounce of additional pleasure from *Robinson Crusoe* or read it one whit more intelligently?' (1994: 283). A generation after Woolf writes these lines, when Ian Watt publishes his seminal *Rise of the Novel* in 1962, speculations about novelistic births in Egypt—or for that matter in Spain—are rare.

One of the most influential moves in literary history was Watt's attempt, at mid-century, to install Daniel Defoe as 'the first key figure in the rise of the novel'—not merely the *English* novel, as Hispanists were surprised to learn, but *the* novel (1962: 83). In an essay published a decade after his influential *Rise*, Watt defended himself by calling attention to the initial 'if' in the opening paragraph of his book: 'if we assume, as is commonly done . . . that [the novel] was begun by Defoe, Richardson and

Fielding, how does it differ from the prose fiction of the past
. . . ?' (1968: 206). Watt recognized, and later admitted to his
readers, that he had been labelled as 'impervious to the legit-
imacy of other previous forms of fiction', and that he had even
been perceived in some literary circles as a picketer 'carrying
a sign which reads "Cervantes Go Home"' (1968: 206–7). By way
of an apologia, he argued that the 'methodological assumption'
in his *Rise of the Novel* had precluded any autonomous treatment
of any forms of fiction other than those of early eighteenth-
century England. The words 'the rise of the novel', Watt had
to admit looked as though he were making 'the much more
unqualified assertion—that the only prose fiction which mattered
began with Defoe'; but such a supposition, he concluded, was
undercut not only by the initial if-clause of his argument, but
also by his 'more modest and casual subtitle: "Studies in Defoe,
Richardson and Fielding"'. (1968: 206)

Despite Watt's self-styled 'spectacle of public penitence' (1968:
212), his 'rise' managed to become firmly institutionalized in
many Anglo-American English departments, even as Hispanism
was downplayed, marginalized, or even banned. As is well
known, the English Department at Harvard University during
the 1950s, when Watt was canonizing Defoe, would not accept
Spanish as a language for their Ph.D. requirements. Watt's
retraction was published as 'Serious Reflections on *The Rise
of the Novel*' in an aptly titled 'Second Thoughts Series' (1968:
205–18). Even more serious reflections are forthcoming on how
this English rise was linked to the discrediting of the Hispanic
world and its legacy.[3] Decades passed before the Wattian rise
of the novel would be viewed as an Anglo-American fiction based
on a *retrospective* canonization of Defoe. When the eighteenth-
century English novel was being institutionalized at the beginning of the nineteenth century, Homer Brown explains, a long
time passed before Defoe was widely granted any major role in
its founding (1995–6: 311). Regretting the lack of 'an adequate
account of how Defoe's novels became so central to the rise of

---

[3] A collection of essays on the origins of American Hispanism, edited by
Richard L. Kagan, is currently in press with the University of Illinois Press. Still in
progress is a large-scale revisionist history, *The Rise of Anglo-American Hispanism,
1612–2000: The Trials of Cervantes and Calderón in the Forging of a Discipline*, edited
and co-authored by Henry W. Sullivan, Charles D. Presberg, Diana de Armas Wilson,
and Steven Hess.

the novel in modern times', Brown wonders—as do I—about
the process of making Defoe 'retrospectively the origin and the
source, and often the only begetter of a genre the properties
of which had been previously developed' (1995–6: 314).

Although the Defoe who 'begat' Robinson Crusoe in 1719
was well aware of Cervantes, my aim here is not to establish a
claim for an earlier 'only begetter'. I wish to argue, instead, for
a fresh understanding of the optic of the New World in the
novels of both writers. Such an understanding may show how
historical discussions of sources and origins remain in the
service of nationalism. More geographical perspectives have been
influencing the remapping of novelistic rises—for example, the
newly minted rise of the Graeco-Latin novel in the Mediterranean of antiquity. Until recently, such perspectives have been
hampered by nationalisms and thwarted by Anglo-American
critical methodologies. The new millennium with its new tech-
nologies has brought an increasing recognition that objects
of knowledge in literary studies—in our case, the novel—are
situated within a vast network of intertextuality, a cross-cultural
and transnational network that demands, for its just assessment,
interdisciplinary methods. In Chapter 3, below, we shall glance
at the rich network of intertextuality that enmeshes Cervantes
and Defoe—both key figures in the rise of their respective
national novels.[4]

3. THE ANGLO-AMERICAN CERVANTES

Most educated readers have entered the new millennium well
disposed to see reality as 'only one of many possible realities'
(Bakhtin 1981: 37)—a vision partly fortified by the 'boom' and
'post-boom' of the Latin American novel, with its comfortable
intertwining of both prosaic and magical realities. Some tradi-
tionalists, however, are still haunted by Watt's legacy: although
his taxonomy of the novel no longer carries any weight, his
generic classification of Cervantes lingers on. In the first of five
passing references to Cervantes, Watt enshrined *Don Quixote*,
along with *Faust* and *Don Juan*, as one of 'the great myths of

---

[4] I echo here Watt's phrase on Defoe as the 'first key figure in the rise of the
novel' (1962: 83).

Western civilisation'—a classification he repeats in his more recent *Myths of Modern Individualism* (1996: p. viii). This classification emblematizes a tendency in the Anglo-American critical tradition to withhold from Cervantes what Coleridge had so easily granted him, namely, the title of novelist. This English tradition pictures Cervantes as writing myth, prose epic, romance, anti-romance, or an indeterminate genre that made possible the English novel, which (as one critic allows) 'could hardly be what it became without him'.[5] Both Michael McKeon and J. Paul Hunter have published major studies of the rise of the novel that address themselves, as their titles make clear, to the English novel. McKeon's monumental study—which argues that the new genre arose in England in response to the profound instability of all literary and social categories—includes an elegant chapter on 'Cervantes and the Disenchantment of the World' (1987: 273–94). Although Hunter acknowledges in his study the desire to say 'something useful about the Spanish tradition, especially Cervantes', he also notes that he does not feel qualified 'to speak comprehensively and authoritatively' about a different cultural tradition (1990: p. xxii). At best, then, this Anglo-American tradition regards Cervantes as 'the great progenitor' of the literary form of the novel that would rise with Fielding and Smollet (Scholes and Kellogg 1975: 233). At worst, it denies Cervantes any role in 'prompting' the later novel, which emerged as a 'new type of fiction' in the eighteenth century. Instancing this latter position is L. G. Salingar, who stoutly maintains that no later novels evolved 'from the promptings expressed or latent in *Don Quixote*', which he insists is a notable example of 'the prose epic' and, like Cervantes's *Persiles*, 'far removed from common realities' (1966: 53–4). Evidently the 'common realities' in Cervantes do not suffice to underwrite the new English novel. James Joyce implied as much in a 1912 lecture delivered in Italian, in which he celebrated Defoe as 'a writer who, two centuries before Gorki or Dostoevski, brought into European literature the lowest dregs of the population—the foundling, the pickpocket, the go-between, the prostitute, the witch, the robber, the castaway'. Although every one of these 'dregs' was present over a century earlier in Cervantes, Joyce somehow saw them as originating with

---

[5] These categories have been proffered, *seriatim*, by Watt (1962 and 1996); Salingar (1966: 53-4); Frye (1976: 179); McKeon (1987: 273); and Hunter (1990: p. xxii).

Defoe, an English author who wrote in 'a truly national spirit', 'without imitating or adapting foreign works' (1994: 320–1).

The politics of priority and nomenclature behind the rise of the novel in Anglo-American criticism, in short, would seem to tell its own story. A study of Magic Realism in contemporary English literature concludes that 'the pragmatic and puritanical Crusoe, not the well-balanced Magical realist couple Sancho/ Quixote, stands at the front door of its house of fiction' (Delbaere-Garant 1995: 261). That house itself, however, is undergoing some serious renovation. In the midst of investigating the initial phase of the institutionalization of the English novel in the mid-eighteenth century, Brean Hammond, for example, has this to say about Fielding's indebtedness:

Fielding's writing is new because it is old. He distances himself from the new species of writing inaugurated by Richardson precisely by allying himself with carefully selected previous practitioners, the most important of whom was Cervantes. The mid-eighteenth century witnessed a surprising concentration of interest in Cervantes, for which Fielding was the most important vehicle. (1998: 4)

The Wattian views on this 'vehicle' are worth rehearsing. In order to fortify his English-only tradition, Ian Watt had to downplay Fielding's title-page avowal that *Joseph Andrews* was written 'in imitation of the manner of Mr. Cervantes' (1987: 2). To that end, Watt dismissed *Joseph Andrews* as 'a hurriedly composed work of somewhat mixed intentions, begun as a parody of *Pamela* and continued in the spirit of Cervantes, and this perhaps suggests that not too much importance should be attached to its Preface' (1962: 251). This suggests no such thing to the editor of the 1987 Norton Critical Edition of *Joseph Andrews*, Homer Goldberg, who attempts to give readers 'some notion of what Fielding took to be "the Manner of Cervantes"':

The interpolated stories of Cardenio, Anselmo, and the other characters Fielding cites in book 3, chapter 1 [have] some direct bearing on Fielding's conception of the novel. Quixote's first adventure after having himself 'knighted' by an innkeeper is a rare instance in which he encounters something like a real wrong to be righted; the account of the battle with the Biscayan is Cervantes's most extended play on the posture of 'true historian'; the Maritornes incident is the prototype of Fielding's final night scene; and Quixote's eloquent defense of poetry anticipates Adams's discourse on Homer in a parallel context. (1987: 344)

In a critical book on the rise of the novel, Watt could safely ignore Fielding's drama *Don Quixote in England* (1734), as well as his fulsome praise of Cervantes as a master satirist.[6] But to ask readers not to attach importance to a Preface haunted by Cervantes seems a desperately exclusionary move. The convention of 'formal realism' that Watt considered to be definitive of the novel is a well-known set of narrative procedures that includes originality, the repudiation of traditional plots, the rejection of figurative language, the use of contemporary names, specificity of time and place, and particularity of individual experience (1962: 13–34). Star-billing is given to this last, a quality that has always seemed to Hispanists not unconnected to Cervantes's practice. Parson Adams is, after all, no more particularized as a bookworm than is Don Quixote.

4. *ROMANCE* VERSUS *NOVEL*

The vigorous challenge to the English 'rise of the novel' thesis has been mounted by classical scholars who have also been involved, since the 1970s, in 'upgrading' the nomenclature of their ancient prose fictions, changing their classification from *romance* to *novel*. Such a change in generic nomenclature—which has considerable resonance for Cervantine studies—is also endorsed in Doody's *True Story of the Novel*. Explicitly responding to the 'parochialism' and 'naiveté' of Anglo-American critics, Doody targets the English separation of *novel* from *romance* as a false distinction that 'has outworn its usefulness' (1996: pp. xvii and 1). Cervantes was writing, of course, sans benefit of this specifically English distinction. In his early modern symbolic order (as is well known to Hispanists), the Spanish term *romance* meant a ballad or the Castilian language itself. And the discursive practices that would come to be known under the Spanish term *novela*—often identified in Cervantes's day with lascivious Italian fictions—were in some tense negotiations with terms like *patraña*, *libro*, or *historia*. Let us recall here a brief history of the distinction between *romance* and *novel*.

---

[6] In the *Covent-Garden Journal*, Fielding had called Cervantes one of 'the great Triumvirate' of satirists, the other two being Lucian and Swift (1988: 73).

The British Hispanist E. C. Riley, author of the indispensable study *Cervantes's Theory of the Novel*, defends the usefulness of the English distinction between these two generic entities, which he acknowledges are difficult to separate. Riley argues that Cervantes 'could not have written *Don Quixote* at all without a keen sense of the difference, and the relationship, between what we now think of as "romance" and "novel"' (1986: 11).[7] That may be true, but can we articulate the difference between these English generic entities any more clearly now than William Congreve did in 1691? The *locus classicus* of this terminological struggle, found in Congreve's Preface to *Incognita*, bears citing in its unmodernized entirety, if only because his progress from 'giddy delight' to the recognition of the 'lye' in romance forms recalls the responses of Cervantes's Canon of Toledo:

> Romances are generally composed of the Constant Loves and invincible Courages of Hero's, Heroins, Kings and Queens, Mortals of the first Rank, and so forth; where lofty Language, miraculous Contingencies and impossible Performances, elevate and surprize the Reader into a giddy Delight which leaves him flat upon the Ground whenever he gives of, and vexes him to think how he has suffer'd himself to be pleased and transported, concern'd and afflicted at the several Passages which he has Read, *viz.* these Knights Success to their Damosels Misfortunes, and such like, when he is forced to be very well convinced that 'tis all a lye. Novels are of a more familiar nature; Come near us, and represent to us Intrigues in practice, delight us with Accidents and odd Events, but not such as are wholly unusual or unpresidented, such which not being so distant from our Belief.   (1970: 27)

Despite Congreve's heroic efforts, a terminological confusion between *romance* and *novel* coexisted across the eighteenth century, when the terms were often used interchangeably. At times the label of *romance* was applied to a species of fiction that was 'excessively improbable, lengthy, boring, and French' (Hammond 1998: 7). This terminological imprecision continued into the nineteenth century, with Sir Walter Scott, to mention one major novelistic practitioner, also using the terms *novel* and *romance* alternately. The distinction was still a concern for Henry James, who in his *House of Fiction* warned against 'clumsy separations' of *romance* from *novel* (1957: 29). To this day the distinction between these two genres remains theoretically

---

[7] For more on the novel–romance binary, see Riley (1980).

inadequate: as Michael McKeon correctly notes, we must always account for 'the persistence of romance, both within the novel and concurrently within its rise' (1987: 3). Or we can stop the accounting, as some classicists would prefer, by simply eliminating the term *romance* from novelistic discourse. In recommending such a move, James Tatum enlists the help of Cervantes, who used the verb form of *novel*—the Castilian term *novelar* ('to novelize') —but no form of *romance* to describe his own fictional practices. While using that verb, Tatum explains, Cervantes 'may or may not have thought that his ancient masters Heliodorus and Apuleius were engaged in the same activity as he was' (1994: 2). According to the leading theorists of Cervantes's day— Scaliger, Tasso, and El Pinciano—the 'activity' Heliodorus had been engaged in was constructing an epic in prose (Wilson 1991: 21–2). The poetics of the novel, or rather its 'prosaics', were as yet unwritten. In his *Voyage of Parnassus* (*Viage del Parnaso*), Cervantes himself provides a clue to the nature of the activity he was engaged in: 'I have opened in my *novelas* a path | through which the Spanish language can | properly represent a folly or madness' ('Yo he abierto en mis novelas un camino | por do la lengua castellana puede | mostrar con propiedad un desatino') (1991*c*: 114). Whatever Cervantes thought he was the first to do in the Spanish tongue, however, he was moving well beyond the Italian 'novella', a form ill-adapted 'to record a convincing alteration of character' (Greene 1968: 246). We can safely argue, in short, that Cervantes was no 'Spanish Boccaccio', as Tirso de Molina had once called him.[8]

5. THE GRAECO-LATIN OFFENSIVE

Although scholars of antiquity have been borrowing Cervantes for their revisionist moves, their real gripe is more personal, more disciplinary: they are challenging the refusal of Anglo-American critics to entertain the claims of Graeco-Latin prose fiction to the status of the novel. Some classicists have launched an acrimonious attack against the 'guardianship' of the novel assumed by American English departments, who have a stake,

---

[8] See Canavaggio, one of Cervantes's most engaging biographers, for Tirso's epithet (1990: 252–7).

as the Latinist Tatum puts it, in 'coopting modernity'. Although claiming 'the novel' for antiquity is problematic, Tatum believes that rejecting such a claim 'may be no less so' (1994: 4). Tatum is not alone in his reclamation project. The Greek scholar Susan Stephens speaks of 'the insidious model of the rise of the novel in the eighteenth century' (1994: 406). As co-editors of numerous Greek 'novels' that pre-date both the Spanish and the English rises by well over a millennium, she and John Winkler have mounted an offensive against what they call the 'pernicious Wattian rise' of the novel, which they see as a project to nationalize a genre through 'fairly narrow bourgeois conventions'. In their introduction to *Ancient Greek Novels*, Stephens and Winkler argue for a 'more up-to-date map of the terrain labeled "novel" ', a map 'drawn to cover everything fictional and in prose from Petronius to the present' (1995: 3). Hunter, for one, would disagree with this generic move: 'making all prose fiction, from all ages and places, into the novel is not a serious way of dealing with either formal or historical issues' (1990: 7).

The grumblings from classicists are much amplified in Margaret Anne Doody's 'truth-telling' study, which argues that the novel is decidedly not the defining achievement of an English middle class but, rather, an ancient form emerging, during the Roman imperial period, from the polyglot energies of 'a motley collection of various peoples living in the Mediterranean basin' (1996: 9). When the English 'cult of realism' appropriated the novel, however, this early prose fiction—the Graeco-Roman novel—was relegated to the trash heap of romance, a despised term, Doody claims, 'reserved for a certain low section of the bookstore appealing to women only' (1996: 15). English critics, she continues, 'do not allow it [the Novel] to be "invented" until the eighteenth century, when the English came on strong' (1996: 2).

I accept Doody's premiss about the control of invention by English critics, although I do not see the genre of romance as being either despised or despicable. But I would no longer apply it to the Greek novels nor, as I once did, to the *Persiles*, which Cervantes himself announced was written to compete with the *Aethiopica*, a Greek novel by Heliodorus. Although Alban Forcione published his pioneering study of the *Persiles* under the title *Cervantes' Christian Romance*, and I have discussed it as a 'Byzantine romance', I would now categorize it, in the manner of Ortega y Gasset, as a 'long exemplary novel' (1961: 115). I do so on the grounds of its contemporaneity (its fictional time is the 1560s), its self-conscious theorizing, its rationalizing of 'miracles', and its avowed imitation of Heliodorus' *Aethiopica* —a work that Daniel Eisenberg, for one, rightly classifies as 'the very antithesis of a romance of chivalry' (1982: 28).

6. THE MULTIPLE RISES OF THE NOVEL

So who now has claim on that mutable and unstable genre we call the novel? Given that the fortunes of the novel have been changing since Cervantes used the verb *novelar*, and that our fractured literary profession is everywhere rethinking its mission, the time seems right for collaborative interdisciplinary study on the novel. We may begin by exploring the links between all the contending 'rises'. For the novel, like the sun, also rises, again and again, in different times and places. It rises in the present but, like any literary genre, it tends to remember bits and pieces of its past. Bakhtin subscribed to a qualified notion of 'multiple origins', as Holquist's introduction to *The Dialogic Imagination* suggests; 'paradoxically', Bakhtin 'perceives the novel as new. Not new when it is said to have "arisen", but new *whenever* that kind of text made its appearance, as it has done since at least the ancient Greeks, a text that merely found its most comprehensive form in Cervantes and those who have come after' (Bakhtin 1981: p. xxvii). This statement downplays the less hospitable side of Bakhtin, the scholar whose multiple rises repeatedly and explicitly exclude the Graeco-Roman novel, because 'in ancient times the novel could not really develop all its potential' (1981: 40). Walter Reed continues in the Bakhtinian tradition, beginning the rise of the novel, in similar fashion, with Cervantes: 'once the masterplot has been established by the novel *Don Quixote*', the novel will be 'born, again and again, whenever polite literature, vulgar fiction and true history forget their proper places and mix it up between the covers, hard covers or paperback ones' (1994: 265).[9] Another proponent of the 'multinational' position, again with different qualifications, is Roberto González Echevarría, who

---

[9] See also Reed (1981: 24).

claims that 'the novel's origin is not only multiple in space but also in time', and that its history is 'not a linear succession or evolution, but a series of new starts in different places'; the only 'common denominator' of these different starts, he concludes, 'is the novel's mimetic quality, not of a given reality, but of a given discourse that has already "mirrored" reality' (1990: 7–8). Even 'multiple rises', as we see, come in multiples.

Whatever qualifications one may bring to the idea of a poly-topic rise, it will entail rethinking the novel in more cooperative ways, as something more than a national commodity. If the whole vexed issue of the rise of the novel is now open for an interdisciplinary discussion, what contribution would Cervantes scholars wish to make to the topic? Wondering what 'beginnings' might mean in a given linguistic system or culture when similar 'beginnings' may be found at different times and in other systems, J. Paul Hunter acknowledges the necessity of knowing several traditions, with their distinctive pasts, in order to understand the beginnings of the novel as a species. Because 'the novel as we know it is not properly described in any single national or linguistic dress', he explains, the history of its beginnings must ultimately 'encompass several converging stories'. Hunter aims to tell only 'one of those stories in some detail', the cultural contexts of eighteenth-century English fiction, and to suggest 'its place in a larger narrative' (1990: 9–10). What 'converging story' would Cervantes scholars wish to make about the beginnings of the novel?

7. THE RISE OF THE CERVANTINE NOVEL

We may start by acknowledging that discussions of origins have become a notoriously bloated critical exercise in Cervantine studies: for example, when does *Don Quixote* as a novel begin? with the hero's second sally? with the adventure of the fulling mills? or with Part 2? Is *Don Quixote* the first novel? Is it the last medieval romance? Or is it some 'half-way house of fiction', as Edwin Williamson envisioned it in a study in which romance as a category gives way, in a progressivist manner, to the novel (1984: p. ix)?[10] Some of the perils of worrying the question of

---

[10] Johnson rehearses these polemics in (Johnson 1990: 23). On the disappearance of romance as a thematic concern in Part 2 of *Don Quixote*, see Riley (1954).

origins are instanced in Stephen Gilman's *Novel According to Cervantes*. At one point Gilman times the birth of the novel from the beginning of Don Quixote's Second Sally (1989: 17); at another, during the adventure of the fulling mills (1989: 60); and at yet another—citing the neo-Kantian philosopher Hermann Cohen—'when love seeks to know its own history' (1989: 31). The shifting origins proposed here for *Don Quixote* may instance what Foucault calls the 'problematics of the origin', the idea that, in modern thought, the origin of things 'is always pushed further back' (1973: 328–35).

Given that issues of origins or beginnings have become so problematic, it would seem futile to argue for a one-time 'big-bang' generic birth of the novel, or for some specific source as its locus of origin. In a study of the topos of the *source* as a locus of origin, David Quint recalls that the notion of prior origins as a criterion for literary prestige was replaced, in the late Renaissance, by the notion of originality. This shift in literary values could be felt—and Quint's example should not surprise Hispanists—when Cervantes asked readers to judge *Don Quixote* 'for its inimitable originality' (1983: 22). Despite this notional shift from origins to originality, claims still abound concerning the source or birth of the novel—whether within a text, a given national literature, Western literature, or world literature.

Discussions about the death of the novel—considered by many an outmoded vestige of a colonial, patriarchal, and bourgeoise industrial world—also abound, especially among those cyber-prophets who can see into an electronic future well beyond Gutenberg's movable type. But such prophecies are not confined to technologically minded postmodern critics. George Steiner's obituary for the European Novel, for example, was vividly countered by Salman Rushdie, who stressed the genre's robust health in India, Latin America, the United States, and even, despite Steiner's gloomy predictions, in Europe (1996: 50). I would add to Rushdie's optimism the widening spatial distribution of *Don Quixote* in the past few years, with new translations in Hebrew, Bulgarian, Chinese, American-English, and French.[11]

---

[11] Translations noted are by, *seriatim*, Skroiski-Landau and Landau; Neikov; Yansheng; Raffel; and Schulman.

Many formative strains have been advanced to account for the rise of the Cervantine novel. Let me cite here some of the most well known: the 'crucial rapprochement between literature and history' (Guillén 1971: 156); 'the erosion of belief in the authority of the written word' (Alter 1981: 956); 'the development of notarial rhetoric' (González Echevarría 1990: 46); the conception of a utopia (Maravall 1991: 182); the enforced 'boredom of the bourgeoisie' (Reed 1994: 268); and even 'hunger' (ter Horst 1995: 172). Although this last would seem to be a social problem generally not suffered by a bored bourgeoisie, Walter Reed links the emergence of the novel to forms of neediness by depicting a bourgeoisie 'bankrupted by the inflation brought on by New World gold and silver, diminished by the expulsion or forced conversion of the Jews, and seduced by the entrenched prestige and power of the aristocracy' (1994: 268).[12] The New World also impinges upon Guillén's theory of the rise of the novel in the sixteenth century, which suggestively emerges 'after the great Florentine historians and the chronicles of the conquest of America' (1971: 156). There is no fundamentally compelling need to privilege any one of the formative strains adduced above for the rise of the Cervantine novel—whether the presence of a utopian humanist class, a bored bourgeoisie, or a hungry peasant class—nor even to think of them as mutually exclusive or competing perspectives. They may all be bundled together as a 'national strand'—a system of multiple formative influences in interaction, all relating to the cultural environment that produced them. The formative influences of the novel, cultural and historical, 'need to be sorted out in detail for each national strand', Paul Hunter wisely notes, 'before moving too quickly to the intertwinings' (1990: p. xxii). One hopes that such national sortings will be part of a common mission to reconceive literary history along new transnational lines.

For the eighteenth-century English novel, Hunter isolates the following cultural and historical issues: 'politics, gender, economics, class, national and regional identity, and shared ambition and desire' (1990: p. xvi). Considering the pivotal roles

---

[12] In an earlier study, Reed noted a trio of other conditions for the novel's rise in Spain, including 'the relative thinness of the Renaissance humanist movement in Spain' (1981: 32).

of Xury and Friday in *Robinson Crusoe,* however, the issue of 'race' must be (and in the last decade has been) added to the above catalogue. Although equally pertinent to the early modern Spanish novel, all of the issues catalogued above are processed differently there. The idea of 'race' that reverberates through early modern Spanish and Latin American social relations, for example, 'is worked out through such discursive practices as *limpieza de sangre* and *mestizaje*' before being codified in the novel (Mariscal 1990: 203). Until recently, most novelistic studies in the academy have tended to focus on specific national traditions and to eschew broadly comparative ones. The time has come, however, to address these last, to set the Spanish next to the English formative influences on the global map. Among the strongest of these influences is the geopolitics swirling around the matter of America—its conquest and colonization by a series of European nations, most indelibly by Spain and England. A comparison of these New World formative influences on the novel has been hampered, however, by the fetishization of national identities. To play down the temporal claims for Cervantes as the 'founding father' of, or for Defoe as the 'first key figure' in, the European novel is to call into question this kind of fetishization.

To sum up, then. If this chapter has further discredited the Anglo-American claims for novelistic firsthood, its aim is not to install Cervantes in Defoe's place as 'father' of the novel. The biological metaphors for the birth of the novel may remain an arresting and even endearing fiction, but they keep readers mired in the kind of paternal genealogies that *Don Quixote* itself eschews. The English-only rise of the novel, which avoided the biological only to fall into the apologetic, was given its final death blows, in the 1990s, by a cluster of classicists who invoked Cervantes in order to fortify their own rightful claims for the Graeco-Latin novel. Not unlike *Don Quixote*'s relation to the Books of Chivalry, the arguments in this chapter have aimed to topple what is almost defunct: the Anglo-American 'novel about the novel'. In its place I would suggest a newer and more cross-cultural 'novel', one that takes into account the rich intertextuality between such figures as Cervantes and Defoe. The chapter that follows sketches out the beginnings of such a project.

3

The Novel as 'Moletta':
Cervantes and Defoe

WHAT Ian Watt enshrined as the first English novel, its own author classified as a history—specifically as 'my History' (Defoe 1994*a*: 258–65). Daniel Defoe's classification of *Robinson Crusoe* generically aligns his work with the 'historia' produced by Cervantes's Arab historian, Cide Hamete Benengeli. Defoe may or may not have been aware that the Spanish term *historia*, unlike the English term *history*, ambivalently signifies both *history* and *story*. His classification of *Don Quixote*, on the other hand, was itself ambivalent. Although at one point Defoe wrote that 'Don Quixot' was a 'famous History . . . which thousands read with pleasure', at another point he called *Don Quixote* 'a just Satyr upon the Duke *de Medina Sidonia*' (1994*b*: 241). Don Quixote himself would have frowned on this reductive classification, given his stricture, mentioned in our Introduction, that satires should address vices rather than people.

The choice of Medina Sidonia, the commander-in-chief of the Spanish Armada, as the target of Cervantes's satire is curious. Defoe may have confused *Don Quixote* with Cervantes's satirical Sonnet 176, 'To the Entry of the Duke of Medina in Cadiz' ('A la Entrada del Duque de Medina en Cádiz'), or he may have wished to suggest, as Ronald Paulson notes, that 'in English eyes [Medina Sidonia] was a Quixote' (Paulson 1998: 34). Turning *Don Quixote* into a satire on Medina Sidonia, however, may support another interpretation: that Defoe did not wish to be compared to Cervantes. Readers should be 'cautious', as Maximillian E. Novak rightly warns, about Defoe's claim that it was the 'greatest of panegyrics' to compare his fiction to *Don Quixote* (1964: 653). When his contemporary Charles Gildon tried to make such a comparison, Defoe vilified him as a 'malicious, foolish Writer' who, 'in the abundance of his gall,' had dared to speak of 'the quixotism of R. Crusoe' (1994*b*: 240–1).[1] One cannot underestimate the wiliness of these protestations, considering that 'Daniel Defoe lifted anything that came his way' (Kernan 1990: 122). Or as one critic put it more charitably: Defoe was 'never more himself' than when 'caught in the act of borrowing, tidying up, or varnishing over the cracks' (Rogers 1980: 134).

1. COLERIDGEAN GERMS

Anyone who sets out to argue that the 'tradition' of the novel begins with *Robinson Crusoe*, then—as did Ian Watt (1962: 92) —would have to sidestep the question of Defoe's indebtedness to Cervantes. Yet this debt was loudly proclaimed by no less a figure than Samuel Taylor Coleridge, whose 1818 lecture on Cervantes posed a novel intertextuality: 'in his Persilis [*sic*] and Sigismunda, the English may find the germ of their *Robinson Crusoe*' (1936: 110). This Coleridgean claim seems to have been resolutely ignored. No critic, at least to my knowledge, has tried to pursue any Cervantine 'germ' in *Robinson Crusoe*, although Coleridge's theory is by no means outrageous. Besides having access to three English versions of the *Persiles* (1619, 1741, 1742), Coleridge may have found his 'germ' in the three German versions he was fluent enough to read (1746, 1782, and 1789).[2]

Numerous points of contact may be established between the theoretical overture to Cervantes's *Persiles*—the Barbaric Isle narrative—and Defoe's *Robinson Crusoe*. Any or all of the following events and motifs in the *Persiles* could have provided the Coleridgean 'germ', never explicitly identified, of Defoe's novel: the arrival, by shipwreck, of European castaways on an island with many New World features; the domestication of

---

[1] Originally published as *The Life and Strange Surprizing Adventures of Mr. D——DeF——of London, Hosier* (1719), Gildon's pamphlet was reissued in 1923 as *Robinson Crusoe Examin'd.* . . . Defoe's *Serious Reflections . . . of Robinson Crusoe* (1720), an allegorical reading of his own *Robinson Crusoe*, was composed under the pressure of Gildon's attacks on him.

[2] A fourth German translation appeared in 1808, but it comprised only Books 1 and 2 of the *Persiles*. See Romero Muñoz's edn. of the *Persiles* for full bibliographical entries of these English and German translations (1997: 80–1).

an island home by one of the castaways; the notable scarcity
of women on the island; the depiction of the local natives as
barbarians and idolaters; the motif of slavery and slave trading; a deep fascination with gold; a convocation of cannibals;
and, finally, a long pilgrimage to and from home, interrupted
by many physical trials and much spiritual agonizing. When
Crusoe speaks of his 'Escape from Barbary' (1994*a*: 165), no
cervantista can forget that the *Persiles* begins with its own harrowing escape from Barbary—from a place called the 'Barbaric Isle'
('Isla Bárbara').

    The escape Robinson Crusoe refers to, however, appears to
have closer links with *Don Quixote* than with the *Persiles*. Crusoe
is running from the 'galling Yoak of Slavery' in the Moorish
seaport of Sallee (now Salé, near Rabat in Morroco), a captivity
that reveals some unacknowledged affinities with *The Captive's
Tale* in *Don Quixote* (1. 39–41), which Defoe may have quarried
for information. A number of passages from *Robinson Crusoe* do,
in fact, seem to have an opportunistic relation to *The Captive's
Tale*—from the hero's ship being surprised and chased by a
Turkish rover, to his captivity as the 'proper Prize' of the rover's
Captain, to his job of looking after his master's 'little Garden',
to his continuous meditations on how to effect an escape from
Barbary (1994*a*: 15–16). Claiming that the story of Crusoe's
captivity is 'the best known instance' of the seventeenth-century
genre of Barbary captivities, one critic allows in a footnote
that 'a century earlier, of course, there is the tale of the captive in *Don Quixote*' (Starr 1965–6: 49). This begrudging nod to
Cervantes's tale makes no mention of its pivotal role in the
subgenre of the captivity narrative, a role quite visible, for
example, in Mrs Rowson's 1794 play titled *Slaves in Algiers* and
based in part on *Don Quixote*.

2. CRUSOE'S HISPANICITY

Criticism of Defoe's novel has been, to a remarkable extent,
'stranded in the utopia of the Protestant Ethic'—where Ian Watt
situated Robinson Crusoe a half-century ago (1994: 299 (1st
pub. 1951)). Although more recent turns in criticism continue
to acknowledge that Protestant utopia in Defoe, they also stress
'his fiction's participation in the economic imperialism and

colonialism of his time, an obvious but nevertheless neglected dimension of his adventure narratives' (Brown 1995–6: 315). This dimension has invited a reconsideration of the travel-book tradition, which embraces such subtexts of *Robinson Crusoe* as William Dampier's popular *New Voyage round the World* (1697). An English pirate and hydrographer, Dampier made available to Defoe a treasury of information about Spanish-American geography, customs, and climate. Dampier sailed on the expeditions that both marooned and rescued the Scottish castaway Alexander Selkirk, who survived five years in solitude on a New World island discovered by, and named after, the Spaniard Juan Fernández. Dampier's claim that 'Goats were first put on the Island by *John Fernando*, who first discovered it in his Voyage from *Lima* to *Baldivia*' (1994: 229) may be behind Crusoe's herd of fictional goats. Apart from Dampier's, other accounts of the marooned Selkirk appeared in print—by Edward Cooke (Captain Cooke) in 1712, by Woodes Rogers also in 1712, and by Richard Steele in 1713.[3] Defoe's indebtedness to the tradition of adventure, trade, or travel narratives has been questioned by critics who see his work as tightly linked to the more nationalized literary subtraditions of Puritan guides and spiritual autobiographies. The arguments for Defoe's use of these Puritan traditions, on the other hand, may be 'overstated' (Downie 1997*b*: 79–85).[4]

In the wake of the travel-book tradition, the discipline of colonial studies has turned an eye on the topographical specificity of Crusoe's island. It is, to begin with, a wandering island. Fernand Braudel identifies 'the original Robinson Crusoe's island' as the Chilean island 'Más a Tierra' (1972: i. 148 n.), one of the two 'Islas Juan Fernández' located some 400 miles east of Santiago. Although reports of a castaway on a Chilean island may have triggered Defoe's plot, his own hero appears to have been tempest-tossed on a Caribbean island. Located at the mouth of the Orinoco river, Crusoe's fictional island has been identified as Tobago. The area around this island, as Defoe's text repeatedly notes, was populated by groups referred to as 'Caribbees', a tribal name earlier deformed by Columbus, as

---

[3] Excerpts of these accounts are repr. in Michael Shinagel's Norton Critical Edition of *Robinson Crusoe* (1994*a*: 227–38).

[4] For some dismissive attitudes to the travel-book tradition, see Hunter (1966: 9–18, 16 n; and 1990: 351–4).

is well known, into the preferred signifier of anthropophagy: *'caníbales'* or cannibals. Peter Hulme and Neil L. Whitehead, whose work has aimed for newer and more nuanced versions of Carib cultural identity—versions of indigeneity 'less wedded to the stereotypes that served European colonialism so stalwartly' (Hulme and Whitehead 1992: 3)—include among those stereotypes the imputations of cannibalism. In Hulme's work on colonial encounters, he specifically aims 'to return *Robinson Crusoe* to the Caribbean' (1986: 176). Coleridge had earlier returned Robinson Crusoe to Cervantes. I would like to merge their insights and return *Robinson Crusoe* to a Caribbean that has a retrievable relation to Cervantes.

Why all this Hispanicity for Crusoe? A few spots of time from Defoe's personal history may shed some light on that question. Even as he was writing *Robinson Crusoe*, Defoe was heatedly urging the South Sea Company, in which he was a stockholder, to erect a British colony on the 'River Oroonoque' (Keane 1997: 99–100), the site of Spanish exploration for almost two centuries. In a brief history of Sir Walter Raleigh published the same year as *Robinson Crusoe* (1719), Defoe explicitly lamented the earlier loss of Guiana to Spain even while claiming—in both an echo of Raleigh and a burst of imperial propaganda for English colonization—that Guiana 'is a Country that hath yet her Maiden-head, was never Sacked, Turned, nor Wrought'. A decade or so later, Defoe was proposing yet another site in South America—'about 120 Miles South of the Rio de la Plata' in the area of Patagonia—where a new and industrious English colony could manufacture woollens.[5] Although Defoe's imperialistic propaganda for promoting new schemes of trade and colonization was ubiquitous—he also regarded Canada and California as viable territories for English colonial expansion— Maximillian E. Novak explains that

> it was in South America that Defoe saw the best opportunity for his nation's enterprise. He was attracted by the gold; by the soil, which he claimed was more fertile than that of the northern colonies; and by the greater density he believed the native population to have. By clothing the natives of the Orinoco, the English woolen industry would find an outlet for all its surplus products. (1962: 141)

---

[5] Both Defoe's history of Raleigh and his imperial schemes for Guiana and Patagonia are discussed by Downie (1997*b*: 87–91).

Defoe's arguments for appropriating parts of South America 'were not entirely without foundation', according to Novak. 'The Spanish claimed all America by right of discovery, but they did not have a large enough population to establish colonies everywhere'. Defoe believed, moreover, that 'Spain was too weak to oppose any enemy in so remote an area' (Novak 1962: 142). Defoe's restless entrepreneurship was projected from his life onto his novels. The relentless pursuit of wealth by the avaricious hero of *Colonel Jack*, for example, is played out in parts of Cuba and Mexico. In both his life and fictions, in short, Defoe was often responding to the diminished but still threatening presence of Spain's empire in the Indies.

In the light of his heavy colonial propaganda for the Hispanic Indies, then, how retrievable is Defoe's relation to Cervantes, who had himself tried to emigrate there? How do we compare the transatlantic negotiations of both novelists? We might begin by noting that their respective novels rise— intriguingly like the ancient novel—out of a multilingual consciousness and on a Bakhtinian boundary line between cultures and languages. Margaret Anne Doody claims that 'the homeland of the Western Novel . . . is a multiracial, multilingual, mixed Mediterranean' (1996: 18). Bending this claim to our purposes, we might say that the 'homeland' of the early modern novel —if the examples used are the *Persiles* and *Robinson Crusoe*— is 'a multiracial, multilingual, mixed' Caribbean. Not only is speaking more than one language typical of the Caribbean, but also, as Rosario Ferré notes, taking over a language is 'a cannibalistic activity'; 'speaking your neighbors' language is a way of becoming them: *Veni, vidi, edi*' (1999: 105). This is precisely what Robinson Crusoe's servant Friday does when he cannibalizes his master's English.

Even childhood readers of Defoe's novel will remember Friday's broken English—phrases like 'Eatee me up!' 'Eatee me up!' (1994*a*: 212), or 'We save the White Mans from drown' (1994*a*: 161). But other linguistic 'cannibals' also appear in *Robinson Crusoe*, such as the young *morisco* ('Maresco') whom Crusoe captures, and who faithfully accompanies his master all along the Guinea Coast until Crusoe sells him to a Portuguese Captain for '60 Pieces of Eight' (1994*a*: 26). This young captive—'my Boy *Xury*', as Crusoe later remembers him—also uses broken English phrases, such as *'we give them the shoot Gun'* or '*Me cut off his Head*' (1994*a*: 27, 20, 22). As early as 1719, Charles Gildon wondered why Xury had to speak 'broken *English*', a language which he 'had no Motive in the World to study', when it would have been 'more natural' to make Robinson Crusoe speak 'broken *Arabick*' (1970: 62).[6] This suggestion is, for various reasons, intriguingly Cervantine. Not only did Cervantes speak 'broken Arabick' during his five-year captivity in Algiers, but also he chose to present *Don Quixote* as a translation from the Arabic, a translation that contains within itself various samples of 'broken Arabick'.

Critical commentary on the broken English of Crusoe's slaves or servants, as Gildon's critique shows, was already emerging during Defoe's lifetime. But no critical studies have focused, at least to my knowledge, on Crusoe's broken *Spanish*, even though he admits, at one point, to speaking with 'as much *Spanish*' as he 'could make up' (1994*a*: 170). Defoe's novel swarms with examples of what Bakhtin calls 'extranational multi-languagedness', a phenomenon that tends to arise when a culture becomes 'conscious of itself as only one among other cultures and languages'—a phenomenon, moreoever, that erodes those systems of national myth 'organically fused with language' (1981: 368–70). The dialogic imagination that Bakhtin considered a precondition for the rise of the novel, in other words, is most intensely stoked in multilingual environments. English, Spanish, and Caribbean languages provide that environment for *Robinson Crusoe*, whose protagonist is a castaway on an island in the Caribbean, an island close to the Spanish mainland. When he is ready to leave his island, it is populated with a mix of Mutineers and Spaniards, the latter portrayed as extremely violent people. By dint of becoming shipwrecked in a geographical zone that the Spanish, rightly or wrongly, considered their 'real world' territorial domain, Crusoe is forced into 'pseudo borrowing' from the Spanish, who have been 'cannibalizing' Caribbean languages for over two hundred years.[7]

---

[6] Charles Gildon, Defoe's first critic and the same contemporary who mentioned the 'quixotism' of Crusoe, thought it more natural to have Crusoe speak broken Arabic, 'which Language he must be forc'd in some Measure to learn' (1923: 62).

[7] 'Pseudo-borrowing', according to the German linguist Herbert Pilch, is a practice endemic among what he calls the 'sesquilingual', his label for Europeans who have mastered one and a half languages.

Even before his twenty-eight years as a castaway, however, Robinson Crusoe was trafficking in Iberian signifiers, always in quaint English spelling, such as calling a fever a 'Calenture', or slave-trading permits from the kings of Spain and Portugal 'Assiento's' (1994*a*: 14, 30). Regarding this latter term—as Patrick J. Keane points out in an illuminating essay on slavery and the slave trade in *Robinson Crusoe*—Defoe was well versed on the subject of trading 'negroes' on the coast of Guinea (1997: 99). Other Iberian signifiers in Defoe's novel—often appearing in italics and sometimes with Crusoe's own handy translations—include *'Maresco'* (*morisco*), 'the *Pico* of *Teneriffe*', *'Ingenio'* ('a Plantation and a Sugar-House'), 'Succades' (*azucados* or sweetmeats), 'Ryals' (*reales* or royals), *'Barco-Longo'* (longboat), 'Cruisadoes' (*crusadoes*), *'Padres'* (priests), and *'Pampeluna'* (*Pamplona*).[8] American signifiers also erupt occasionally across this English novel: 'Amozones' (Amazon River), 'Oronoque' or *'Oroonooko'* (Orinoco River), 'Savana's' (*sabanas* or 'Meadows'), *'Canoes'*, and *'Carribees'*.[9] Soon after his third year on the island, Crusoe constructs a dugout canoe or *'Periagua'* (1994*a*: 92), an Anglicization of *piragua*. Corominas's Spanish dictionary notes that this term, from the Caribbean language ('de la lengua caribe'), was first set down in 1535 by Oviedo, who explained that the *caribes* used the word *piraguas* for their large canoes or 'canoas'. At one point Robinson Crusoe uses the word 'Moletta', a false cognate for the Spanish term *mulata*, to describe what he did *not* look like after living in his tropical island for several years: 'As for my Face, the Colour of it was really not so *Moletta like as one might expect from a Man not at all careful of it, and living within nine or ten Degrees of the Equinox'* (1994*a*: 109). Unlike Crusoe's face, however, the novel he inhabits, with its pronounced linguistic hybridity, is, in fact, *very* 'Moletta like'.

When false cognates such as *'Moletta'* are dropped into an English-language fiction, readers may turn to various common conventions to explain them—for example, simplicity, rusticity, or even a comic intention. The South African writer J. M. Coetzee usefully pressures these conventions by examining not only how English is used to represent imagined foreign speech

---

[8] These Iberian references may be found, *seriatim*, in Defoe (1994*a*: 16, 21, 27, 139, 140, 200, 204, 207, 209).
[9] These Caribbean references may be found, *seriatim*, in Defoe (1994*a*: 32, 32 and 155, 72, 119, 155).

—his own various examples are the speech of an Afrikaans or a Zulu consciousness—but also what intentions lie behind, or what myths are being validated by, such a practice (1988: 115–35). The same has yet to be done for Defoe's cultural linguistics, his representation of imagined foreign speech. What myths, for instance, are being validated by Crusoe's ostentatiously broken Spanish? What intentions might lie behind this kind of defensive ad hoc practice? The 'novel' about the English novel would have us believe that the Reformation, empirical philosophy, the Protestant work ethic, the rise of the middle class, and English individualism all combined to produce *Robinson Crusoe*. Until recently, no 'Molettas' have ruffled the Puritan readings of this novel.

3. 'IMPERIAL MIMESIS'

Robinson Crusoe's pseudo-borrowing from the Spanish may reinforce the reputation of English as a promiscuous language during the eighteenth century, as well as the reputation of England as an imperial imitator. Apart from Crusoe's broken Spanish, various other Iberian shards appear in *Robinson Crusoe*. The image of a shipwrecked hero who has 'in a clear Day discover'd the Main, or Continent of *America*' (1994*a*: 161) blatantly gestures to Christopher Columbus. Crusoe's governorship of his island ('They all call'd me Governour') may have its roots, as Michael McKeon astutely suggests, in Sancho Panza's governorship of his island, both 'ruling class' scenarios about political power and compliance (1987: 319, 334). But far more striking than either Crusoe's post-Columbian 'discovery' of America or the Cervantine 'roots' of his governorship is his rhetorical imitation of the Spanish against themselves. Robinson Crusoe seems to have read his Las Casas, specifically the Spanish Dominican's inflammatory *Brevísima relación*—his 'very brief account' of Spanish atrocities in the New World. Written in 1542–3 but published in Seville in 1552, this text was translated, before the end of the century, into Dutch (1578), Latin (1579), French (1579), English (1583), and German (1597). The English translation of Bartolomé de Las Casas's treatise, available to Defoe since 1583, was titled *The Spanish Colonie, or Briefe Chronicle of the Acts and gestes of the Spaniards in the West Indies,* *called the newe World, for the space of xl. yeeres.* Another English translation appeared in 1656 by Milton's nephew John Philips, who feelingly rendered the title of las Casas's treatise as *the Tears of the Indians* (Gibson 1971: 73–7).

This treatise was a pivotal text for Spain's European enemies, who used Las Casas's humanitarian campaign on behalf of the Indians to construct a centuries-long Anglo-Dutch 'Black Legend' ('leyenda negra') excoriating Spanish cruelties.[10] In an illustrated Latin edition of Las Casas's *Brevísima relación* published in Frankfurt in 1598, the expatriate Flemish publisher Theodore de Bry disseminated vividly engraved images of Spanish atrocities across the whole of Europe. After the death in 1616 of Richard Hakluyt, the historian of Elizabethan expansion, his unpublished papers came into the hands of Samuel Purchas, whose 1625 edition of *Hakluytus Posthumus* or *Purchas his Pilgrimes* included a section on Las Casas pointedly titled 'Books of Cruelty done in the Indies'. Daniel Defoe could have encountered Las Casas's text, in short, in its original Spanish version, in English or Latin translations, in graphically illustrated editions, or within accounts of English explorations. Given his biographical interest in Sir Walter Raleigh, Defoe would surely have known the passage in *History of the World* (1600) where Raleigh, anxious to have the English supplant the Spanish in the New World, contemplated sending on to 'the Inga' a copy of 'The Bartol: de las Casas booke of the Spanish crueltyes with fayr pictures' (1820: vi. 120–33).

Robinson Crusoe's exploitation of, and contributions to, the 'Black Legend' are remarkably vivid. Indeed, his imitation of Las Casas's fiery discourses constitutes a remarkable moment of 'imperial mimesis'—to borrow Barbara Fuchs's incisive phrase for a cultural and literary phenomenon that also functions as a potent rhetorical weapon.[11] With this calculated mimesis, Crusoe joins his voice to the huge chorus of anti-Catholic Europeans who had been trying, for over a century, to break the Spanish monopoly on American colonization. Crusoe's appropriation of Las Casas merits citing in its entirety, not only for its

---

[10] In 1914, Julián Juderías, a conservative official of the Spanish Crown, would belatedly name and defensively describe what he considered an anti-Spanish propaganda campaign. See Gibson (1971) for an instructive synopsis of this campaign.
[11] Fuchs's *Mimesis and Empire*, portions of which I was privileged to read in manuscript, is forthcoming from Cambridge University Press.

self-congratulatory rhetoric, but also because it remits us to the
discourse of cannibalism that may have provided, or at least
contributed to, the Coleridgean 'germ' of *Robinson Crusoe.*

Deliberating about whether or not to attack some 'twenty or
thirty naked Savages' who 'eat humane Flesh', Crusoe eventually decides against the act because these people have done
him no injury and, therefore, it would not be just to fall upon
them (1994*a*: 123–4). More to the point, such an act would
'justify the Conduct of the *Spaniards* in all their Barbarities
practis'd in *America,* where they destroy'd Millions of these
People, who however they were Idolaters and Barbarians,
and had several bloody and barbarous Rites in their Customs,
such as sacrificing human Bodies to their Idols, were yet, as to
the *Spaniards,* very innocent People' (1994*a*: 124). Thus far,
Crusoe could be recycling the arguments of Montaigne in
'Des cannibales', which suggested, as is well known, that the
Europeans were more cannibals than the cannibals. But when
Crusoe alludes to the abhorrence of 'the *Spaniards* themselves'
toward their own New World atrocities, his tirade clearly alludes
to, and even appears to paraphrase, Las Casas's attack on his
own countrymen. The act of 'rooting' all these 'innocent' New
World peoples out of their countries, Crusoe declares,

is spoken of with the utmost Abhorrence and Detestation, by even
the *Spaniards* themselves, at this Time; and by all other Christian
Nations of *Europe,* as a meer Butchery, a bloody and unnatural Piece
of Cruelty, unjustifiable either to God or Man; and such, as for which
the very Name of a *Spaniard* is reckon'd to be frightful and terrible to
all People of Humanity, or of Christian Compassion. (1994*a*: 124–5)

Throughout this impassioned passage—which cannibalizes and
telescopes Las Casas's devastating *Brevísima relación*—Robinson
Crusoe meticulously mimes the great defender of the American
Indians against the Spanish colonists in order to set himself and
his nation above both. Crusoe concludes his attack by calling
Spain 'particularly Eminent for the Product of a Race of Men,
who were without Principles of Tenderness, or the common
Bowels of Pity to the Miserable, which is reckon'd to be a Mark
of generous Temper in the Mind' (1994*a*: 125).

Keeping in mind those 'Bowels of Pity', let us compare the
novels of Cervantes and Defoe for their enactment of what
Crusoe calls those 'bloody and barbarous Rites'. What kind

of direction does the New World trope of cannibalism take in
its transnational and cross-cultural itinerary from Cervantes
to Defoe, from Spanish to English imperialism? The direction, to be graphed below, seems to tally with the state of the
empire of each writer as he novelizes. Soon after the decline
of the Spanish empire, the English begin anticipating their
own imperial era—an age of colonization and lucrative oceanic
trading monopolies. By the seventeenth century, England
would surpass Spain and Portugal in the acquisition of fluid
wealth, the force behind mercantile prosperity. The discourse
of cannibalism appears to function as a barometer of these rises
and falls. Whereas Cervantes deploys a rebarbative episode of
ritual cannibalism as a conventional satirical topos for political
ends—to *demonize* imperial evolution—Defoe uses the grosser
representation of gustatory cannibalism as a 'tool of empire',
in William Arens's phrase, as a narrative to *support* imperial
evolution.[12]

4. RITUAL CANNIBALISM IN CERVANTES

The proclivities of Caribbean cannibals were well known to
Cervantes, as may be seen by the comic curse he puts into the
mouth of Pedro de Urdemalas, the titular character of a *comedia*
who has been to the Indies and returned penniless: 'May bad
cannibals eat you!' ('¡Cómante malos caribes!') (1991 *d*: ii. 651).
The cannibals in Cervantes's *Persiles*, as what follows will show,
are bad cannibals, although not because they eat people. The
New World hallmarks of these cannibals are unmistakable:
they trade in gold and pearls, fight with bows and arrows, communicate by signs or through a kidnapped female interpreter,
and sail about in rafts constructed with *bejucos*—a specifically
Caribbean (*taíno*) signifier to be discussed in Chapter 4, below.
Cervantes's cannibals live on a 'Barbaric Isle' located somewhere
(and thus nowhere) in Europe and yet also in America. As
locative and evasive as La Mancha, that strategically 'forgettable'
site that opens *Don Quixote*, the Barbaric Isle is a meeting place

---

[12] Arens's influential 1979 book, *The Man-Eating Myth*, inaugurated the contemporary debate about cannibalism: does it or doesn't it really exist? The jury is
still out on this one.

for the topographical dualism that inaugurates the *Persiles*: Europe versus the New World. Like Thomas More's Utopians —who tend their English gardens somewhere off the coast of Amerigo Vespucci's Brazil—Cervantes's cannibals straddle both sides of an imperial divide: they inhabit the discursive ground of two mutually contradictory topographies and two mutually incompatible signifying worlds.

This kind of unstable habitation will not surprise anyone familiar with American readings of Shakespeare's *Tempest*, as forcefully instanced by Peter Hulme (1986), who highlighted the play's transatlantic colonial discourse. Aiming for a simultaneous description of *all* the relevant colonial contexts of *The Tempest*, including those of Ireland and the Mediterranean, Barbara Fuchs asks her readers: 'When is America not America? When it is Ireland, or North Africa, or Europe itself or the no-man's land (really every man's *desired* land) of the Mediterranean in-between' (1997: 62, 45). I would invert Fuchs's generative question in order to further contextualize the opening of the *Persiles*. When is Europe not Europe? When it is a barbaric island located somewhere in between European and American discourse. The cannibals who live on this barbaric Cervantine island are themselves a compromise formation, existing only within discourse and well beyond the bounds of representation. In this they resemble Shakespeare's Caliban, whom Peter Hulme depicts as being the ground of two discourses, English and American.[13] Unlike Caliban, however, Cervantes's cannibals are explicitly sutured to the custom of ritual cannibalism. They practise a kind of cardiophagy or 'heart-ash cannibalism' whose probable source, Inca Garcilaso de la Vega, is addressed in Chapter 8, below.

An extremely complex sign, the cannibalism in the *Persiles* is of the cooked—we might even say the *burnt*—variety. Cervantes's cannibals ritually swallow a drink made with ashes of the charred hearts of sacrificed males. These cannibals, in fact, sacrifice and consume *only* males, perhaps following a hearsay New World tradition described in 1500 by Amerigo Vespucci: 'non mangiano femmina nessuna'.[14] The historiographer Peter

---

[13] I am indebted to Hulme's insightful discussion of Shakespeare's *Tempest* (1986: 88–134).

[14] Vespucci's description of cannibals, in a letter dated 18 July 1500, may be found in Levillier's edn. of *El nuevo mundo* (1951).

Martyr reiterated this food prohibition in 1511, when he testified that eating women was considered, by New World cannibals, 'impious and obscene': 'Mulieres comedere apud eos nephas est et obscenum.'[15] The cannibals in the *Persiles* consume powdered male hearts as a way to foretell the father of their forthcoming Messiah, a man destined to be a super-imperialist—a world conqueror (1969: 57). This is a far cry from the 'survival cannibalism' represented in Cervantes's *Numancia*, where the besieged Numantines—'barbarians' fighting for their liberty against an aggressor Roman empire—are given orders to kill and dole out the dismembered bodies of Roman prisoners in order to nourish the besieged.[16] In contrast to this Cervantine allegorical drama, the cannibalism in the *Persiles* is connected to the initiation of, not the resistance to, empire. Instead of giving us cannibals who are *other*—either as frightful savages or as pitiable victims of European imperialism—Cervantes represents them as great empire builders themselves. By sidestepping virtually every identification given them by European categories of thought and cultural presuppositions, Cervantes's cannibals cause the kind of disturbance that, as Michel de Certeau argues in *Heterologies*, calls into question the whole symbolic order (1986: 70).

Cervantes, in short, scrambles the European binary that placed imperialism on the side of civility and cannibalism on the side of barbary to produce—in the spirit of Sancho Panza's basin-helmet ('baciyelmo')—a tribe of imperial cannibals. Imperialism here meets in cannibalism the figure of its own desire. This conflation would seem to be a postmodern and post-colonial practice—what Peter Hulme, in a different context, calls 'the self-reflective analysis of imperialism as itself a form of cannibalism' (1998: 5). Cervantes aligns himself with both Montaigne and his most important source, Jean de Léry, in suggesting that cannibalism is a phenomenon equally at home in Europe or the Americas. As Jean de Léry had wryly put it, 'it is not necessary to go to America to see such monstrous things'.[17] Unlike Montaigne, however, Cervantes

---

[15] Martyr's gendered eating prohibition is in the first 'Decade' of the 1511 *De orbe novo*. See Petrus Martyr de Angleria (1966: 40–1). See also Martyr (1912: 63).

[16] See Frederick A. de Armas's classic (1998) study of the epic elements in *La Numancia*.

[17] Cited by Forsyth (1985: 30).

does not idealize his cannibals. The ritual cannibalism in the *Persiles* denounces, even demonizes, cannibals—not as man-eaters but as world conquerors—as men who 'utterly consume your cities' (to borrow a phrase from Marlowe's *Tamburlaine*). Virtually on his deathbed, then, Cervantes is telling the Spaniards an allegory about themselves as imperialists.

5. GUSTATORY CANNIBALISM IN DEFOE

Defoe is also telling his countrymen a story about themselves, but a more self-congratulatory story. Where Cervantes suggested the need to look within to understand why a tribe of cannibalizing barbarians should behave like imperial Spaniards —why these cannibals were every inch a projection of European territorial fantasies—Defoe entirely eschews this kind of bracing self-reflection. All readers remember the classic moment when Robinson Crusoe finds 'the Print of a Man's naked Foot on the Shore' and is overwhelmed with fear, shock, and even insomnia: 'I slept none that Night', he tells his journal (1994a: 112). Some three years later, Crusoe encounters the traces of a cannibal barbecue on the beach—'Skulls, Hands, Feet, and other Bones of humane Bodies'—a discovery that makes him vomit 'with an uncommon Violence' (1994a: 119–20). What is Defoe up to here?

Upholding tribal or national pieties often requires the construction of 'otherness', which is why Defoe relocates cannibalism 'out there'—represents it as a barbaric practice on some Caribbean outpost of the empire, well beyond the reach (to cite Crusoe himself) of 'people of Humanity, or of Christian compassion'. Crusoe invokes cannibals, in short, as an image of what English society is *not*. Indeed, he is very explicit about this distinction between 'Us' and 'Them': 'I . . . gave God thanks that had cast my first Lot in a Part of the World [England] where I was distinguish'd from such dreadful Creatures as these' (1994a: 120). Not unlike the Spaniards' own earlier discourses on cannibals—Peter Martyr, for instance, had depicted them as 'barbarians' and 'monsters' (1912: 63)—Crusoe's prayer of thanks here instances the kind of arrogant European conscience that attempts to consolidate itself by imagining a savage other. Crusoe's imperial narrative of 'dreadful' cannibals, in fact, fortifies the sanctimonious tissue of myth and self-infatuation that, until the end of World War II, would disfigure England's career as a colonial power. We English can never *be* cannibals, Crusoe suggests, but neither should we *kill* cannibals, since that would equate us with the Spaniards. At pains to differentiate the English from their Spanish competitors, Crusoe raises the cannibals to put down Spaniards. This upgrading of cannibals represents a remarkably transparent about-face, given that earlier in the same episode Crusoe had impugned them as 'Savage Wretches' and 'dreadful Creatures'. In his more Lascasian mimetic mode, however, he calls them a 'very innocent People' when compared 'to the *Spaniards*' in America (1994*a*: 120 and 124). Crusoe creates a very handy hierarchy here, with the 'compassionate' English at the top, the 'innocent' Caribbean cannibals in the middle, and the 'frightful and terrible' Spaniards at the bottom. These English attacks on the pitiless Spaniards (those men lacking in 'Bowels of Pity') were a commonplace by the time Defoe was writing. As early as the 1580s, Hakluyt had represented the Spaniards, in a strikingly orientalist comparison, as having 'executed most outrageous and more than Turkish cruelties in all the West Indies' (1935: 212). The colourful grammar of Hakluyt's phrase, may, in fact, have haunted Defoe, whose 1702 poem 'A Reformation of Manners' includes a high-minded attack on slavers for their 'more than *Spanish* Cruelty' (Keane 1997: 102).

Crusoe's imitation of Las Casas rings hollow because of the conflict between Crusoe's spiritual and imperial longings. Not only does he represent himself, at various points in his narrative, as lord, master, governor, majesty, and emperor of his domains, but also, as the leader of an 'Army' of eight men, Crusoe fashions himself, via an Italian superlative, as their *generalissimo* (1994*a*: 192). His overdetermined rage against the cannibals suggests that he is projecting his own territorial desires onto these figures. Every inch an imperialist—a would-be slave trader, a proto-capitalist, and a mini-conqueror—Crusoe can still invoke all the evangelical pieties. James Joyce famously identified Crusoe as 'the true symbol of the British conquest', portraying him as a figure who embodied 'the whole Anglo-Saxon spirit': 'the manly independence; the unconscious cruelty; the persistence; the slow yet efficient intelligence; the sexual apathy; the practical, well-balanced religiousness; the calculating taciturnity' (1994: 323). Marthe Robert adapted this view of Crusoe to present him as a symbol of the British novel, a genre she personified as a lawless 'conqueror' and an adventurous 'colonizer'. Robert's heroic simile—her comparison between an expanding, appropriating, and monopolizing genre and the English 'imperialistic society from which it sprang' (1980: 4)— could also be applied to earlier imperialistic societies, such as the Roman or the Spanish ones. The manly, religious, and taciturn qualities of Robinson Crusoe—the hero of England's 'conquering' genre—may also be found in Cervantes, although less in his Europeans than in his cannibals.

Although both Cervantes and Defoe were fictionalizing cannibalism in the colonial world, Cervantes was writing at the end of an exhausted and bankrupt Spanish empire, an empire 'waiting for the barbarians' (which he would handily supply). Defoe, on the other hand, was writing at the beginnings of a nascent English empire, an empire whose 'Principles of Tenderness' did not exclude the lucrative practice of becoming 'a *Guiney* Trader' (1994*a*: 15), Crusoe's prospective career before his two-year captivity in the Muslim-held Maghreb. Decades later he will berate himself for having tried, while a planter in the 'Brasils', to resume that aborted career:

and what Business had I to leave a settled Fortune, a well stock'd Plantation, improving and encreasing, to turn *Supra-Cargo* to *Guinea*, to fetch Negroes; when Patience and Time would have so encreas'd our Stock at Home, that we could have bought them at our own Door, from those whose Business it was to fetch them. (1994*a*: 141)

Crusoe's 'ORIGINAL SIN', as the text trumpets it in capitals, was not in *buying* negroes but in having sailed off to *fetch* them (1994*a*: 141). It was this 'sin' that led to his shipwreck. When he talks about doing 'wrong', Patrick Keane writes in a discussion of slave traffic that connects Crusoe to Defoe, it is not a moral error (1997: 99).

6. 'SPHANISHED' EMPIRES

Almost three centuries have passed since Crusoe vomited over those cannibal traces—long enough for the rise and fall of both the English empire and the Wattian theory of the novel that helped sustain it. The idea that Cervantes and Defoe were instrumental in the rises of their respective national novels is by now a commonplace. The idea that two texts as different as the *Persiles* and *Robinson Crusoe* would rise and converge—that the first may have provided the 'germ' of the second—is scarcely a commonplace, but neither is it novel: Coleridge aired it some 200 years ago—to a deaf audience, it would seem. The idea that these two texts—emerging out of different nations, languages, and religions—would converge in some insular Caribbean mindscape is perhaps novel but remains inert until we unpack the trope of cannibalism shared by Cervantes and Defoe. Whether ritually swallowing the ashes of human hearts, as in Cervantes, or 'inhumanely' feasting upon 'humane Bodies', as in Defoe, these cannibals serve as rapacious projections of European fantasies of consumption. But they also serve to show us what Antonio Benítez-Rojo calls 'the glorious cannibalism of men and of words, *carib, calib, cannibal, Caliban*' (1992: 13). The different European nationals who claimed to have encountered cannibals in the Caribbean—*and* in the novels that rose and converged there—did, in fact, have to eat each others' words.

To sum up, then. This chapter has tried to suggest Defoe's indebtedness both to Cervantes and to an Iberian culture whose imperial primacy had 'sphanished'—to borrow a coinage from Joyce's *Finnegans Wake*—but whose traces were still dominant in the Caribbean when Crusoe was shipwrecked there. In addition, and with the support of Coleridge, I have tried to indicate how deeply both Cervantes and Defoe were indebted to the Caribbean, and to its alleged cannibals, in their attempts to 'novelize' about their respective imperial cultures. Imagery of the New World proliferates in, as well as motivates, these narratives that will struggle to become the modern novel—an expanding, expropriating, and monopolizing genre in both its Spanish and English beginnings.

4

Some Versions of Hybridity:
cacao and *Potosí*

THIS chapter will pick at one thread in the Spanish 'national strand' of the novel: the cultural and literary metaphor of hybridity. If, indeed, the novel rises at multiple times and places in history, as suggested in the previous chapters, let us consider why the genre rises with special vigour in locations of culture that tolerate, and sometimes even value, hybridity. The main focus of this chapter is the phenomenon of hybridity in Cervantes's two long novels, which I hope to elucidate with some theoretical glances backwards and forwards—at the Graeco-Latin novel in antiquity and at some versions of hybridity emerging from the heated debates within colonial and post-colonial theory in our day. After examining one of Cervantes's most striking linguistic hybrids—his coinage of a phrase juxtaposing the Aztec term *cacao* with estimates of value among Spain's 'nation' of gypsies— we shall turn to the various uses, in his two novels, of an idiom newly constituted during his lifetime: 'to be worth a *Potosí*' (*valer un Potosí*). In both of these expressions, Cervantes uses New World terms for currency—one in Nahuatl, the other in Aymara—to enrich Old World utterances about worth. The result is a Cervantine hybrid, a cross between two different linguistic configurations which is sometimes, but not always, asymmetric. A close look at these two hybrids paves the way for a survey of hybridity in *Don Quixote* and the *Persiles* respectively.

1. HYBRIDITY, TRANSCULTURATION, HETEROGENEITY

The arguments that follow presume neither a historical nor a theoretical coverage of hybridity, a concept deriving from the discipline of biology to become a post-colonial entity and, in some quarters, an anti-colonial strategy. As a metaphor for the cross between two different biological or botanical species, hybridity has become a familiar term in cultural history and politics. Given its frequent use in discussions of racial identity, it is often entangled with belligerent value judgements. At present hybridity jostles with a cluster of related but by no means similar concepts, all carrying their own ideological baggage: *mestizaje*, creolization, bastardy, in-betweenness, syncretism, mongrelization, alterity, transculturation, neoculturation, and heterogeneity. Homi Bhabha's uses of hybridity, to be addressed later in this chapter, remain the most influential, and perhaps the most controversial, within Anglo-American post-colonial studies.

Both hybridity and its related categories, however, have received intense theoretical scrutiny from distinguished Latin American thinkers such as Antonio Cornejo Polar, Nestor García Canclini, and Ángel Rama. These categories feature prominently in recent attempts to produce a theoretical apparatus that will do justice to the profound conflicts in Latin American cultures and literatures. Over two decades ago, Cornejo Polar proposed the category of 'heterogeneity' to describe historical processes rooted in these cultural and literary conflicts (1982: 67–85). His concept of 'heterogeneity' has been described, with emphasis added, as the semiotic acts emerging from real world heterogeneity and implying 'the *profound and honest comprehension of the alternative culture*' ('la comprensión *profunda y honesta de la cultura alternativa*') (Bueno 1996: 34). Along with the other categories mentioned above—all provisional modes for thinking about the effects of cultural crossovers—heterogeneity has been the target of many recent polemics.[1]

Another category that has also received sustained reflection among Latin America thinkers is *transculturation*, a related and belated neologism coined in the 1940s by Fernando Ortiz as a substitute for the demeaning anthropological concept, hatched in North American universities, of 'acculturation'. The process

[1] See the recent *homenaje* for Cornejo Polar titled *Asedios a la Heterogeneidad Cultural*, which contains an impressive cluster of theoretical essays on cultural and literary heterogeneity.

of transculturation, which involves the transfer of cultural con-
tents and practices from one culture to another, requires some
retooling when applied to literary works, a task handily explained
in Ángel Rama's important work on narrative transculturation
(1985: 32–56). Walter Mignolo opts for transculturation over
hybridity, although he shares the concept of 'spaces in between'
with Homi Bhabha (1995: p. xvi)—a concept that Cervantes,
as I hope to show in what follows, shares with them both.
Transculturation is also the preferred term for Doris Sommer,
who claims that it distinguishes 'the unresolvable, often violent
tension among cultures in conflict from the neat resolutions of
difference suggested by such ideal concepts for *costumbrismo*
as syncretism, hybridity, or *mestizaje*' (1996: 121–2). Unlike the
'violent tension' that Sommer finds in transculturation, however, Cornejo Polar claims that the concept is not problematic
enough, that it implies a synthesis of contradictions, a 'more or
less unproblematic unity' ('una unidad más o menos desprob-
lematizada') (1996: 55). In a densely argued and much cited
article, Cornejo Polar calls for the formulation of a theoretical
category that would make sense of discourses in which 'the
dynamics of multiple crossovers would *not* function syncretically
but, on the contrary, would emphasize conflicts and alterities'
('las dinámicas de los entrecruzamientos *no* operan en función
sincrética sino, al revés, enfatizan conflictos y alteridades') (1996:
55). It is precisely in this context that Cornejo Polar invokes
García Canclini's theory of hybridity, which de-emphasizes
('desenfatiza') the syncretic function (1996: 55). Elsewhere he
celebrates García Canclini's theory, which acknowledges different
historical forms of hybridity, for 'its immersion in history' ('su
inmersion en la historia').[2] Despite these polemics over nomenclature, it is clear that most Latin American thinkers today rightly
eschew any culturalist uses of the term *hybridity* that celebrate
either the unities or the pieties.

Bakhtin's important contributions to the concept of hybridity are also deeply immersed in history—largely the history
of the novel—although instead of emphasizing conflicts and
alterity they emphasize dialogue. To what degree Bakhtin's

---

[2] This passage is from Cornejo Polar's last paper—'Mestizaje e hibridez: Los ries-
gos de las metáforas. Apuntes'—presented at the XXI Conference of the Association of Latinamerican Studies (LASA) in Guadalajara, Mexico, in Apr. 1997, and
distributed through e-mail by José Mazzoti of Harvard University.

unsystematic thinking would enrich any of the above polemics remains to be seen. Although Cornejo Polar complained in 1988 that the use of Bakhtinian theory had caused almost all Latin American authors to be 'carnivalized' (1989: 46), he later allowed that Bakhtin's category of dialogism might help to sharpen ('afinar') his own literary perspectives on heterogeneity (1996: 55). Rita de Grandis, who discusses Bakhtin's discursive concept of hybridity in relation to García Canclini's theory, sees hybridization as a process and a condition for both thinkers: in Bakhtin's case, it is a linguistic condition; in García Canclini's, a condition of popular culture and its symbolic goods (1997: 294). Bakhtin's analysis of the novel as a hybrid formation could provide, de Grandis claims, 'a fertile field' ('un campo fértil') for the development of hybridity by post-colonial critics (1997: 292). Such a development, one hopes, would be more open to reciprocal influences. Perhaps it would include some further 'transculturation' between Anglo- and Latin-American critics of hybridity, with the former citing García Canclini in the same spirit of enquiry as the latter cite Homi Bhabha.

This chapter uses the term *hybridity*, not only because of its immersion in history but also because of its reliance on dialogue. Although the term embraces cultural as well as linguistic mixtures, I am concerned in this chapter with intentional linguistic practices that sometimes, though not always, smuggle in racial or religious issues. The patterns of hybridity invoked sporadically in connection with Cervantes, or with his classical novelistic precursors, are deeply immersed in history. But as what follows will show, some of these patterns are also dispersed in geography—specifically in American locations of culture that make them inseparable from colonial studies. These Cervantine patterns are not especially celebratory nor harmonious. They do not function, in a syncretic way, to fabricate resolution or to forge consensus. One argument of this chapter is that patterns of hybridity work, rather, to forge novelistic discourse— that they are, indeed, the inescapable cultural condition of it.

In a persuasive polemic against the 'phantom category' of Commonwealth Literature, Salman Rushdie discusses the 'transnational, cross-lingual process of pollination' just now taking place among deprived minorities living in powerful countries, a process that he rightly claims is 'not new'. Looking for commonalities in this kind of literature, Rushdie instances the

work of a Muslim Russian writer, Fazil Iskander, which 'finds
its parallels', he concludes, in the work of Cervantes (1991:
68–9). It is something like this transnational, cross-lingual
pollination process that I am affiliating with hybridity. What
Rushdie responds to in Cervantes is the discourse of a writer
who articulates a between-world condition in early modern
Spain, who creates a space of representation where, as the examples in this chapter will show, Spanish wealth is metaphor-
ized by indigenous American signifiers—*cacao* and *Potosí*—and
connected to poverty, exploitation, and even police torture.

2. HYBRIDITY IN THE GRAECO-LATIN NOVEL

Patterns of hybridity have an ancient history and have been stud-
ied under different names. Margaret Anne Doody reminds us
of the term *Alexandrian*, which 'stands for that which is racially
mixed, impure, and cosmopolitan' (1996: 8). The term itself
was resurrected by the young Nietzsche, who lamented that his
own age was 'entangled in the web of Alexandrian culture'.
Nietzsche found a handy target to vilify in the perpetrator
of what he considered the artful bourgeois lies of the Greek
novel: 'Alexandrian man, who is at bottom a librarian and
a corrector of proofs' (1956: 109–10). Alexandrian writers,
however—Heliodorus, Apuleius, and others—served as avowed
models for Cervantes. Preoccupied with the progressivist
argument that *Don Quixote's* earliest readers were resistant to its
cruelties, Nietzsche overlooked the Alexandrian to focus on the
depressive aspects of Cervantes's novel: 'Today we read *Don
Quixote* with a bitter taste in our mouths, almost with a feeling
of torment and would thus seem very strange and incompre-
hensible to its author and his contemporaries: they read it with
the clearest conscience in the world as the most cheerful of
books, they laughed themselves almost to death over it' (1967:
66). Even granting Nietzsche his age of bitterness, this is a romantic fantasy of a unified reading culture in Cervantes's day.
The author of the apocryphal sequel to *Don Quixote*, Alonso
Fernández de Avellaneda, certainly read *Don Quixote* 'with a
bitter taste' in his mouth, given his subsequent attack on
Cervantes for being crippled, old, and friendless (1980: 3–5).
Early modern readers who knew anything about Erasmus and

More would have been alert to the ironies of the serio-comic genres, the kinds of literature that challenged both the cheerfulness and clear conscience that Nietzsche tries to project onto the era. As a writer who specifically turned to the 'bourgeois lies' of the Greek novel as a model—and whose works disclose a startling degree of fondness for mixed and impure forms— Cervantes could be fittingly catalogued under the rubric of Alexandrian man. The Alexandrian web deplored by Nietzsche, moreover, is fast becoming a world wide web.

Although he did not use the term 'Alexandrine', Bakhtin tried to theorize manifestations of hybridity in lower Italy during the Hellenistic era, noting its 'hybrid culture and hybrid literary forms', its 'bilingualism' and even 'trilingualism' (1981: 63). In Bakhtin's depictions of the long prehistory of novelistic discourse, he sees it as a consciously structured hybrid of languages that 'always developed on the boundary line between cultures and languages', and that constituted itself as a genre through, among other things, a multilingual consciousness (1981: 50). This consciousness emerged at points of cultural and linguistic intersection throughout the whole Hellenistic world, as Bakhtin notes, in 'centers, cities, settlements where several cultures and languages cohabited, interweaving with one another in distinctive patterns' (1981: 64). Pondering that cohabitation of different languages in certain sites of antiquity, one wonders whether bilingualism was even then a suspect quality, whether it had those 'overtones of deceitfulness' that twentieth-century sociolinguistic studies have found in it (Cohen 1975: 7). If so, bilingualism would affiliate itself naturally with the genre of the novel, especially during the early modern period, when the great critical task for many readers, as thematized in *Don Quixote*, was to separate fiction from lying.

Despite all his acknowledgements of a multilingual consciousness in the Hellenistic world, in the end Bakhtin withholds the term *novel* from what he calls antiquity's 'pre-novelistic discourse': 'the ancient world', he concludes, 'did not succeed in generating forms and unities that were adequate to the private individual and his life' (1981: 110). Although ancient novelistic discourse—Apuleius and Petronius are his examples—'prepared the ground for the novel', Bakhtin argues that it 'could not at that time gather unto itself and make use of all the material that language images had made available' (1981: 60).

Elsewhere Bakhtin claims that 'the Greek novel only weakly embodied this new discourse that resulted from polyglot consciousness' (1981: 65). The novel's potential 'came to light only in the modern world' with *Don Quixote,* which represents, in Bakhtin's somewhat rigid teleology of progress, 'the classic and purest model of the novel as genre' (1981: 40, 324).

Bakhtin's tendency to see the ancient novel as a static entity —as having no potential for growth, change, or evolution—has been strongly contested by various scholars, who see him as indulging, on this issue, in a version of 'pastoralism' (Doody 1996: 2), or as reducing all the events in Greek novels 'to a mere parenthesis' (Konstan 1994: 11). Although I agree with these judgements, I am less concerned here with Bakhtin's generic nomenclature for Greek fictions than with his prescient descriptions of the hybrid culture underwriting the pre-novelistic discourse of the Hellenistic world. Hybridity is a startling feature of the Greek novel *Ethiopika,* the major and avowed subtext of Cervantes's *Persiles*—advertised in the Prologue to the *Novelas ejemplares* as 'a book which dares to compete with Heliodorus' ('libro que se atreve a competir con Heliodoro'). Indeed, Doody was not excessive in regarding Cervantes as 'perhaps the world's most attentive reader of Heliodorus' (1989).

On the Latin front, Bakhtin was more aware of Cervantes's familiarity with Apuleius, another writer displaying a hybrid consciousness. Bakhtin acknowledges that *The Golden Ass* was the main subtext of Don Quixote's famous battle with the wineskins, an Apuleian shard that noisily interrupts the priest's reading of *The Curious Impertinent* (*El curioso impertinente,* 1. 35) (Bakhtin 1984*a*: 209 n.). But fragments of Apuleius also appear in various other places in the Cervantine canon, as, for example, in the antidote of roses mentioned in *The Colloquy of the Dogs* (*El coloquio de los perros*), a prescription that handily reverses a metamorphosis: 'I only wish', Berganza tells Cipión, 'that it were as easy as the one noted by Apuleius in *The Golden Ass,* which consists in merely eating a rose' ('quisiera yo que fuera tan fácil como el que se dice de Apuleyo en *El Asno de oro,* que consistía en solo comer una rosa') (1975*b*: ii. 294). Another affinity between *The Golden Ass* and *Don Quixote* was remarked by Thomas Mann, who astutely suggested that Cervantes's 'extraordinary tale' of the braying ass-men in *Don Quixote* (2. 25 and 2. 27) might be 'a reminiscence' of the Graeco-Roman representational world of Apuleius, in which the ass, like Sancho Panza, is repeatedly beaten for braying (1965: 450). Yet another Cervantine homage to Apuleius, this one quite unambiguous, is found in the Countess Ruperta episode of the *Persiles*, a grotesque chivalric recycling of the Cupid and Psyche story in *The Golden Ass*.[3]

Speculating on why the Greek novels are 'all too often located in non-Greek lands, populated with non-Greek characters, and preoccupied with non-Greek cultures', Susan A. Stephens and John J. Winkler conclude, in their edition of *Ancient Greek Novels*, that a 'fascination with the "other" may lie at the heart of the novel form or somewhere along its periphery' (1995: 18). Like the ancient novel, which arose within an expanding multilingual empire, the Cervantine novel also rises through a fascination with the 'other', sometimes located on the fringes of Spain's own national preserve—gypsies, Basques, *moriscos*— sometimes in its American colonies. Also like the ancient novel, the Cervantine novel—the *Persiles* even more than *Don Quixote* —rises from these 'polyglot energies' and positions itself on the border between multiple cultures and languages. Although not the only instances of linguistic hybridity in Cervantes, this chapter focuses on two New World signifiers specifically concerned with spheres of economic activity: the Mexican *cacao* and the Andean *Potosí*.

3. IMPORTING *CACAO*

To determine when a foreign word becomes 'integrated' into a native language is always problematic, and it is certainly not the aim of our argument. What interests us here is not *when* but *where* the American term *cacao* arrives. Cervantes imports the term to insert it into the lexicon of his fictional gypsies. The great Spanish lexicographer Sebastián de Covarrubias Orozco, Cervantes's contemporary, never mentions *cacao* in his *Tesoro* (1611). Nor is the word to be found in the various collections of proverbs (*refraneros*) or dictionaries of *marginalismos* of the Spanish Golden Age. Joan Corominas's modern critical-etymological dictionary, however, derives *cacao* from the Nahuatl term *kakáwa*, and traces the phrase *no valer un cacao* exclusively back to

---

[3] See Wilson (1994).

Cervantes's *La gitanilla,* explaining it through the use of *cacao* as coinage ('moneda') in Mexico (1991: i. 719). That no other writer is mentioned in this entry suggests, although it does not prove, that Cervantes provides the earliest use of the phrase in Golden Age literature. What can be proved with some certainty is that his transgressive use of loan words from across national and cultural borders intensifies after the 1605 publication of *Don Quixote,* Part 1.

A glance at the specific use Cervantes makes of *cacao* in *La gitanilla,* the liminal novella of his *Exemplary Novels (Novelas ejemplares,* 1613), may be instructive, as it emblematizes both the linguistic hybridity and the American reach of his longer novels. Alban A. Forcione notes that the anthropological comments of the gypsy elder ('gitano viejo') in that novella—his remarks on how the gypsies practice 'much incest but no adultery' ('aunque hay muchos incestos, no hay ningún adulterio')—are modelled on the truant sexual desires of 'a tribe of south American Indians described in a contemporary chronicle of exploration' (1982: 189). South American Indians may also have provided the subtext for the ceremonial execution of Andrés Caballero's mule in Cervantes's story, which includes burial with all its trappings 'in the style of the Indians' ('a uso de indios')—a custom that, as Jorge Campos notes, may point to 'the Peruvian huacas' ('las huacas peruanas') (1947: 395). But it was the Aztecs who gave Cervantes the currency he needed to depict a more surprising phenomenon than marriage and burial customs: the gypsy custom of disdain for torture.

Cervantes's gypsy elder offers readers a vivid example of hybridity when he invokes Aztec currency to explain his culture's stoic, even dismissive, attitudes to police brutality or to rowing in the galleys: 'neither having the lash tickle our backs nor paddling water in the galleys is worth one cocoa bean to us' ('[ni] el mosqueo de las espaldas, ni el apalear el agua en las galeras, no lo estimamos en un cacao') (1975*a*: i. 74–5). This utterance of the Nahuatl word *cacao* as a coin of exchange nods to the multilingual consciousness-raising that occurred during the age of Iberian conquest. In his study *Quixotic Scriptures,* Elias L. Rivers has discussed the mixing of Spanish and native languages in Latin America, a phenomenon he calls 'diglossic [or triglossic] symbiosis' and regards as 'a basic sociolinguistic situation in significant areas' of the continent (1983*b*: 139–40). More recently Martín Lienhard discusses 'linguistic diglossia' ('*diglosia linguística*'), which he sees as an asymmetric practice of bilingualism, given the 'unequal social prestige' of two languages within colonial situations (1996: 72–9). Cervantes's phrase 'it's not worth a cocoa bean to us' ('*no lo estimamos en un cacao*') is diglossic but not, it would seem, asymmetric. In this utterance the more 'prestigious' language of Castilian is being deployed by a marginated culture, Spanish gypsies, who invoke Nahuatl, the language of an equally marginated American culture, to describe their victimization.

Spain's inner and outer 'others', in short, are harnessed together here in a potential transatlantic dialogue about values. Such a dialogue had been a century in the making. Long before Cervantes's fictional gypsies were invoking the cocoa nugget to show their disdain for both torture and money, the Milanese humanist and historiographer Peter Martyr had celebrated *cacao* in *De Orbe Novo*, a text available to Cervantes, as the ideal currency because it made gold worthless: 'cocoa gives to the human race a useful and delightful drink, but also prevents its possessors from yielding to infernal avarice, for it cannot be piled up, or hoarded for a long time' (1912: ii. 112). In a later book, Martyr explains how 'rewarding' it is to hear what a 'happy currency' ('foelici moneta') the New World inhabitants use: 'for they have money which I call *happy*, because they obtain it by merely scratching the earth, and because neither the envy of the avaricious nor the terrors of war cause it to return to its subterranean hiding-place, as happens with gold or silver' (1912: ii. 354–5). When Cervantes's gypsies allude to this 'happy' currency in Nahuatl, readers are asked to consider two different linguistic domains of interaction. But Cervantes's gypsy elder does not merely compare an indigenous American to a peninsular minoritarian language group. He uses the phrase *no valer un cacao* to show Spaniards—both in and out of his text—the disdain of the gypsy 'nation' for the police who hound them and the judges who sentence them to the galleys.

Spain had been legislating against its 'egipcianos'—the legal and etymological term for its reviled gypsies—since 1499, in a series of stern proclamations and in a language very close to the stereotypes rehearsed at the opening of *La gitanilla*, which are catalogued after a telling expression of doubt: 'it would seem that' ('parece que') (1975*a*: i. 3). As one of the most recalcitrant elements of Spain's body politic, the gypsies were subject to surveillance, torture, and repeated expulsions. They were also discursively positioned outside the national teleology. The entry on *gitanos* in Covarrubias's *Tesoro*—published in 1611, during the expulsions and a few years prior to Cervantes's fictions about gypsies—vilifies them not only as 'manifest thieves' ('ladrones manifiestos') but also as a 'lost and vagabond race, restless, deceitful, lying' ('gente perdida y vagabunda, inquieta, engañadora, embustidora') (1994: 590–1). Covarrubias also documents that the gypsies are 'severly punished' in Spain ('los castigan severamente'), the men being ritually thrown into the galleys ('a galeras') (1994: 591). In the wake of Cervantes's fiction, however, these reviled peoples could also be classified as a nation (he explicitly calls them 'esta nación') involved in some curious transatlantic coalitions with Mexican Indians. Cervantes's hybridizing move establishes a bond between Spain's internal gypsies and her ultramarine *indios*. Even as they import *cacao* into their lexicon, Cervantes's gypsies are searching the New World for resistant values to the Old World. Through this cultural alterity—which complicates the reigning cliché that gypsies were, as Covarrubias summed it up for the age, a 'wretched peoples' ('ruin gente') (1994: 591)—Cervantes intervenes in one of the crucial debates of the postmodern: the ethics of using stereotypes to locate the 'other', the marginal person, in a position of inferiority. By having his fictional gypsies look to America for a currency to describe their defiance of the Spanish authorities, Cervantes punctures the stereotypes that portray them as 'manifest thieves' of silver and gold—of those less 'happy' peninsular currencies.

4. MINING *POTOSÍ*

Compared to Cervantes's use of the Nahuatl term *cacao*, his borrowings of the Aymara term *Potosí*—a New World signifier that quickly became an idiom—seem at first sight more conventional.[4]

---

[4] I thank Verónica Salles-Reese, whose expertise on the viceroyalty of colonial Peru extends to Andean languages, for confirming the term's derivation from Aymara, specifically from 'putukh' or 'potojsi', which means 'noise' (*ruido* or *estruendo*). The phoneme *potoj* does not exist in Quechua. See the entry on 'putukh', in Bertonio (1984: 178).

A scrutiny of the bounty produced by *Potosí*, the most productive and, for the Andean Indians who worked it, the most deadly silver mine of the early modern era, may help to contextualize the seemingly ornamental or idiomatic uses of the image in Cervantes's novels. In a long historical account of 'American Silver', Fernand Braudel discusses, in copious detail and with multiple charts, how the Indies 'disgorged' their riches into Spain and from there, in the first cycle, to the Netherlands, a distribution centre for Germany and northern Europe. In its second cycle, American silver moved into Italy and then, via the Italy–China axis, across the Orient (1972: i. 476–517). The role of the German banking family of the Fuggers in the imperial routes of these American precious metals should be of special interest to Cervantes scholars, given Don Quixote's uncharacteristic reference, during the Cave of Montesinos episode, to the Fuggers (2. 23). Before that dream vision, Don Quixote had wanted to be a chivalric knight—an Orlando or an Amadís. When the Enchanted Dulcinea asks him for a loan of six *reales* to lighten her hardships, however, Don Quixote expresses the wish to be a Fugger in order to remedy them ('que quisiera ser un Fúcar para remediarlos', 2. 23). Because this desire is deviously connected to the American silver mines, it deserves a closer look.

The family of the Habsburgs had been indebted to the moneylending Fuggers since 1487–8, some three generations before they secretly bankrolled the imperial coronation of Charles V. Jacob Fugger—head of the fanatically Catholic, anti-Semitic, and anti-Lutheran banking family at the time of the coronation—reminded the Pope in a famous letter, reprinted by Rodolfo Puiggrós, that he could have just as easily made Francis I emperor of Germany (1989: 178). By way of thanks for helping him to become Holy Roman Emperor-designate, Charles V enriched the coffers of the Fuggers with the first shipment of gold that Cortés sent him, without the Aztecs ever knowing, as Puiggrós puts it, that their defeat subsidized the election 'of the sovereign of the world' ('del soberano del mundo') (1989: 178). That was only the beginning of the Fuggers' lucrative connections with the New World. In 1531 the family contracted with the Spanish Crown for the governorship and one-fifth possession of all lands discovered within eight years between the Straits of Magellan and Peru—for which Anton Fugger received the title of *adelantado*—a project that came to

nothing, partly because of the resistance of the Spanish conquistadores to being supplanted. But although conquest and colonization proved impossible for the Fuggers in South America,
Charles V enabled them to receive 'the lion's share' ('la parte
leonina') of the mines of the New World, including *Potosí*, by
leasing to them the Spanish mines of Almadén (Puiggrós 1989:
183). These peninsular mines produced mercury, indispensable
for the new high-volume methods of refining American silver.
Mateo Alemán, the author of *Guzmán de Alfarache*, inspected
the Almadén mercury mines in 1593 and, in a secret report,
painted a dire portrait of the treatment of the galley slaves sent
to labour there (Bleiberg 1985). Anne J. Cruz elaborates on
both the report and the conditions in the mines: the 'hellish
scenes of back-breaking labour', 'the overseers' whippings',
and, above all, 'the painful body sores and extensive brain dam-
age inflicted by mercury poisoning' (1999: 80). The mines of
Almadén were located in the province of Ciudad Real, a territory well known to Cervantes and mentioned in both *The
Colloquy of the Dogs* (*El coloquio de los perros*) and in Part 2 of *Don
Quixote*. If Cervantes were aware of the conditions of these
mines—from hearsay, if not from Alemán's report—then making his hero aspire to be a Fugger, one of the thriving lessees
of the toxic mercury mines, borders on the grotesque.

Beyond its connections to Don Quixote's dream vision of
becoming a banker instead of a knight, American silver furnished
Cervantes and his age with a new idiom for great wealth—'to
be worth a *Potosí*' (*valer un Potosí*). The silver mine of *Potosí* was
discovered in 1545 in Upper Peru (roughly modern-day Bolivia),
two years before Cervantes was born and sixty years before the
references to it begin appearing in his novels. In 1550, the
Dominican friar Domingo de Santo Tomás described the mine
in a letter from Chuquisaca (La Plata) to the Council of the
Indies: 'Some four years ago, to complete the perdition of this
land, there was discovered a mouth of hell, into which a great
mass of people enter every year and are sacrificed by the greed
of the Spaniards to their "god". This is your silver mine called
Potosí'.[5] In his long description of the mine and of the hardships endured by the 'wretched Indians' who worked it, this same

---

[5] See Hemming (1970: 369–70) for this citation from Rubén Vargas Ugarte's
Historia del Perú, Virreinato (1551–1600) (Lima: 1949), 36–7.

friar included a passage that resembles not only Don Quixote's many paeans to 'la libertad', but also his peppery discourse against compulsion ('fuerza') when he first encounters the galley slaves (1. 22). Reminding his monarch about the difference between slaves and free men, Domingo de Santo Tomás makes a prescient claim:

No one who knows the meaning of liberty can fail to see how this violates reason and the laws of freedom. For to be thrown by force into the mines is the condition of slaves or of men condemned to severe punishment for grave crimes. It is not the law of free men, which is how Your Highness describes these poor people in your provisions and ordinances. (cited in Hemming 1970: 370)

A very different attitude to 'reason and the laws of freedom' would be available to Cervantes some forty years later, in José de Acosta's *Historia natural y moral de las Indias*, published in 1590 and so enthusiastically received that it was almost immediately translated into six European languages—French, Italian, German, English, Dutch, and Latin (O'Gorman 1962: p. xi). Some thirteen chapters of this worthy Jesuit's chronicle focus on precious metals in the Indies, with one chapter devoted to the discovery of the mine at Potosí and to the changes that this discovery brought to the area. The desire for silver turned Potosí from a cold, windy, and sterile red-coloured mountain into a boom town, as Acosta describes it, with a dense population —over 100,000 inhabitants by 1600—accustomed to finding abundant luxuries in the plazas: 'fruits, preserves, gifts, an excess of wines, silks, and galas' ('frutas, conservas, regalos, vinos excesivos, sedas y galas') (1962: 149). Other luxuries not mentioned by Acosta included the town's many theatres and dance academies, casinos and brothels. Although he conventionally uses the term 'greed' ('codicia'), and even feelingly cites Pliny on 'the hunger for money' ('la hambre del dinero'), Acosta actually sees the discovery of Potosí as providential, as ordained by Divine Providence for the happiness ('felicidad') of Spain (1962: 149; 157). Indeed, Acosta finds it fitting that the greatest wealth known to have existed in the world would remain hidden until it could be manifested during the glorious reign and within the empire of Charles V (1962: 151). In this Jesuit's 'moral history', then, the hand of Providence provides the Spanish crown with 'the treasure of the Indies' ('el tesoro de

Indias') to wage war against the enemies of the 'Holy Faith' ('Santa Fe') (1962: 154). Needless to say, this providential reading does not find its way into Cervantes.

Acosta provides a long and riveting description, filled with measurements in 'estados', so that his reader will understand how hard men work to find silver in the 'entrails of the profundity' ('entrañas del profundo')—a bodily metaphor echoed in Cervantes's later depiction, in the *Persiles*, of the treasure hidden 'in the entrails of *Potosí*' ('las entrañas de Potosí', 338). Acosta's description is made even more compelling by the fact that the Jesuit chronicler suffered a bout of vertigo when he himself descended into the mine, no doubt during a fact-finding tour for his *Historia*. The miners who descend into 'the entrails' of *Potosí* must negotiate everything in the dark, Acosta writes,

knowing little or nothing about when it's daytime or nighttime; and since these are places never visited by the sun, not only is there perpetual darkness but also great cold, and an air very dense and alien to human nature, and thus newcomers turn dizzy, as happened to me, feeling nausea and stomach pains.

sin saber poco ni mucho cuándo es día ni cuando es noche; y como son lugares que nunca los visita el sol, no sólo hay perpetuas tinieblas, mas también mucho frío, y un aire muy grueso y ajeno de la naturaleza humana, y así sucede marearse los que allá entran de nuevo, como a mí me acaeció, sintiendo bascas y congojas de estómago. (1962: 156)

Illuminating their toil with candles, the miners hack at the heavy metal, carrying it on their backs while ascending up a long series of precarious ladders made from twisted cowhide and wooden slats. Although Acosta acknowledges that he is describing a nightmare—'a horrible thing that merely to think on sets one's teeth on edge' ('cosa horrible y que en pensalla aun pone grima') (1962: 156)—this Jesuit priest and chronicler never quite focuses on *who* exactly is working the mines of *Potosí*.

Cervantes may have known about Fray Domingo de Santo Tomás's moving protest against forced labour in the American mines. He very likely knew about Padre Acosta's hellish descriptions of *Potosí*. And he certainly did know about the location of the wealth of *Potosí* in the 'entrails' of a mountain in South America. The descriptions of *Potosí* by the above clerical chroniclers—as a place of 'perpetual darkness' and as a 'mouth of Hell'—remind us of Don Quixote's descent into the Cave of Montesinos, although Cervantes's hero categorically refuses to allow Sancho and the humanist guide to call the place infernal —'You call that Hell?' ('¿Infierno le llamáis?', 2. 22). The mines of *Potosí* come to mind again during Sancho's doubly-parodic accidental descent, en route home from Barataria, into a pit outside the ducal estate. It is difficult, in short, *not* to find some dark linkages in these almost contemporary portraits of such a costly catabasis.

When, in Part 2 of *Don Quixote*, the distressed Dueña Dolorida describes Clavileño, the wooden horse that Merlin constructed, she quite neutrally observes that its present owner Malambruno uses it for his travels, flying one day to France, the next to *Potosí* (2. 40). That the Welsh Merlin is here considered a French wizard and linked to a Peruvian mine becomes less gratuitous when we consider Merlin's own cavernous abode in Carmarthen. This abode is described as a mine worked by the 'huge toile' of sprights in Spenser's *Faerie Queene* (3. 9), a nearly contemporary text that, unlike Cervantes's novels, loudly advertises its complicity with colonialism. A less fantastic and more economic reference occurs when Don Quixote wonders how to reimburse Sancho for the lashes undertaken toward the disenchantment of Dulcinea: 'the mines of *Potosí* would not suffice to pay you' ('las minas de Potosí fueran poco para pagarte', 2. 71). The *Persiles* again alludes to the American silver bonanza when a wounded count, after marrying a portionless young woman on his deathbed in order to enrich her, claims that even if he possessed the great fortunes 'hidden in the bowels of the earth in *Potosí*' ('que encierran las entrañas de Potosí'), he would honour her in the same way (338).

In the context of judging the criteria we possess for whether some alien idea has been assimilated, Sir J. H. Elliott wonders whether assimilation has finally been achieved 'when new impressions and new information have become so routine that they have ceased even to be discussed'. As an instance of this assimilation, Elliot mentions the Spanish expression for extreme wealth, *vale un Potosí*, which 'has become so commonplace that its original American connotations are effectively forgotten' (1995: 399). They certainly seem to have been forgotten in a ballad by Góngora in the *Romancero de Palacio*, a poem in which a Petrarchan blason mechanically compares the throat and bosom of a desired woman with 'the silver of *Potosí*' ('la plata de Potosí').[6] But were the American connotations forgotten by more anti-Petrarchan writers like Cervantes? The very fact that invocations of *Potosí* were becoming routine and commonplace makes us vividly aware that, in the symbolic order of Cervantes's characters, excessive wealth—for centuries indicated by inert comparisons to the classical figures of Midas or Croesus —could now be signified by the problematic image of an American mine. The American topos did not entirely replace the oriental one, however, or at least not in poetic appropriations of the Indies from Boscán to Quevedo: 'it would be misleading', Elizabeth B. Davis explains, 'to give the impression that the oriental code of wealth had become extinct in Peninsular poetry'. Quevedo, as Davis shows, continued to use both the Oriental and American codes (1989: 52). So, for that matter, did Cervantes, although his oeuvre cites Midas only five times, far less often than *Potosí*. But when Don Quixote imagines a silver mine in Peru as an insufficient reward for Sancho's sacrificial self-flagellation—for a punishment devised by a ducal class of Spaniards powerful enough to dole out islands—the careful reader cannot forget that the original American connotations of *Potosí* involved other victims of sacrifice.

Herman Melville is one American reader of Cervantes who seems to have understood this sacrificial element. A loaded image of *Potosí* finds its way into his chivalric recycling of Cervantes. When the weary and dejected narrator of 'The Piazza', the liminal story in *The Piazza Tales*, sees through the medium of a rainbow a house at the top of a mountain in Massachusetts that he renames 'Charlemagne', he claims that 'it glowed like the Potosi mine' (1987: 3–5). Riding out on a quest toward this radiant spot, Melville's narrator pointedly identifies himself with Don Quixote, whom he calls 'the sagest sage that ever lived' (1987: 6). When the narrator reaches his destination—the shining house at the end of the rainbow—he discovers it to be the rotting cottage of an impoverished couple: a seamstress called 'Marianna' and her brother, a man 'fagged out' from working, the tale infers, in the local coal mines (1987: 9). The house

---

[6] 'Otro [Romance de Luis de Góngora]' is in a miscellany of 16th-cent. poems newly edited by Labrador Herraiz, DiFranco, and Bernard (1999: 57).

that glows like *Potosí* is discovered to be a sham, the impoverished abode of an exhausted coal miner. The wheel of influence
—from *Potosí* to La Mancha to Mt. Greylock—has come full
circle, returning the mine and its devious connections with
chivalry back to America. Cervantes's assorted uses of *Potosí*, the
indigenous name of a mine found in the Bolivian *altiplano* two
years before his birth, is but an isolated instance of the artistic
possibilities of polyglot discourse. It prepares us to consider in
more general and more theoretical terms, however, the workings of hybridity across his two novels.

5. HYBRIDITY IN *DON QUIXOTE*

Posing the question 'What is hybridization?', Bakhtin branches
out into various answers, all of them useful for his reading,
if not necessarily ours, of Cervantes. According to Bakhtin,
hybridization is an intentional novelistic device in which 'a
mixture of two social languages' occurs within the arena of a
single utterance. More specifically, 'an intentional hybrid is
precisely the perception of one language by another language,
its illumination by another linguistic consciousness' (1981:
358–9). Bakhtin's discussion of hybridization, however, tends to
focus on heteroglossia—on the rich mixture of different speech
communities, the internal stratification of different social speech
types within one national language. Cervantes's *Don Quixote*
—so goes the Bakhtinian argument—is a text 'which realizes
in itself, in extraordinary depth and breadth, all the artistic
possibilities of heteroglot and internally dialogized novelistic
discourse' (1981: 324). Cervantes is celebrated here, in short,
largely for his heteroglot talents. Although Bakhtin does not
cite any textual passage to document his claims for Cervantine
heteroglossia, he could no doubt have enlisted Sancho's proverbs, the Duchess's elevated speech, or the Cousin's humanist
jargon as examples of the concept. There is no question that
Don Quixote shows an extraordinary understanding of the many
different 'languages' simultaneously existing within single cultures or speaking communities—between classes, between generations, and between the sexes. A dense heteroglossia appears
at the very beginnings of Cervantes's novel, to cite only one example, with the first women Don Quixote meets on his initial

sally, two 'public prostitutes' ('rameras públicas') accompanying some muledrivers en route to Seville (1. 2). These prostitutes, whom Don Quixote renames with the honorific titles of 'Doña Toloso' and 'Doña Molinera', cannot understand a word of his 'retóricas', his pseudo-chivalric utterances. Even though they are all speaking the same national language, Don Quixote, as the text explains, is 'not understood by the ladies' ('no entendido de las señoras'), who belong to a very different speech community (1. 2).

Although much more could be said about heteroglossia to supplement Bakhtin's meagre negotiations with the text of *Don Quixote*, I am largely concerned here with polyglossia, that is, with the presence of two or more *national* languages as they interact within one single cultural system. The interactions between radically different languages—between Castilian and Nahuatl, to recall our *cacao* example—show us Cervantes's more global reach. 'Only polyglossia', as Bakhtin reminds us, 'fully frees consciousness from the tyranny of its own language and its own myth of language' (1981: 61). This kind of polyglot consciousness emerges with surprising vigour in Cervantes. In *Don Quixote*, for example, readers encounter over a half-dozen languages: Spanish, Arabic, Turkish, German, Italian, Basque, and the multitongued lingua franca. Don Quixote himself feels obliged to give Sancho a little lesson in the Arabic derivations of a cluster of Spanish words:

The word *albogues* comes from the Arabic, like all the words in Spanish that begin with *al*, namely *almohaza, almozar, alhombra, alguacil, alhucema, almacén, alcancía*, and others of the same sort, though not too many others; our language has only three words borrowed from the Moors that end in the letter *i*, and these are *borceguí, zaquizamí, and maravedí*. The words *alhelí and alfaquí* are clearly recognized as Arabic, as much because of the *al* at the beginning as the *i* at the end.

Y este nombre *albogues* es morisco, como lo son todos aquellos que en nuestra lengua castellana comienzan en *al*, conviene a saber: *almohaza, almorzar, alhombra, alguacil, alhucema, almacén, alcancía* y otros semejantes, que deben ser pocos más; y solos tres tiene nuestra lengua que son moriscos y acaban en *i*, y son *borceguí, zaquizamí* y *maravedí; alhelí* y *alfaquí*, tanto por el *al* primero como por el *i* en que se acaban, son conocidos por arábigos. (2. 67)

The above passage shows Cervantes's working familiarity with Arabic, the language of a *morisco* community suffering exile even as he writes. This exile is discussed during one of the most flamboyant polyglotic encounters in Cervantes. All readers of *Don Quixote* remember the delightful picnic on the grass, enjoyed by Spaniards, Moors, and Germans, and replete with six flowing wineskins and with caviar—'a black food which they say is called *cabial*' ('un manjar negro que dicen que se llama cavial', 2. 54). The Germans are identified by Ricote as a band of pseudo-pilgrims on the road for profit: they immediately ask Sancho to give them 'Geld! Geld!' ('¡Guelte! ¡Guelte!'). Their custom is to visit the sanctuaries of Spain, 'which they consider their Indies' ('que los tienen por sus Indias', 2. 54). Even here— in the midst of German caviar and Iberian wines—Cervantes invokes the great wealth of America, linking the Indies to Spanish sanctuaries that can be exploited for money. Enactments of polyglossia in this episode are intense. The German pilgrims want unification with the Spanish people, a sentiment they express in the lingua franca of the Mediterranean—'Español y tudesqui, tuto uno: bon compaño'—to which Sancho replies, '¡Bon compaño, jura Di!' (2. 54).

The picnic suddenly turns serious, however, when Ricote the Moor—who appears disguised as a German or Dutchman— speaks not in Arabic but in the 'purest' Castilian, a language full of arabisms, about the Philip III's recent Expulsion Decree. Almost 300,000 *moriscos* or bilingual Spanish Moors were driven into exile between 1609 and 1613, a radical and tragic surgery performed on Spain's body politic that Carlos Fuentes, for one, wryly assesses as a 'colossal blunder': 'this counterproductive act practically ruined the middle classes of Valencia and Aragon, who had lent money to the Moors, and the nobility, who had leased land to them; it even threatened to diminish the Inquisition, now bereft of more than a quarter of a million heretics to persecute' (1992: 164). Cervantes's representation in the Ricote episode of a bilingual, even trilingual, consciousness is part of that cross-lingual process that alienates notions of unitary national myths, of monocultural patriotism. The only real 'patriot' in this episode is Sancho, who refuses to help Ricote dig up his buried treasure because he believes he would be helping his king's enemies. But neither does Sancho, who prides himself on being an Old Christian peasant, betray his old neighbour: 'Be satisfied that I won't turn you in' ('Conténtate que por mí no serás descubierto', 2. 54). Nor, we assume, will

Sancho turn in his new caviar-carrying German friends en route to exploit their own private 'Indies'. It is easy to forget that this painful episode, one of the richest manifestations of transcultural hybridity in *Don Quixote*, is part of a 'history' putatively written by Cide Hamete Benengeli, an Arab historian who seems far more concerned with narrative constraints than with political ones. This episode, however, is politically loaded: a Muslim historian represents a lively encounter between an Old Christian Spanish peasant and a disguised exiled Spanish Moor in the company of some opportunistic German Christians—all of them peacefully sharing a meal, al fresco, while Spain burns.

Ricote the Moor's praise of Germany as a tolerant country that enjoyed religious freedom was seized on by Thomas Mann, who felt 'a patriotic pride' upon reading this passage. In a series of notebook entries written during his 1934 'maiden voyage' to the New World—in which he portrayed himself as 'most surprisingly in act to repeat the voyage of Columbus' (1965: 432) —Mann took along, as 'the chosen companions' of his trip, 'four little orange linen volumes of *Don Quixote*' (1965: 429). Among the multiple responses to Mann's shipboard reading, his view of the episode of the Moor Ricote bears citing. The German novelist stresses Cervantes's artistic dilemma in justifying the national policy of persecution even while sympathizing with the persecuted. The episode becomes, for Mann, a 'shrewd mixture' of both 'blameless submission to the great Philip III' and 'the most lively human sympathy for the awful fate of the Moorish people, who, attacked by the Edicts of the King, are sacrificed to the supposed interests of the state and driven into misery without regard for individual agony' (1965: 456). Ricote's exilic lament, as Mann rightly argues, gives the lie to his statements about the inspired justice of the King's Edicts of Expulsion:

Wherever we are, we weep for Spain, where, after all, we were born and raised; nor have we found, anywhere else, the welcome our miseries long for, and even in Barbary and in all the places in North Africa where we expected to be eagerly and and bounteously received, there above all we have been most reviled and mistreated.

Doquiera que estamos lloramos por Expaña, que, en fin, nacimos en ella y es nuestra patria natural; en ninguna parte hallamos el acogimicnto que nuestra desventura desea, y en Berbería, y en todas las partes de África donde esperábamos ser recebidos, acogidos y regalados, allí es donde más nos ofcnden y maltratan. (2. 54)

Mann's reading of the Ricote episode, together with his repeated remarks of the love of exiles for their homelands, may have been influenced by his own feelings of homelessness as he sailed west to confront a 'towered city of giants'— his phrase for 'the skyscrapers of Manhattan' (1965: 464). Not all readers will agree with Mann's vision of Cervantes as 'a poor and dependent writer' who 'had all too much need to prove his loyalty' (1965: 457), but they must acknowledge the exceptionally rich hybridity, the international mix, of the Ricote episode. This chapter alone (2. 54) mingles references to Spain, Germany, France, Italy, Africa, and, by metaphor, the Indies.

In a study of *Don Quixote*'s 'linguistic perspectivism', written in 1948 but still indispensable, Leo Spitzer glances at Cervantes's tendencies to create this kind of hybrid world. After commenting on the 'highly daring' coinage of 'basin-helmet' ('baciyelmo') —which he believes Cervantes 'automatically' transferred from the pattern behind 'designations of hybrid animals'—Spitzer goes on to mention an equally daring hybrid construction in *Don Quixote*. In an essay that moves from polyonomasia to polyetymologia to polyglottism, Spitzer cites the polyglot habits of the characters in the interpolated *Captive's Tale*, who speak Castilian, Arabic, Turkish, and bits of lingua franca, also known as a 'bastard tongue' ('bastarda lengua') or a 'mixture' ('mezcla') of the above languages plus French, Italian, Portuguese, and Greek (1948: 64). Although Spitzer calls attention to the 'hybrid world of Mohammedans and Christians' in *Don Quixote* (1948: 63), he does not explain how that world both frames and disturbs the whole novel. Although the locations and preoccupations of both parts of *Don Quixote* seem resolutely Spanish —give or take some Florentine aristocrats, French pirates, German pilgrims, Calabrian renegades, and Moorish or *morisco* father–daughter pairs—the narrative that contains them is not. Strategically filtered through the pen of an Arab historian, and then 'translated' into Castilian by a freelancing *morisco*, the story of a born-again Christian knight crosses and recrosses language boundaries to find its fictional linguistic 'source' in Arabic, in a commissioned translation from the language of Spain's defeated enemy, a translation that obliterates its 'source'.

This talk of a foundational fiction brings us to Cervantes's recycling of the 'lost manuscript topos'. Let's look again at the remarkable episode in which the reader-editor-narrator of *Don*

Quixote discovers, in the Toledo market place, the 'original' of the novel we are reading:

One day when I was in the Alcaná at Toledo, a boy came by, selling some notebooks and other old documents to a dealer in silks, and since I'm always fond of reading, even the scraps of paper in the street, it was perfectly natural for me to pick up one of the notebooks the boy was selling, which I saw was written in what I recognized as Arabic characters.

Estando yo un día en el Alcaná de Toledo, llegó un muchacho a vender unos cartapacios y papeles viejos a un sedero; y como yo soy aficionado a leer, aunque sean los papeles rotos de las calles, llevado desta mi natural inclinación, tomé un cartapacio de los que el muchacho vendía y vile con carácteres que conocí ser arábigos. (1. 9)

The reader-editor-narrator admits that although he could recognize, he could not read these Arabic characters, and that he needed for the task a special kind of translator, a 'morisco aljamiado': 'so I went looking about for some Spanish-speaking Moor who would read it to me, and it wasn't difficult to find exactly the kind of translator I was looking for' ('anduve mirando si parecía por allí algún morisco aljamiado que los leyese, y no fue dificultoso hallar intérprete semejante', 1. 9).

This anonymous *morisco* translator brings to light some of the class conflicts and cultural alterities that Cervantes's writing enacts under the rubric of hybridity. He begins by translating the title, for both the narrator and ourselves, as the 'History of don Quijote of La Mancha, written by Cide Hamete Benengeli, Arab historian' ('Historia de Don Quijote de la Mancha, escrita por Cide Hamete Benengeli, historiador arábigo', 1. 9). But the *morisco* translator does not believe everything he reads. He considers a later chapter in *Don Quixote* as 'apocryphal' ('apócrifo'), for instance, because Sancho speaks well beyond his limited abilities about remarkably subtle things (2. 5). Beyond Sancho's amusingly heated altercations with his wife over their family's future, what is extraordinary about this chapter is that it depicts a bilingual *morisco* judging the speech of a monolingual Christian peasant, finding it wanting, but still feeling 'professionally obliged' to translate this chapter ('por cumplir con lo que a su oficio debía', 2. 5). The translator rightly regards as 'apocryphal' the kind of talk in which Sancho aspires to his seeing his daughter become a countess, to having grandchildren who will be called 'gentlemen' ('que se llamen "señoría"'), or to negotiating his lowly situation, of both birth and poverty, to the heights of prosperity (2. 5). Our initial response is to laugh at the aristocratic aspirations of the illiterate Sancho. But Cervantes brings us back, again and again, to the uppity ways of the translator, making us reflect on why a Spanish Moor born into the socially suspect status of impure blood, a poor man happy to freelance for wheat and raisins would not wince at—and may even wish to censor—Sancho's social climbing. But as a professional, the translator completes the job. The rest is history, literally: *Don Quixote* presents itself as a history at least twice removed from its author. Readers are finally offered a reconstructed Spanish translation of an Arabic version of a Spanish 'true story'.[7]

Bakhtin's claim that any 'distancing of the posited author or teller from the real author' in the European novel is 'a heritage from *Don Quixote*' (1981: 312) needs to be reassessed. Generalizing about how the speech of certain narrators in Pushkin, Doestoevsky, Leskov, as well as some narrators in Symbolist and post-Symbolist prose, 'is always another's speech', Bakhtin explains that

in every case a particular belief system belonging to someone else, a particular point of view on the world belonging to someone else, is used by the author because it is highly productive, that is, it is able on the one hand to show the object of representation in a new light (to reveal new sides or dimensions in it) and on the other hand to illuminate in a new way the 'expected' literary horizon, that horizon against which the particularities of the teller's tale are perceivable. (1981: 312–13)

While this discussion of the benefits of authorial distancing is instructive, this technique is not necessarily, or at least not exclusively, Cervantes's legacy to the European novel. In his fine anatomy of this distancing strategy, Bakhtin does not mention that the African Apuleius also used 'another's speech', and that, in fact, his use of it may have influenced Cervantes. A native of Madaura who learned Attic Greek as a child in Athens but was later trained in Rome to speak Latin, Apuleius chose a Greek narrator to relate a Grecian story in Latin. Readers receive a

---

[7] For a detailed analysis of this pivotal trip to the market place, see Parr's *Anatomy* (1988: pp. xx ff.), which launches the important question of whether *Don Quixote* is narrated by an 'unreliable narrator' or a 'mock-chronicler'.

mixed invitation—a Latin invitation to begin a Greek fable
—at the threshold of *The Golden Ass*: 'Fabulam Graecanicam
incipimus' (1965: 4).

Cervantes outdoes Apuleius not by being the first to cross
language boundaries with a posited author, but by strategically
choosing this author, and even his translator, *from across official
enemy lines*. Both of these fictional figures come from a race
of deprived minorities who would be forcibly expelled from
Spain, in the wake of the royal Expulsion Decree mentioned
above, four years after the publication of Part 1 of *Don Quixote*.
Long before the expulsion, however, Spanish Moors managed
to provide a handy categorical slot for assimilating the New World
peoples, as shown by the spectacularly racist passage in López
de Gómara's history about the rumoured lifestyle of American
Indians in the province of Esmeraldas: 'they live like sodomites,
speak like Moors, and look like Jews' ('viven como sodomitas,
hablan como moros y parecen judíos') (Porras Barrenechea
1955: 230). That an official historian of imperial Spain, a
nation so stridently invested in monoglossia, would choose to
disseminate such an absurd confusion of languages (that the
South American Indians 'speak like Moors') was almost prescient.
A blending of Moors and Indians was actually played out in parts
of the New World in dramatic performances that included a
'Moors and Christians' ('moros y cristianos') cycle, a tradition
still persisting in parts of Latin America today. In such performances, as it happens, indigenous peoples appear to be 'celebrating the victory of Christians over infidels'.[8] Not only were the
Moors handily slotted as Americans, but also their Berber
homelands were sometimes equated with the New World. In
Fray Diego de Haedo's history of Algiers, for example, Barbary
becomes a kind of America. Haedo vividly describes how, in
twenty or thirty days, Algerian pirates can steal from Mediterranean islands and the whole coast of Spain what Spanish
merchants in the Indies must earn at great risk of life. These
corsairs have made Algiers the richest city in the Levant. With
good reason, Haedo concludes, the Turks call Algiers 'their Indies
and Peru' ('sus Indias y Perú') (1929: 87–8).

What kind of hybridity, then, do we encounter in a translation
from the language of a defeated enemy? Does Cide Hamete

---

[8] For more on these oppressive facts, see Wachtel (1977).

—endearing 'Muslim philosopher' ('filósofo mahomético', 2.
53) and possible kinsmen to the amorous *morisco* muleteer at
Juan Palomeque's inn (1. 18)—function as a sign of Christian
Spain's cultural debt to Islam, a debt which the nation grafted
onto itself even while hounding its Moors and *moriscos?* Certainly
this cultural debt is invoked in *The Captive's Tale*, not only in
the lingua franca spoken between Arabs and Christians—
called a 'mixture' ('mezcla') or a 'bastard tongue' ('bastarda
lengua')—but also in the mixed marriage of the tale's protagonists, issues taken up in the scrupulous critical attention lately
given to *The Captive's Tale*. Michael Gerli specifically celebrates
the 'miscegenation' in *The Captive's Tale*, which he sees as rewriting Spain's stubborn foundational fiction of the Reconquista
(1995: 40–81).[9] In both parts of *Don Quixote*, then, we witness
the emergence of a hybrid national narrative that pries open
the nostalgic past of Spain's Reconquista—of 1492 and all that
—to the history of marginality, as well as to the narrative subjectivity, of the defeated Moors. Once readers enter this page
of history, they are compelled to wonder why on earth, and even
in earthly fictions, would an Arab such as Cide Hamete wish
to write a history of a madman who mimics Spain's colonial
ideologies and, in the process, empties its chivalric narratives
of their national and imperial authority. Focusing on Cide
Hamete from the site of hybridity, we note that he appears—
indeed, he is strategically presented—as a figure of ambivalence,
as a Muslim who swears 'like a Catholic Christian' ('como cristiano católico', 2. 27). A new look at the hybrid narrator of *Don
Quixote* is in order, a study that will examine him afresh, not
only as the 'lying' Moor of narratological studies, but also as a
counter-narrator of the nationalist pedagogy.

6. HYBRIDITY IN THE *PERSILES*

All the hybrid forms present in Cervantes's earlier work may
be retrospectively understood through the *Persiles*, which rises
from the same kind of 'polyglot energies' found in the ancient
novel to position itself on the border between multiple cultures
and languages. Cervantes's last novel takes *translatio* in both senses

---

[9] For other indispensable essays on this episode, see Allen (1976), Garcés
(1989), McGaha (1996), Murillo (1981), Percas de Ponseti (1996 and 1999), Diane
Sieber (1998), and Smith (1993).

of the word—as literary translation and geographic movement
—even further than *Don Quixote*. Crossing many national frontiers, the *Persiles* is itself without nation. It is also without a national
language. Although we are informed that we are reading a translation, we are never told from what language the *Persiles* is
supposed to be translated (159). And although the original
is in Castilian, that language is never privileged. The novel's
Icelandic hero is presented to us, in Castilian, as virtually
incapable of speaking that language ('no muy despiertamente
sabía hablar la lengua castellana', 70); its Frislandic heroine
cannot understand Castilian at all; and its large cast of characters are multi-languaged. They speak English, Norwegian,
Polish, Irish, Danish, Lithuanian, French, Italian, Portuguese,
Castilian, Valencian, Arabic, a *lengua aljamiada* (Spanish written
in Arabic consonants), and a kind of 'barbaric' language for
which Cervantes provides a polyglot translator, to be discussed
in the Conclusion. One of the most intriguing uses of linguistic hybridity, at least for the purposes of our New World argument, falls to the narrator of the *Persiles*, who uses a strange word
in the opening chapter—*bejucos*—for the 'vines' tying up a raft
somewhat implausibly designed to sail in the North Sea (52).
Instead of the conventional Castilian signifiers available for these
vines, the narrator chooses a word of Caribbean origins, specifically a Taíno (*taíno*) word, which he may have accessed through
various popular historiographers of the Indies, Fernández de
Oviedo, or López de Gómara.[10]

The representation of this wildly polyglot world in the *Persiles*
begins with its opening word, 'Voices' ('VOCES'). A barbarian
is 'giving voice' to his anger, screaming into an underground
dungeon commands that nobody understands ('de nadie eran
entendidas articuladamente las razones que pronunciaba', 51).
When the hero is pulled out of the dungeon, he immediately
addresses some grateful words to Heaven. Because these are 'said
in a different language' ('dichas en differente lenguaje'), the
barbarians, in turn, are mystified. Readers are immediately thrust

---

[10] *Diccionario de Autoridades*: 'BEJUCO, del taíno de Santo Domingo. 1a doc.: 1526.
Los más antiguos cronistas (Oviedo, Las Casas) escriben *bexuco*; también en el *Persiles*
I, cap. I, ed. Schevill, p. 3. Friederici, AM. Wb. 86'. The *Taíno* language has been
assigned by linguists to the Arawakan family and traced back to the middle of the
Amazon Basin. About the time of Christ, *Taíno* speakers moved into the West Indies
from the Guiana coast. See Rouse (1987: 293–312).

into a world of polyglossia, where communications take place by signs, some of them terrifying. One of these non-verbal exchanges—when a barbarian aims a monstrous bow and arrow at Periandro-Persiles, making signs that he might shoot him in the chest (53)—would seem to be a shard from the Indies. One thinks of Cabeza de Vaca's fearful captivity near Matagorda Bay, in today's Texas, with Indians, as he relates it, who 'aimed arrows at our hearts every day, saying that they wanted to kill us' ('nos ponían cada día las flechas al corazón, diciendo que nos querían matar') (1989: 135). In the *Persiles* the language between the barbarians and the Europeans is conducted 'by signs' ('por señas') or via a translator (53). The language between the Europeans themselves, however, is like Babel, or as Otmar Hegyi's marvellous formulation puts it, like 'Algerian Babel'.

Another hybrid manifestation found in the *Persiles* is structural. The novel repeats an operation, specifically a 'labor of suturing', that Michel de Certeau—writing about Jean de Léry's *Histoire d'un voyage faict en la terre du Brésil* (1578)—claims is 'repeated hundreds of times throughout ethnological works' (1988: 219). In these works, a structural breakage of space first appears as an oceanic rift 'between the Old and the New World', in which 'tempests, sea monsters, acts of piracy, [and] "marvels"'—regarded as 'the visible marks of alterity'—are narrated (1988: 218). The breakage is further manifested as a 'combination of Western forms that seem to have been cut off, and whose fragments seem to be associated in unexpected ways' (1988: 219), in other words, as a kind of hybridity. Where Jean de Léry writes about his encounter in America with hybridity—for example, with a four-footed animal called a *tapiroussou* that is 'half-cow and half-donkey', 'being both of the one and of the other' (1988: 219)—Cervantes writes about fictional barbarians who are half-European and half-American. In this writing, Cervantes reiterates what de Certeau calls 'a picture covered with countless broken mirrors in which the same fracture is reflected (half this, half that)' (1988: 219). The effect of such a narrative allows us to deduce, in short, that 'over there'—that part of the world which seemed to be entirely other—no longer coincides with otherness. Alterity is thrown out of skew by such a displacement, the whole operation dismantling what de Certeau calls the 'dangerous' bipolarity that 'truth is over here while error is over there' (1988: 221).

7. HYBRIDITY AS HERESY

Aiming to reconnect the analysis of hybrid and 'impure' forms with their actuality, Edward Said claims that the 'whole notion of a hybrid text' was 'one of the major contributions of late twentieth-century culture' (Wicke and Sprinker 1992: 249). The notion may be new but the text itself is not. In a discussion of Martorell's *Tirante El Blanco*—a book highly praised during the scrutiny of Don Quixote's library (1. 6) and receiving increasingly appreciative commentary in our day[11]—Margaret Anne Doody notes 'the tendency of the novel to represent international mixes and the bringing together of people of different races and cultures' (1996: 210). This tendency, an ancient one, seems to have appealed to Cervantes in his work of 'novelizing', as the Alexandrian subtexts of his novels demonstrate. Various scholars have nodded to Cervantes's strong interest in mixed and impure cultural forms of languages, races, genres, or genders—what we may call his Alexandrian complex. In a 1960s article on the episode of Maese Pedro's puppet show, for example, George Haley noted its 'hybrid form' as its 'most striking feature' (1965: 152). Some twenty years later, Anthony Cascardi wrote that 'the mixing of kinds which occurs in [*Don Quixote*] is not literary alone: the order of natural kindness is also transgressed in the realm of material objects (the *baciyelmo*) and the sexes (the bearded waiting-women of Part II)' (1986: 42). George Mariscal—who believes that Cervantes's interest in mixing 'may have extended to questions of race and ethnicity'— has written about the *mestizaje* or 'miscegenation' in the *Persiles* as 'an imagined hybridity with a far-reaching resonance given that such a process was already taking place outside the fictional realm in America and elsewhere' (1994: 196). Elsewhere, Mariscal has persuasively situated 'the mestizo family' in the *Persiles*— Antonio, Ricla, and their children—within the broader framework of the Spanish colonial enterprise in America (1998: 207–9). In a more visionary moment, Mariscal predicts the emergence, in this new millennium, of a different disciplinary model, one interested in understanding Spanish culture within its historical conditions of hybridity. This model 'would put an end to the artificial division between peninsular and Latin American studies, something to be greatly desired' (1998: 213).

[11] See e.g. Aylward's instructive study of Martorell's *Tirant Lo Blanch*.

The present book—a small attempt to bridge this long-standing division—underwrites this new model.

All Cervantes's 'mestizo' moments—his forms of linguistic, sexual, racial, generic, and cultural hybridity—are resurfacing with astonishing vigour at present. Salman Rushdie's recent defence of the novel heralds the emergence of a new postcolonial novel—cosmopolitan, transnational, interlingual, and cross-cultural—an offshoot of the 'hybrid formation' described by Bakhtin (1981: 268). Simultaneously contesting George Steiner's 'obituary' for the whole genre and the old 'imperial map' in his head, Rushdie insists on the robust health of the novel today—in Latin America, India, the United States, and even in Europe. There is no 'crisis', he claims: 'The novel is precisely that "hybrid form" for which Professor Steiner yearns: it is part social inquiry, part fantasy, part confessional; it crosses frontiers of knowledge as well as topographical boundaries' (1996: 50). This kind of description and defence of hybridity makes us understand why Rushdie elsewhere acknowledges Cervantes as one of his literary 'parents'. At least two of the other members of Rushdie's 'polyglot family tree', Melville and Kafka, have also acknowledged Cervantes in their own writings (1991: 21). Melville, as noted earlier in this chapter, showed how chivalric posturing cannot finally occult the shabby realities that prop up quixotic dreams. Although Cervantes questioned an earlier and different imperial map than the one now being undermined by Indo-British fiction writers, he shares a 'family' resemblance with these writers that merits further attention.

If 'hybridity is heresy'—as Homi Bhabha puts it in one of his various complex discussions of the notion[12]—then Cervantes is a certifiable cultural heretic. His writing presciently taps the historical and cultural dimension of what Bhabha calls the 'Third Space', a space of enunciations, an 'alien territory' where contraries are assimilated and an instability created which 'presages powerful cultural changes' (1994c: 38–9). Rough mappings of Bhabha's alien territory have been multiplying across the 1990s: in Gianni Vattimo's sense of 'worlds and communities [that] present themselves explicitly as plural' (1992: 60); in Tobin Siebers's sense of places based on the inclusion of differences

---

[12] This particular equation is from Bhabha's 'How Newness Enters the World' in *The Location of Culture* (1994a: 225). But see also Bhabha's complex explorations of hybridity elsewhere in that text, e.g. in 'By Bread Alone' (207–9), and in 'Signs Taken for Wonders' (102–22).

(1994: 20); or in Susan Stephens's sense of the space created in the ancient Alexander Romance, in which the foundational fictions of 'two separate cultures are given equal prominence and equal value' (1995). Bhabha claims that theoretical recognition of this 'third space of representation' is a precondition for mapping a new transnational culture, a culture based on the articulation of a hybridity where difference would not be coded as hierarchy (1994a: 221). Addressing the issue of hierarchy, he elsewhere proposes a cultural construction of the western nation as 'a form of living . . . more hybrid in the articulation of cultural differences and identifications—gender, race, or class—than can be represented in any hierarchical or binary structuring of social antagonism' (1990: 292). This kind of hybridity, in Bhabha's dense sense of the term, is not merely 'a question of the admixture of pre-given identities or essences', nor is it a form of living that strangely forgets the history of a nation's past (a forgetting he calls 'the minus in the origin') (1990: 310). Hybridity has become 'the perplexity of the living as it interrupts the representation of the fullness of life; it is an instance of iteration, in the minority discourse, of the time of the arbitrary sign' ('the minus in the origin'). Through hybridity, in sum, 'all forms of cultural meaning are open to translation because their enunciation resists totalization' (1990: 314).

As the above testifies, hybridity has become far more complex theoretically than earlier critical discussions about its presence in the Graeco-Latin or the Cervantine novel. Many of the postmodern representations of hybridity, however—as a non-binary structuring, as a disruptive perplexity, as an instance of minoritarian iteration—are foreshadowed in Cervantes's novels. At one point, during a moment of social if not ideological pathology, Cervantes even thematizes the whole concept by having a character depict himself as a 'place', specifically, as an uncharted space of representation for hybridity. When warned that his endless storytelling is fatiguing his listeners, the last of Cervantes's protagonists, the garrulous hero of the *Persiles*, interrupts his narration with this prescient comparison: 'I am like this thing they call place, which is where all things fit, and nothing is out of place' ('Yo soy como esto que se llama lugar, que es donde todas las cosas caben, y no hay ninguna fuera del lugar', 227). The novel rises at different times and in different places, whenever a writer, in search of a world elsewhere, tries to imagine that capacious, transgressive, and hybrid place anew.

5

'Scorpion Oil': The Books of Chivalry

WHEN Charles V delivered his famously testy Easter Monday speech of 1536—an address to Pope Paul I, his cardinals, and the ambassadors of Europe—he was responding to the King of France's leagues and agreements with the Turks or 'infidels'. The imperial Ottoman threat was a constant anxiety to the Spanish King. In 1529, even as he was preparing for his papal coronation as Emperor of the Holy Roman Empire, Algiers was captured by the Turks. In 1534, a Turkish armada took Tunis from the Spaniards. In 1541, Charles V would mount an unsuccessful expedition against Algiers with an enormous convoy that included, among other distinguished old soldiers, Hernán Cortés. In the 1536 speech in question, however, this last event was still on the horizon. Enraged that the King of France was conspiring with the Turks, the enemies of both Spanish and French Catholicism, Charles V concluded his speech with this proto-quixotic oath:

Therefore, I promise your Holiness, in the presence of this sacred college and of all these knights here present, if the king of France wishes to meet me in arms, man to man, I promise to meet him armed or unarmed, in my shirt, with sword and dagger, on land or sea, on a bridge or on an island, in a closed field, or in front of our armies or wherever and however he may wish and it be fair.[1]

The high chivalric discourse of this regal *desafío* is, of course, familiar to all readers of *Don Quixote*. One need only recall the mad knight's formulaic challenge to Cardenio in defence of Queen Madásima's chastity. Anyone who claims that the Queen slept with Maestro Elisabad is lying like a great villain, Don

---

[1] Madariaga cites this speech in *Spain* (1942: 43–4). His 'Notes and Appendices' claim his source to be 'Professor de los Ríos's booklet: *Religión y Estado en la España del Siglo XVI*' (1942: 462).

Quixote shouts at Cardenio, 'and I will make him know it, on foot or on horseback, armed or unarmed, by night or by day, or however he chooses' ('y yo se lo daré a entender a pie o a caballo, armado o desarmado, de noche o de día, o como más gusto le diere', 1. 24).

The correct protocol for these challenges is not lost on Don Quixote. He knows the laws of chivalry well enough to recognize that the hero of an old ballad about Zamora, Don Diego Ordóñez de Lara, had overstepped them in formulating his own challenge: 'for there was no need to challenge the dead, the town's water supply, its foodstuffs, or its unborn children' ('porque no tenía para qué retar a los muertos, a las aguas, ni a los panes, ni a los que estaban por nacer', 2. 27). But although Don Quixote stridently identifies himself with the fictional figures of his favourite books—chivalric heroes such as Lancelot or Amadís or Reinaldo de Montalbán—various highly visible flesh-and-blood models were also available, as the above speech by Charles V suggests, for him to imitate.

These models were heavily invested in chivalry. To celebrate his son's birth in 1527, for example, Charles V laid on 'tourneys and ventures like those described in *Amadis*, but far more daring and accomplished than those in the book' (Kamen 1997: 2). Deeply invested in Spain's reincarnation as a chivalric nation, both royals, father and son, were fond of mounting tournaments on a large scale. In 1551, for example, Philip organized a grand tourney in Torrelobatón, where over 100 men jousted against each other for two weeks (Kamen 1997: 50). Like his father, Philip became a devotee of 'the rites of chivalry', if not quite 'for the rest of his life', as Henry Kamen claims, at least until after his father's death in 1558. The mourning service held for the dead King Charles in Brussels was a characteristically chivalric affair, dominated by all the 'regalia and colour of the knights of the Golden Fleece' (1997: 2, 6, 71). But these rites and displays of chivalry, and the careers of some of the historical figures who practised them, ranged well beyond European ceremonies for celebrating births or mourning deaths.

Don Quixote himself gestures toward a chivalric American career when, in a discussion of the violent origins of the surname Vargas y Machuca ('Clubber'), he mentions the descendants of Diego Pérez de Vargas, a Spanish knight famous for clubbing down Moors with the bough of an oak tree (1. 8). Among these descendants was Bernardo de Vargas Machuca (1557–1622), known for his refutation of Bartolomé de las Casas. Six years before the publication of Part 1 of *Don Quixote,* Vargas Machuca had written a handbook for Spanish soldiers in the Indies— *Milicia y descripción de las Indias* (1599). Territorial acquisition was the unabashed motto of Vargas Machuca, as witnessed by the notorious legend on the frontispiece of his handbook, where invocations to the sword and compass were followed by a shameless string of exhortations: 'More and more and more and more' ('Más y más y más y más'). This handbook provided soldiers in the Indies with the standard formula for taking possession of an Indian village. Dressed in full armour and sword in hand, the would-be conquistador was to pronounce, while in high dudgeon ('arrebatándose de cólera'), the following words to justify his expropriation: 'if anybody tries to counter this, let him step into the field with me, where I shall do battle with him, of which he may be assured, because in its defense I offer to die now and forever more' ('si hay alguna persona que lo pretenda contradecir, salga conmigo al campo, donde lo podrá batallar, el cual se lo aseguro, porque en su defensa ofrezco de morir ahora y en cualquier tiempo').[2] The comical stentoriousness of this document notwithstanding, it shows the propensity of chivalry—even at the turn of the seventeenth century— to underwrite territorial claims. Although the field has moved from Europe to the Indies, Vargas Machuca's invitation to a duel recycles the same rhetoric used by Charles V some sixty years earlier in the century. Instead of an audience of courtiers and cardinals, however, the challenger in the Indies would be surrounded by a circle of uncomprehending natives.

1. THE 'ENCHANTED' CONQUISTADORES

The family resemblances of these ritual challenges make it clear that chivalry—a medieval and feudal institution—was still an empowered discourse during Spain's age of conquest and colonization. The discourses of chivalry not only remained intact

[2] See Gonzalo Menéndez Pidal, *Imagen del mundo hacia 1570* (Madrid, 1944), 12; cited by Testa (1986: 67–8).

until well into the sixteenth century, but many of them also gained strength through a transatlantic crossing. In the 1520s, for example, Hernán Cortés 'takes on the lineaments of the chivalric', as José María Rodríguez García argues, in his second letter to Charles V. Beginning with a rhetoric of disinterested self-sacrifice that occults any mercenary motivation, Cortés vows to have Moctezuma 'imprisoned or dead or subjugated to Your Majesty's royal crown' ('que lo habría preso o muerto o súbdito a la corona real de Vuestra Majestad') (Rodríguez García 1997: 481). Cortés is operating here in 'a universe of chivalric inter-personal relations based on abstract qualities such as valor, virtue, and trust'. Aptly describing these relations as 'the traditionally enchanted chivalric relations', Rodríguez García claims that Cortés's universe of courteous enunciations constitutes the ideology of *cortesanía* (1997: 500 n., 491, 476). I would add that Don Quixote alludes to this very ideology when, in a discussion of the frenzy of various historical figures for fame, he invokes the risky exploits of 'the very courteous Cortés in the New World' ('el cortesísimo Cortés en el Nuevo Mundo', 2. 8). Only a deluded madman would give 'that oppressor of men' ('ille hominum oppresor')—to use Las Casas's understated phrase for Cortés (1958: 306–8)—the label of 'very courteous'. But why did Cortés tap into the medieval discourses of chivalry? How did sixteenth-century Spanish culture produce and regulate these popular discourses? And what, in turn, were their cultural effects? This chapter aims to show how the chivalric discourses of the above figures—kings, conquistadores, and fictional knights—were both intertwined and intercontinental.

Don Quixote has recently been assimilated, in studies of spiralling scholarly confidence, to the historical figures of the conquistadores. One scholar claims that it is easy for twentieth-century readers to see Don Quixote as 'a comic incarnation' of 'the conquistador mentality of Golden Age Spain' (Skinner 1987: 54). Another calls Cervantes's hero an 'aspiring' and even 'divinely inspired' conqueror, a figure who embodies 'what is great and what is insane about Spanish imperialism' (Higuera 1995: 1–2). Such recent New World axes of identity for Don Quixote are an intrepid development from older constructions, which invoked some rhetorically preposterous connections between Don Quixote and the 'quixotic' conquistadores— figures themselves identified with the heroic characters in the dominant fictional genre of the sixteenth century: the *libros de caballerías*. I have translated this prosaic literary kind as the Books of Chivalry to avoid the Anglo-American penchant, not adopted by other European literary languages, for separating the novel from romance (Doody 1996: 1 and 487 n.). My literal translation also avoids what Daniel Eisenberg calls 'the unfortunate confusion caused by the different meanings of the word "romance" in English and Spanish' (1982: 2). After sampling the representational practices that hover over the above-mentioned interrelated trio—Don Quixote, the conquistadores, and the heroes of the Books of Chivalry—I shall argue that Cervantes's hero not so much 'incarnates' or even 'aspires to' the conquistador mentality as that he 'mimics' it, that he plays the role—both by the book and to the hilt. Harold Bloom suggests this kind of mimicry when he writes that Don Quixote is 'neither a madman nor a fool, but someone who plays at being a knight-errant' (1994: 127–35). My own reading, less ecstatic and less Romantic than Bloom's, borrows some recent insights on mimicry that address, from various colonial and post-colonial perspectives, the contingencies of identity formation. In his 'sane madness', Don Quixote plays at being not only a knight errant but also a conquistador. One political theorist even regards Don Quixote, if only on the basis of his occasional imperial flights, as 'the greatest novelistic portrait ever penned of an important kind of would-be conqueror' (Higuera 1995: 185). How does Don Quixote's adopted surname, then, turn into an adjective for New World conquerors?

2. THE 'QUIXOTIC' CONQUISTADORES

Because of its long and transnational history, the term *quixotic* stubbornly resists definition. Attempts to define it run the gamut from *admirably idealistic* or *romantically exalted* to *wildly delirious* or *hopelessly hallucinated*. The term took an interesting lexical swerve during the first half of the eighteenth century, when it acquired some of its more demeaning aspects. E. C. Riley explains that when *Don Quixote* began to be admired for its satire and its irony—when it began to be understood as a burlesque epic and a parody, even a caricature, of the chivalric hero—then the words 'quijotada' and 'quijotesco' entered the lexicon 'with a depreciatory significance' ('con un significado despectivo') (1990: 226). Although not instanced by Riley, Herman Melville uses the term '*Quixotism*' in this depreciatory sense when he depicts in his log-book, in an 1857 entry, the manias of an anti-Semitic Yankee whose 'Puritanical energy' is linked to his 'preposterous' ideas (Leyda 1951: ii. 549). But I am less interested here in the application of the term *quixotic* to eccentrics than to conquistadores, whose energy, it is safe to say, was not Puritanical. The connections between the term *quixotic* and the New World conquerors is triangulated, obsessive, and preposterous, as what follows will show.

A generation before any post-colonial notions of mimicry were circulating, Don Quixote's status as a sterile imitator had been proposed from a metaphysical perspective. In a classic study of the history of triangular desire in novels beginning with Cervantes, René Girard famously fulminated against the condition, which he regarded as a highly 'contagious' ontological sickness (1965: 98). Girard's startling vision of Don Quixote as an essentially sick man, a character whose reigning desire is 'to be another', may have prepared us to entertain Don Quixote as a mimic man, a character whose strategic vocation is to mime another. There is triangulation, as well, in this kind of mimicry. Don Quixote imitates the same fictional chivalric heroes who motivated the conquistadores. By a kind of synchronic retaliation, then, the conquistadores are obsessively identified as 'quixotic'. Two discursive domains intersect here: chivalry, the feudal institution whose available and automatic language Don Quixote aims to revive, and imperialism, the more contemporaneous, and more American, institution to which his exploits often allude. Although this intersection has become more visible in the present climate, Cervantes's complex responses to the practice of 'ocean chivalry'—William H. Prescott's notion of what the conquistadores were doing in the New World (1873: i. 216)—remain undertheorized.

What William Prescott was doing in the New World, however, is a much clearer story, one whose understanding may reduce the number of banalized American readings of Don Quixote as a 'Man of La Mancha'. Richard L. Kagan has enlightened the kind of influence that Prescott, a nineteenth-century Harvard-educated gentleman historian, brought to bear on American historical scholarship of Spain. A better understanding of 'Prescott's paradigm' helps to explain what Kagan rightly calls the inability of Americans 'to associate Spain with anything except the pathetic figure of Don Quixote tilting at windmills' (1996: 444). Based on the Protestant prejudices of his age, Prescott offered an approach to Spanish history through the lens of United States history. Seen through this Prescottian lens, Spanish national character appeared as a causal factor in a long history of economic backwardness and social decline. Kagan's eye-opening study of certain entrenched stereotypes about Spain—begun by Prescott but fully operative in the professionalization of American history and surviving until the 1960s —concludes that 'such rigid thinking is increasingly a thing of the past', that its decrease has been accompanied 'by the understanding that imperial power is rarely long-lasting' (1996: 445). Unfortunately for earlier readers of both Spanish history and its cultural products—including Cervantes's novels—that understanding was not part of the Prescott package.

Beyond inaugurating the always exalted and often stereotyped writing of Spanish history in the United States, Prescott may have also launched some preposterous links between Don Quixote and the conquistadores. It is instructive to look at the relations between these figures from the rhapsodic perspective of Prescott, who availed himself of the one in order to describe the other: 'What wonder, then, if the Spaniard of that day, feeding his imagination with dreams of enchantment at home and with its realities abroad, should have displayed a Quixotic enthusiasm,—a romantic exaltation of character, not to be comprehended by the colder spirits of other lands!' (1873: ii. 59). Elsewhere and in the same breathless language, Prescott celebrates the 'bold spirit' of the Spanish conquistador who, 'not content with the dangers that lay in his path, seemed to court them from the mere Quixotic love of adventure' (1873: ii. 45). Prescott's highly Romantic writing, as these citations make clear, disguises the economic realities of conquest and colonization to represent the New World enterprise, instead, as a kind of glorious adventure tale.

Nowhere is this more evident than in the following effusion, where Prescott compares the chivalry of 'romantic Spain' with the more 'civil' spirit of enterprise of 'our own Puritan fathers', who with the true Anglo-Saxon spirit, left their pleasant homes across the waters, and pitched their tents in the howling wilderness, that they might enjoy the sweets of civil and religious freedom. But the Spaniard came over to the New World in the true spirit of a knight-errant, courting adventure, however perilous, wooing danger, as it would seem, for its own sake. With sword and lance, he was ever ready to do battle for the Faith; and, as he raised his old war-cry of 'St. Jago', he fancied himself fighting under the banner of the military apostle, and felt his single arm a match for more than a hundred infidels! It was the expiring age of chivalry; and Spain, romantic Spain, was the land where its light lingered longest above the horizon.   (1873: iii. 60–1)

More to our point here, however, Prescott construes his New World 'cavaliers' as displaying 'quixotic' qualities long before Don Quixote himself does. Cervantes's hero lends his adopted surname, in short, to behaviour that anticipates him by over a century. Although Prescott's formulation was preposterous— in the rhetorical sense of *prae-postere*, the scheme of putting the cart before the horse[3]—it was also seductive: the notion of the conquistadores as 'quixotic' seems to have taken hold in the popular imagination. Not only would they still all be characterized, a century later, as participants in the 'delirious dream of Don Quixote' ('sueño delirante de don Quijote'), but at least one of them, Francisco de Pizarro, would be celebrated for the 'quixotic words' ('palabras quijotescas') that he vented on the Isla del Gallo (Pedro 1954: 78–80). Because the 'delirious' aspects of the conquest have been marked and remarked, it may be useful to consider delirium as a discourse that supposedly strays 'from a presumed reality' to a knowledge ensnarled by 'the paths of desire' (Kristeva 1986: 307). Insofar as Prescott's writing has ensnarled the paths of Spanish history, it, too, may be called 'delirious': his historical portrait of 'cavaliers' crossing the ocean for the 'mere Quixotic love of adventure' discloses his own desire more than the reality of either the conquistadores or Don Quixote.

As for the application of the term 'quixotic' to the conquistadores, that practice shows no sign of abating. Fernando Arrabal's recent psychobiography of Cervantes, for example, celebrates Columbus for the 'quixotic enterprise that inspired

---

[3] The figure of *praepostere* is variously known as *reversio, inversio, anastrophe, epanastrophe*, and *hypallage*.

Cervantes' ('quijotesca empresa inspiradora de Cervantes') (1996: 153). In a more measured characterization of Columbus as 'a kind of Quixote a few centuries behind his times', Tzvetan Todorov discusses some of some of the Admiral's temperamental tics (1984: 11). Although Todorov does not apply these traits to Don Quixote, Cervantes's hero does, in fact, share a number of them with Columbus: a credulous and overheated imagination; an alertness to the appearances of enchantment; a fondness for the ceremonies of naming; an intellectual arrogance based on prescience instead of experience; a penchant for adjusting the data, as well as challenging the humanity, of messengers bearing unwelcome intelligence; a proclivity for imposing oaths on other people; and an injudicious bookishness. As the first of many conquistadores whose 'quixotic' words and deeds are located in events prior to Cervantes's time, Columbus exemplifies how the later text of *Don Quixote* has altered some influential readings of the earlier historiography of the Indies. America, it would seem, had been exceedingly hospitable to 'quixotic' careers long before Don Quixote existed. That hospitality was grounded on the printed book, specifically on a large corpus of books tied to institutionalized forms of power and funded by a common set of discursive memories. These books could move, persuade, and, in certain cases, unhinge their readers.

3. REMEMBERING THE *AMADÍS*

Critical discussions of the conquistadores often reference their proclivity for the same books that crazed Don Quixote. The conquistadores 'remember the Amadís', Stephen Gilman writes, because 'their impetus and vocation are of the same stuff as Don Quijote's' (1961: 110). Although this remark overlooks the better part of his avowed vocation—'to defend damsels, shelter widows, and succour orphans and needy people' ('para defender las doncellas, amparar las viudas y socorrer a los huérfanos y a los menesterosos', 1. 11)—Don Quixote shares the impetus of the conquistadores to seek fame and adventure, to light out for newer worlds. Let's take a closer look at the books that the conquistadores supposedly remember. The discursive properties of the Books of Chivalry—usefully catalogued in Daniel Eisenberg's study of the elements commonly found in the genre (1982: 55–74)—had been codified long before Cervantes's invective against them. Rather than categorizing them as an essentialist and timeless genre, or as shards of the Old French Romances, I shall discuss them as a peculiarly Spanish and specifically sixteenth-century kind of prose fiction that encoded, as Carroll B. Johnson puts it, a 'ruggedly masculine, superphallic world of armor, lances, and horses' (1993: 88). If the Books of Chivalry had some roots in medieval feudal discourse, however, they also had branches that stretched across the Atlantic. As a genre, these books flourished for close to a century in both Spain and its colonies, their greatest popularity in Castile coinciding with the reign of Charles V (1517–55) (Eisenberg 1982: 40–1). Beginning with *Amadís de Gaula*—which appeared in at least one, if not several, editions before 1508, the year of the first surviving edition—some fifty different Books of Chivalry were published across the century in Spain and Portugal, many of which were either hand-carried or exported to the colonies.[4]

The role of these books in the production of Castilian identity —in the cultural representation of Spain to the Spanish—was most potent during the Caroline period, which coincided with the age of conquest. Like most literary genres, the Books of Chivalry were codified forms of thought. They originated in crucial and recurrent real-life situations, which were institutionalized, across time, into patterns of ritualized response to Spain's social order. The genre of the Books of Chivalry— which propped up the ideology of the Castilian ruling class, if not of Castile itself—brought to light many of the constitutive features of the aristocracy, reaffirming its social hierarchies, its chivalric ideals, and its imperial schemes. In reproducing and reinforcing these ruling class values, this popular genre actually structured the readers who experienced it. If Castile's inaugural Book of Chivalry, *Amadís de Gaula*, is a codification of the discourses of hegemony that 'repeat' the values of the ruling class, then remembering the *Amadís* is, to say the least, a conservative gesture. Don Quixote remembers the *Amadís*, however, within a text that repeatedly announces its intentions

---

[4] For these publication facts on the Books of Chivalry, see Chevalier (1976: 64–5). Among the many excellent studies of the genre, see esp. Daniels (1992), Eisenberg (1982), Mancing (1982), Riquer (1973), Rodríguez Prampolini (1948), Roubaud (1998), Sieber (Harry) (1985), Thomas (1952) and Urbina (1988).

to destroy precisely that kind of fiction. *Don Quixote* parodies the Books of Chivalry with such a high degree of affectionate malice that, in the end, the novel frees itself from the 'stuff' of its chivalric subtexts. But it never frees the critic from rethinking the process of this parodic liberation: not only the moves required to dislodge the Books of Chivalry from an aristocratic culture that cherished them as a representational practice, but also the role of Don Quixote in parodically repeating and systematically undermining *Amadís de Gaula* and its multiple sequels.

Books have their fates, as Terence long ago remarked ('Habent sua fata libelli'). And the Books of Chivalry were fated, before their decanonization, to produce at least three major psychological upheavals that concern our argument: one and the same genre would give the conquistadores their delirious dreams, Cervantes his fictional plot, and Alonso Quijano a psychotic turn. Readers who wish to ponder these three different responses to one literary kind—delirium, creativity, and psychosis—must remember that it was also the fate of these books to be reviled, in both Spain and its New World colonies, long before Cervantes thematized their demolition. They were reviled, above all, for lying. These books were a problem for readers engaged in the arduous sixteenth-century process of becoming conscious of fiction as a practice distinct from both history and lying. The Canon of Toledo gestures to the difficulties of this process at the end of a long speech reiterating the position, both moral and ecclesiastical, on the Books of Chivalry as harmful to the republic: 'Lying fictions must be wedded to the intelligence of those who read them' ('Hanse de casar las fábulas mentirosas con el entendimiento de los que las leyeran', 1. 47).

4. FEAR OF LYING

With the inauguration of the Books of Chivalry as a Castilian prose genre, New World chroniclers were no longer obliged to call upon God—as Dr Diego Álvarez Chanca had done in his letter to the Cabildo of Seville describing Columbus's Second Voyage—to witness the truth of their reports. Dr Chanca, a physician to the fleet and a figure given more to botanizing than theorizing, winds up his eyewitness account anxious that readers would find him prolix or given to exaggeration. But as God is his witness, he swears to his readers, he has not strayed 'one iota from the bounds of truth' ('una jota de los términos de la verdad') (1988: 72–4). After the arrival of the Books of Chivalry, chroniclers could invoke these fictions, instead of God, to witness what lying—really shameless lying—would look like. Wishing to deny any connections between the Books of Chivalry and their accounts of the New World, writers would routinely continue, in the spirit of peninsular invectives, to vilify the genre. The virulent sixteenth-century attacks in Spain on the Books of Chivalry tended to stress their toxicity. B. W. Ife provides a colourful catalogue of censorious attacks on the genre, which was variously described as 'filth', 'excrement', 'infection', 'gangrene', and—in the colourful 'poison topos' favoured by the age—as 'scorpion oil' ('aceite de escorpiones') (1985: 15). The attacks on the Books of Chivalry degenerated into a 'series of topoi' such as the above, commonplaces repeated 'by various moralist writers who had no direct knowledge of the works they attacked' (Eisenberg 1982: 45). The censoriousness of these moralists is enacted in Part 1 of *Don Quixote* most notably by the Canon of Toledo, who rails at length about, and even manages to personify, the Books of Chivalry:

For my part, I find them pleasant enough reading as long as I don't allow myself to think that they're all lies and nonsense, but as soon as I recognize their real nature, I toss even the best of them against the wall—and I'd even toss them into the fire, if one were handy, which they deserve for being cheats and liars and beyond the pale of common human nature, like the creators of new sects and ways of life, who allow the ignorant masses to take all their crazy lies as truth.

De mí sé decir que cuando los leo, en tanto que no pongo la imaginación en pensar que son todos mentira y liviandad, me dan algún contento; pero cuando caigo en la cuenta de lo que son, doy con el major dellos en la pared, y aun diera con él en el fuego, si cerca o presente le tuviera, bien como a merecedores de tal pena, por ser falsos y embusteros y fuera del trato que pide la común naturaleza, y como a inventores de nuevas sectas y de nuevo modo de vida, y como a quien da ocasión que el vulgo ignorante venga a creer y a tener por verdadera tantas necedades como contienen'. (1. 49)

The Canon of Toledo recognizes the appeal of these books in an image that gestures to the cartographic impulse so prevalent in his age: only somebody 'barbaric and untutored' ('bárbaro e inculto'), he sniffs, could take satisfaction in reading about how 'a tall tower full of knights goes sailing off to sea . . . and tonight it will be in Lombardy and the next day in the land of Prester John of the Indies' ('una gran torre llena de caballeros va por la mar adelante . . . y hoy anochece en Lombardía, y mañana amanezca en tierras del Preste Juan de las Indias', 1. 47).

In Part 2 of *Don Quixote*, Don Diego de Miranda, also known as the Man in Green ('el caballero del Verde Gabán'), takes a similar moral stance, refusing to allow any Books of Chivalry to cross his threshold. The world has been filled with tales of these fake knights errant, he claims, 'much to the harm of good morals and to the discredit of truthful books' ('tan en daño de las buenas costumbres y tan en perjuicio y descrédito de las buenas historias', 2. 16). In between the publication of Parts 1 and 2 of Don Quixote, Covarrubias's *Tesoro* (1611) summarily defines the *libros de caballerías* as fictions providing 'much entertainment and little benefit' ('mucho entretenimiento y poco provecho').

The habit of regarding the Books of Chivalry as a genre of lies that required suppression began early and was carried across the Atlantic. Although fond of reading Books of Chivalry during his siestas, Charles V did not consider them fit reading for his transatlantic subjects. On 4 April 1531, he had his queen, acting as sovereign in his absence, publish a royal decree prohibiting exports of the genre to the Indies, since 'this is bad practice for the Indians and something with which it is not well for them to be concerned' (Leonard 1992: 81). Further instructions from the Queen to the viceroy of Mexico five years later, in 1536, suggest that the earlier ban had been ineffective and required repetition. Seven years later, in 1543, the ban was once again reissued, this time by Prince Philip, who forbade all entry into the Indies of 'profane and imaginative' books 'such as those about Amadis and others of this type of lying histories'— a ban that again seemed to be more 'honored in the breach' than the observance (Leonard 1992: 83). Noting that Spaniards in the colonies 'managed to read around the ban', Barbara Fuchs usefully explores the metropolitan motivations for the censorship: anxiety that the Indians, once they realized that the Books of Chivalry lied, would cease to believe in religious books, for example, the Bible (Fuchs, forthcoming). A more realistic anxiety might have been that the Indians, once they became familiar with the Books of Chivalry, would begin to behave like chivalric knights—much as the Indians depicted in Ercilla's *Araucana* behave, a trait discussed in Chapter 7, below.

Just before the appearance of the second royal ban, Gonzalo Fernández de Oviedo, Spain's official chronicler of the Indies, loudly divorced his work from the Books of Chivalry in his *Historia general y natural de las Indias* (1535): 'I do not recount the nonsense of the books of Amadís nor those that depend on them' ('no cuento los disparates de los libros de Amadís ni los que dellos dependen') (1851–5: i. 179). Oviedo was well acquainted with all that lying nonsense, given the earlier publication of his own *Don Claribalte* (1519), a chivalric work that earned him the status of America's first novelist. A similar notion of the Books of Chivalry as lies or fables that need to be separated from historical truth motivates Pedro de Castañeda Nájera, who advertises himself, in his chronicle of the Coronado expedition (1540–2), as a reliable and dependable author who does not write fables like those found in the Books of Chivalry (1940: 276). Bernal Díaz del Castillo similarly debunks the genre in chapter 151 of his 'true history' of the conquest of New Spain (*Historia verdadera de la conquista de la Nueva España*) (c.1568; pub. 1632), where he refuses to become prolix about the day-to-day carnage of 'many Mexicans' ('muchos mexicanos') because 'it would resemble the books of Amadís or Chivalry' ('parecería a los libros de Amadís o Caballerías') (1980: 346). Even at the start of the 1590s—a decade in which, due more to royal edict than to loss of popularity, no Books of Chivalry are published (Eisenberg 1987: 34)— the New World Jesuit historian José de Acosta still worries that Spanish readers might confound his history of the Indies—*Historia natural y moral de las Indias*—with one of the detested Books of Chivalry. Acosta's readers still needed to be reminded, it would seem, that the world of the American Indians was not at all like 'the fabulous stories cooked up in the Books of Chivalry' ('las patrañas que fingen los libros de caballerías') (1962: 278).

Although both 'true' and 'fictive' modes of writing interpenetrate in the Chronicles of the Indies, their writers—in the mode of Cide Hamete—ritually insist on the truthfulness of their texts. If these chroniclers are aware that 'the boundaries between fiction and nonfiction are not laid up in heaven', as

Bakhtin wryly puts it (1981: 33), their aim is scarcely to advertise such earthly incertitudes. The New World chroniclers could scarcely anticipate, say, Hayden White's well-known account of the poetics of historiography—which sees the writing of history as a literary or 'fiction making' operation encoding cultural anxieties—an account that has not gone uncontested (1973: 82–5).[5] Although we may assume that the chroniclers were scarcely appealing to this kind of demystified postmodern reader, someone keenly aware of an author's selection and emplotment of historical events and situations, Cervantes often seems to be addressing just such a reader. While Don Quixote serves as a cautionary tale of both the psychic dangers of reading overwrought fictions and of their power to compel belief, the text that contains him does not privilege history over fiction. History and fiction remain inextricably linked in *Don Quixote*, which repeatedly thematizes the compromised nature of *all* historical accounts—whether by Old or New World historians. Cide Hamete, the pseudo-chronicler of *Don Quixote*, makes frequent facetious statements about the 'truth' of his remarkable 'history'. Although he is introduced to readers as a putative 'liar', his tireless self-presentation as a 'veracious historian' may, in fact, encode some cultural anxieties about his status as a Moor, affiliated with a community fated to undergo forced expulsion between the publications of Part 1 and Part 2 of *Don Quixote*. Cervantes's sceptical or perspectival view of truth, in short, anticipates many ideas about the complicity between 'truth' and power so intensely discussed in the postmodern. But Cide Hamete's obsession with questions of truth also looks back to a legion of earlier models of 'true histories', including *La Araucana*, to be discussed in Chapter 7, below.

5. BOOKS AND THEIR PATHOLOGIES

What many sixteenth-century historiographers of the Indies had tried to put asunder—the 'lying' Books of Chivalry and their own 'truthful' chronicles of Spain's imperial exploits— would be put together again by various post-Romantic American writers. In 1828, for example, the fanciful and sentimental

[5] See e.g. Momigliano 1981: 267–8.

Washington Irving asserts, in his biography of Columbus, that the stories of the conquistadores are both incredible *and* true: 'The extraordinary actions and adventures of these men, while they rival the exploits recorded in chivalric romance, have the additional interest of verity' (1868: iii. 14). In 1843, William Prescott, in turn, compares the deeds of the conquistadores to the fantastic exploits in the Books of Chivalry. Prescott could count on the renewed interest in Arthurian chivalry then gripping his Anglo-American reading public: Alfred Lord Tennyson had just published his chivalric blockbuster, 'Morte d'Arthur', the year before. According to Prescott, the spirit of enterprise which 'glowed in the breast' of the sixteenth-century Spanish cavalier was 'not inferior to that of his own romances of chivalry' (1873: ii. 47). This comparison between the conquistadores and their reading materials foreshadowed a critical trend beginning in the 1920s with a series of major scholars—Henry Thomas, Torre Revello, Rodríguez Prampolini, and Irving Leonard—who would link, in one way or another, the Books of Chivalry to the 'enterprise of the Indies' ('empresa de las Indias') (Adorno 1992: pp. xxviii n. 1, and xxxv n. 32).

A number of other twentieth-century scholars have reiterated the notion that the exploits of the New World Spanish explorers were influenced by the Books of Chivalry. Alan Deyermond, for example, writes that 'Spanish and Portuguese explorers were often inspired by, and formed their expectations on, the model of what they read in the romances, while the chroniclers of discovery and conquest wrote in similar terms; there is no doubt that life to some extent copied literature, as it always does' (1971: 162). Ramón Iglesia claims that 'the shadow of the books of chivalry projects itself over the enterprise of the conquistadores' ('la sombra de los libros de caballerías se proyecta sobre la empresa de los *conquistadores*') (quoted in Gilman 1961: 110). Juan Francisco Maura, an editor of Cabeza de Vaca's *Naufragios*, characterizes the sixteenth century as a time when the fantastic events related in the Books of Chivalry 'did not differ much from what was happening in the New World' ('no se diferenciaba mucho de lo que estaba aconteciendo en el Nuevo Mundo') (1989: 41). On a more cautious note, Daniel Eisenberg acknowledges the harmony of the Books of Chivalry 'with the spirit which led to the conquest and colonization of the New World', although he questions 'the degree to which the romances were a cause of the New World exploration and conquest' (1982: 42). As this chapter argues, there can be no Talmudic knowledge about the degree of influence of the Books of Chivalry—or of any cultural production—on the conquest of America. All we can say is that the genre was deeply implicated in the the enterprise of the Indies.

Evidence of this implication appears in the Spanish frenzy for renaming, part of the ceremonial act of possession that included the effacement of native toponyms. Beginning with Columbus, who renamed six islands during his first voyage, the practice reached new heights in Bernal Díaz's *Historia verdadera*, which cites hundreds of cases of renaming in New Spain. In two notable cases the toponyms given to American territories were taken directly from the Books of Chivalry: 'Patagonia' from a tribe of savage monsters in *Primaleón*, and 'California' from a kingdom of Amazons in *The Exploits of Esplandián* (*Las sergas de Esplandián*), the fifth book of the *Amadís* cycle and a prominent book in Don Quixote's library. Of the multiple books instrumental in crazing Cervantes's hero, the *Sergas de Esplandián* was the first to be consigned to the bonfire during the inquisition of Don Quixote's library (1. 6). Published before 1510 by Garci Rodríguez de Montalvo, this book introduced Europe to a tribe of Amazons living on a fictional island called California. The inaugural appearance of California as a toponym begins with Montalvo's enticing address to the reader: 'You should know that on the right hand of the Indies there was an island, named California' ('Sabed que á la diestra mano de las Indias hubo una isla, llamada California') (1950: 539). Irving A. Leonard's 1949 classic, *Books of the Brave*, considered the case of the Amazons to provide the 'most compelling demonstration' of the links between the conquistadores and the Books of Chivalry (Adorno 1992: p. ix).

Leonard's arguments merit close attention for their attempts to document the negative influence of the Books of Chivalry on the conquistadores, though not to justify their more ruthless exploits.[6] Although his title—*Books of the Brave*—appears to reinforce triumphalist notions about the glorious achievements of

---

[6] 'Careful readers take exception to the notion, implicit in chapter 1 [of *Books of the Brave*], that the conquistadors' consumption of tales of chivalry as "men of their times" could be used to explain or even to justify their roles in wars of enslavement and destruction' (Adorno 1992: p. x).

Spain's conquistadors, Leonard also responded to some of their less glorious impulses. Many soldiers loitering about Sevilla while awaiting their sailing orders to the Indies, he argued, bought copies of the *Sergas de Esplandián*, the fifth book of the *Amadís* cycle, on sale in the *talleres* of the Cromberger press in Sevilla in 1510. The *Sergas* exemplified, for Leonard, 'the highly seasoned fiction' that inflamed the imaginations of the conquistadores and 'distorted their conceptions of the lands they were to penetrate' (1992: 96). Reading the *Sergas* in camp and then discussing it on the march seems to have also inflamed the acquisitive imaginations of these soldiers: 'the ruthless confiscation of the treasures of Montezuma, of Atahualpa, and of other victims of Spanish greed owed not a little to the imaginative quill of the storytelling regidor of Medina del Campo' (1992: 34–5). This remark is strongly in the humanist tradition of Juan Luis Vives, whose *De Officio Mariti* (1529) found the 'fables' of Tristan, Lancelot, Amadís, and Arthur harmful because they 'kindle and stir up covetousness' (Ife 1985: 14). Leonard mentions the 'points of coincidence' between Montalvo's portrait of the Amazons of California and Francisco de Orellana's later discovery of the Amazon river, allowing that Orellana's indebtedness to the *Sergas* remains 'a matter for speculation' (1992: 60). On the Cervantine front, Jorge Campos notes the appearance of both Juan de Orellana and Francisco de Pizarro in the *Persiles* (bk. 3, ch. 2), figures he regards as well-known 'in all the world' ('en todo el mundo') (1947: 403). The figures that appear in the *Persiles* are actually the descendants of the two famous, and contemporaneous, conquistadores. Cervantes's retrievable relation to Orellana, however, is also a matter for speculation. Toward this end, then, let us rehearse the discovery that gave the Amazon river its name and Cervantes his loaded allusions to the Orellana and Pizarro families.

6. ORELLANA AND THE NEW WORLD AMAZONS

In 1542 an expedition of some fifty-six men led by Francisco de Orellana, a lieutenant of Pizarro, inadvertently travelled more than 2,000 miles down to the mouth of the great river to be called the Amazon. It was the first such journey by Europeans, and one of the participants, the Dominican friar Gaspar de Carvajal, recorded some of its incidents.[7] On the feast of St John the Baptist, the friar-chronicler reports, God willed that the unfailing Amazons should finally materialize. On rounding a bend of the huge river, the Spaniards saw a large cluster of shining white villages that they identified as the 'dominion of the Amazons' ('señorío de las amazonas'); forewarned of the coming of the Spaniards, however, the natives of these villages plunged into the water to confront them in a hostile mood ('no con buena intención') (Carbaxal 1992: 257). A serious battle took place, the Spaniards shooting with crossbows and heavy matchlock guns, the Indians raining arrows on them. The narrating friar was himself struck by an arrow that penetrated his torso, and only the thickness of his clerical habit saved him. Notwithstanding his wounded state, and the later loss of an eye, the friar-chronicler managed to eyewitness some ten or twelve Amazons who had come down for this battle:

they were fighting at the head of the Indians like female captains, and they fought so vigorously that the Indians never dared to turn their backs on them, and anyone who did so they clubbed to death. These women are very white and tall, with long hair braided and wrapped around their heads, and they're very muscular and walked about stark naked, only their shameful parts covered, with bows and arrows in hand, each as war-like as ten Indians.

andaban peleando delante de todos los indios como capitanas, y peleaban ellas tan animosamente que los indios no osaban volver las espaldas, y al que las volvía delante de nosotros le mataban a palos. Estas mujeres son muy blancas y altas, y tienen muy largo el cabello y entrenzado y revuelto a la cabeza, y son muy membrudas y andaban desnudas en cuero, tapadas sus vergüenzas, con sus arcos y flechas en las manos, haciendo tanta guerra como diez indios. (Carbaxal 1992: 258)

By the time of their retreat, communications between the Spaniards and a kidnapped interpreter had considerably improved. Working through the medium of a word-list, the Captain managed to understand the captive Indian, who seems to have communicated an impressive number of facts about these

[7] Citations from the 'edición facsimilar' of Fr. Gaspar de Carbaxal's *Relación del descubrimiento . . .* (1992) will be parenthetically documented in my text. English translations are my own, although readers may wish to consult Lee's 1934 translation of 'Carvajal's Account'.

Amazons: that they lived a seven-day journey away; that they were so numerous they populated some seventy villages; that their houses were built not of straw but of stone; that they owned a great abundance of gold and silver, including eating utensils in these metals; that they had many gold and silver idols in the form of women; that they dressed in very fine wool clothing, in blankets girded about them from the breasts down; that they wore crowns of gold on their heads; that their hair reached down to the ground at their feet; that they were carried about the land on camels; and, finally, that they were not married but that they bore children.

This last fact seemed to intrigue the Spaniards. When they asked the Indian interpreter the predictable question—how these women could become pregnant, given that they were 'not married nor with any men living among them ('no siendo casadas ni residir hombre en ellas')—he obligingly explained that *sometimes* these women did consort with men (Carbaxal 1992: 262). 'When they feel sexual desire' ('Cuando les viene aquella gana'), the interpreter continued, the Amazons assemble a great horde of warriors and go off to make war on a very great overlord. They bring back to their territories whatever men they desire, and after they find themselves pregnant ('se hallan preñadas'), they send the men back to their own lands; and when the time comes for delivery, 'if they have a male child, they kill him and return him to the father, and if a female child, they rear her with great solemnity and teach her war-like things' ('si paren hijo le matan y le envían a sus padres y si hija la crían con muy gran solemnidad y la imponen en las cosas de la guerra') (Carbaxal 1992: 262). Gáspar de Carvajal's chronicle of the discovery of the Amazon river Amazons, who supposedly practised an especially cruel brand of male infanticide, closes with a little cautionary tale, allegedly told him by some local male natives: 'that whoever visits the territory of these women will go as a young man and return aged' ('que el que hubiese de bajar a la tierra de estas mujeres había de ir muchacho y volver viejo') (Carbaxal 1992: 265).

Orellana and his exhausted companions returned to civilization from 'the country of these women' at the end of the year 1542. On 20 January 1543—exactly one month after witnessing their arrival in Santo Domingo—Gonzalo Fernández de Oviedo wrote a twenty-four-page letter to Cardinal Pietro Bembo in Italy.

In this letter, Oviedo called the Marañon river, formerly the *Mar Dulce* visited by Vicente Yáñez Pinzón in 1500, the 'River of the Amazons' ('Río de las Amazonas'). An Italian translation of Oviedo's letter, included within Ramusio's collection, furnished Europe with its first account of this epic journey into the interior of South America.[8] Although Oviedo had earlier rejected the possibility of Amazons in the Caribbean, dismissively noting that all accounts of them were based on the mere testimony of *indios*[9]—he was in fact the first chronicler to affirm their existence in South America. Orellana's journey was ending just as Charles V was signing, in November 1542, the famous New Laws inspired by Bartolomé de las Casas, which were confirmed in Valladolid in June 1543. That the Spanish government seriously intended to enforce these New Laws is documented by the contract they issued to Orellana in 1543, ordering that 'no harm be done to the Indians', who were 'human beings and subjects' (Kamen 1997: 30). As is well known, the New Laws provoked a tide of rebellion among the Spanish colonists in America and were revoked in 1545.

Although these events occurred several years before his birth in 1547, that Cervantes knew some of the particulars of Orellana's discovery is obliquely suggested in the *Persiles*, in the long interpolated story of Feliciana de la Voz (bk. 3, chs. 2–5). In this tale, a young mother suddenly and urgently gives away her newborn son to its father, who, in turn, hands it over into the care of two historical figures with names closely linked to the Amazon legend: Don Juan de Orellana and Don Francisco Pizarro. This gesture adds an American dimension to the Feliciana story and moves me to a strong reading of its components. Cervantes's literary rendering of Feliciana's strange postpartum behaviour may qualify as a civilized and Christianized shard from the Amazon legend discussed in the Orellana chronicle—where women bear children outside marriage and give away their male offspring to the fathers. In the *Persiles* story, the newly delivered mother is explicitly depicted as unattached,

---

[8] Oviedo's letter is discussed by Gerbi (1985: 167). Oviedo would also insert a version of Gáspar de Carvajal's chronicle into the second part of his *Historia general de las Indias*, a text not published until 1851.

[9] Reputed sightings of Amazons drove Oviedo to multiple revisions of a chapter in his *Historia general y natural de las Indias*, revisions that dealt with Núñez de Guzmán's sighting, and later recantation, of Amazons. See Myers (1992: 523–30).

a happily temporary lapse, to her male offspring: 'what is even more significant', Cervantes writes, 'no natural love moved her to recognize the child—the newborn being a boy' ('lo que es más de considerar, el natural cariño no le movía los pensamientos a reconocer el niño, que era varón el recién nacido', 297).

Although Cervantes's story of Feliciana de la Voz needs no Amazonian subtext to explain the marked absence of mother love depicted in its heroine, the presence of such a subtext is fortified by Cervantes's relationship to the historical figures named in the *Persiles*: Don Francisco Pizarro and Don Juan de Orellana. Although they have different surnames, both were sons of Don Fernando de Orellana, the 'real life' magistrate of Trujillo in 1607, and his wife Doña Francisca Pizarro. A number of scholars have suggested that Cervantes's episode of Feliciana was an artistic rendering of 'real-life' events between Doña Feliciana de Cervantes de Gaete—a female member of the Extremadura branch of the Cervantes family—and Don Pedro de Orellana; that the couple was married in Trujillo on 21 March 1615; and that the bride was related to Miguel de Cervantes. It is clear that the kinship ('parentesco') between the Pizarros, the Orellanas, and the Extremadura branch of the Cervantes family will continue to exercise early modern scholars and critics.[10] The complicated itinerary of Americana that ends with the Orellana allusions in the *Persiles*, in sum, began with one of the most influential Books of Chivalry, the *Sergas de Esplandián*. This fictional narrative prefigured the New World Amazons that Orellana's exploratory party would then sight—or more likely hallucinate—decades later. When Cervantes gave the *Sergas* a place in *Don Quixote*, installing the fictional California Amazons in his hero's library, and when he gave Orellana and Pizarro a role in the *Persiles*, he provided readers with a whole network of speculative but tantalizing American connections.

Cervantes never tells us about Don Quixote's response to the copy of the *Sergas de Esplandián* found in his library. To speculate about the effect of a book on a single fictional character —especially a figure 'so movingly inflexible' as Don Quixote (Greene 1968: 264)—is perhaps easier than to consider the same

---

[10] For unedited documents on the Pizarros, see Astrana Marín (1948–58: vi. 519; vii. 431–33, as well as his app. 27 on pp. 746–50). See also Avalle-Arce's long footnote on these kinships in his edition of *Persiles* (1969: 288 n.), as well as Romero Muñoz's footnote in his more recent edition of *Persiles* (1997: 457–8 n.).

book's effect on a community of real-life conquistadores. The effect of a long military struggle, by land and sea, of Europe's finest Christian knights against the California Amazons would have enthralled Don Quixote during his pre-manic reading bouts. His avowed pudicity, however, would have been offended by the Amazons' practice of mating randomly and feeding their unwanted male infants to their pet griffins—a gruesome and patently fabulous detail from Montalvo's *Sergas*. But Don Quixote would no doubt have celebrated the final defeat and domestication of those anti-Dulcinea figures, the California Amazons, by Montalvo's heroic knights. His mimicry of militant European knighthood, in short, would have remained inflexible.

What Montalvo's *Sergas*—or for that matter, any of the Books of Chivalry—contributed to the mass psychology of the conquistadores is another and more evasive story, one that will always remain open to speculation. Books and culture play off each other in ways that are hard to codify. There is no way to plug the Books of Chivalry into an equation and see what effect they had on the psychology of the conquistadores. The assertion that the fictions of popular culture contribute to group psychology tends to gain support during violent times like our own, when, for example, the links between media violence and aggressive behaviour are being tirelessly researched. Although the Books of Chivalry serve as a mirror of, as well as a window on, Cervantes's culture, the difficulties of measuring their precise influence on that culture is thematized in *Don Quixote* itself. The long itinerary that Tzvetan Todorov takes through 'projective psychology' concludes that readerly reinterpretation will be controlled by cultural constraints—by the commonplaces or notions that members of a given social group will 'deem plausible' (1990: 39–49). But *Don Quixote* shows how members of the same readerly community cannot arrive at any consensus on questions of 'truth' in the Books of Chivalry, how they respond in wildly different ways, moreover, to notions of plausibility. The same fire that melts the butter hardens the egg. The same books that craze Don Quixote lead Dorotea, who knows and imitates them expertly, out of a wilderness of seduction and betrayal. Traditionally blamed for Don Quixote's amusing madness, the Books of Chivalry may also be praised for his disruptive mimicry.

7. THE MIMIC MAN

In calling Don Quixote a mimic man, I do not mean to agitate
the English line of descent of mimic men, which can be traced
through such writers as Kipling, Forster, and Naipaul. It is not
only the discourse of English colonialism, however, that speaks
in a forked tongue. Civilizing missions have epic intentions
that often produce texts rich in the traditions of irony and
mimicry, texts distinguished by a 'comic turn from the high
ideals of the colonial imagination to its low mimetic literary
effects' (Bhabha 1994b: 85–7). Although never invoked in Homi
Bhabha's theories of mimicry, Don Quixote—written toward the
end of a century-long civilizing mission that left many visible
traces in its text—instances this comic turn with astonishing
precision. There are, of course, major differences between the
English and Spanish civilizing missions, including their respective colonial ideals, which in Spain were feudal and chivalric.
'We should not forget', Peter Russell remarks in an untroubled
tribute to the conquistadores, 'that even the narrow and militant
chivalric ideals of fifteenth-century Spanish knights in their way
made some important offerings to the history of the Renaissance.
It was, for example, men sustained by such ideals who had the
energy and stubbornness to find and conquer the New World'
(1964: 58). Don Quixote identifies with these idealistic knights
in an ambivalent way. Although technically on the side of the
colonizers, he is imaginatively on the side of the colonized. In
his mimicry he anticipates Daniel Dravot, the British colonial
in Kipling's 'The Man Who Would be King', who goes 'mad
in his head' as 'king' of Kafiristan, even entertaining chivalric
aspirations to become 'a Knight of the Queen' (n.d.: 164).
Don Quixote's mimicry is not unlike, and may even have
influenced, Kipling's enactment of mad colonial chivalry.

   To bend Homi Bhabha's instructive formula to our purposes
here, Don Quixote is 'almost the same, but not quite' a conquistador
(1994b: 86). As a mode of colonial discourse, Bhabha's mimicry
—also known as 'colonial imitation' or 'colonial mimesis'—has
a double vision. It is, to begin with, a system of subject formation,
a 'complex strategy of reform': mimicry desires 'a recognizable
Other' whose sense of personal identity will be 'almost the same,
but not quite' that of the conquering caste. The underlying premiss of a mimic man is that he can never exactly reproduce

the dominant values. Don Quixote emits inexact and insane reproductions of chivalric values that bond him to other nostalgic Spaniards of his day. Although Cide Hamete speaks of 'the long lost and almost moribund order of knight errantry' ('la perdida y casi muerta orden de la andante caballería', 1. 28), when Don Quixote lights out across La Mancha, chivalry is still alive and well in royal sectors and, as suggested earlier, among the conquering caste in the Americas.

Beyond producing recognizable but not identical others, mimicry is also 'the sign of the inappropriate, a difference or recalcitrance' that poses a threat to the authority of colonial discourse (1994*b*: 86). This discourse and its power, as Bhabha claims elsewhere, are never 'possessed entirely by the colonizer' (1983: 200). Modes of mimicry appear throughout *Don Quixote* as strategies of reform, signs of recalcitrance, and menaces to authority. Whenever these modes surface, they violently shake up the political status quo. Don Quixote's liberation of the galley slaves (1. 22), for example, is explicitly depicted as a threat to, and a disruption of, the King's disciplinary authority. The knight's pseudo-chivalric mimicry in this episode—his high dudgeon against a king who would 'force' men to row in the galleys—profoundly disturbs the aims of imperial Spanish culture. Although he is cruelly stoned for his salvific impulse, the episode stresses the discordancies between crime and punisment in the early modern Spanish penal system (1. 22). Reading this episode as a 'political parody', Anne J. Cruz sees Cervantes as craftily censuring the practice of condeming criminals to the galleys (1999: 80). A different kind of menace to authority appears in the episode of Maese Pedro's puppet show (2. 26), in which members of the Carolingian ruling class are displayed as puppets, inverting the popular notion that only colonized people are puppets or marionettes. In this episode Don Quixote, the would-be knight, ends up maiming all the puppet-knights, beheading some and wounding others. Although he pays in cold cash for his misplaced rescue mission, a restitution aimed at reviving Maese Pedro's puppeteering career, careful readers understand the symbolic spectacle of a 'de-nosed Melisendra' ('Melisendra desnarigada', 2. 26).

Perhaps the most disrupting effect of Don Quixote's chivalric mimicry may be found in his offer of an ínsula to Sancho—a 'gift' whose implications will be unpacked in Chapter 6, below.

The novel's very first allusion to Sancho mentions him as a 'poor villager' ('pobre villano') seduced into Don Quixote's service by the knight's promise to win some island and leave his squire there as its governor (1. 7). This empty promise of an island functions as a parody of a feudal topos found in the Books of Chivalry: in *Amadís*, for example, the protagonist made his squire Count of Ínsula Firme. When Sancho, as a dupe of the Dukes, is finally installed as governor of a landlocked 'ínsula' —a parody-island from the Books of Chivalry—the power of the Spanish ruling classes receives its most satirical treatment. In renouncing the sham governorship of Isla Barataria in order to return home to his village in La Mancha, Sancho also renounces his squirely mimicry of the ideology of chivalry, which the corrupt aristocracy are themselves mimicking.

This kind of ideology at work in a colonial context appears in V. S. Naipaul's history of *El Dorado*, which provides an instructive portrait of how the Spaniards in the New World—'paying for their history, the centuries of Muslim rule and the slow cleansing of their land'—remained committed to 'an outdated code of chivalry' (1973: 43). This commitment is documented in a case study of Antonio de Berrío, a chivalric conquistador who arrived in the Indies in 1580, eventually to become governor of the Island of Trinidad. Naipaul, who consults a variety of chronicles to show exactly how Berrío 'is made to look like a man from another age' (1973: 43), never mentions Cervantes. But Berrío may have served as a model for Cervantes when he began to fashion his own cultural nostalgic, Don Quixote. Indeed, Cervantes may have even crossed paths with Berrío in the early 1580s, when the American conquistador was running between the court and Seville in order to help his wife, María de Oruña, the niece of Gonzalo Jiménez de Quesada, to claim her inheritance. When Cervantes married Catalina Salazar in the mid 1580s, he joined an interlaced family tree that actually included the Quesadas and the Berríos. These family ties are intriguing, if only because they portray the extended Quesada family, in the words of a Colombian historian, as 'the ultimate refuge of knights errant' ('el último refugio de los caballeros andantes') in Spain (Arciniegas 1998: 1247).[11] We need not invoke these transatlantic genealogies, however, to recognize

---

[11] See Arciniegas (1998: 1246–51) for the genealogies of these families.

that Antonio de Berrío and Don Quixote—one a historical conquistador, the other a fictional would-be—are united by a shared and stubborn commitment to the same abstract cognitive structure: the outmoded ideology of chivalry.

8. GENERIC CLEANSING

Don Quixote mounts a five-pronged attack on the Books of Chivalry: through satire, parody, irony, generic transgression, and intention—this last the avowed wish to topple 'the ill-founded machine' ('la máquina mal fundada') of a whole genre. The official censor of Part 2 of *Don Quixote*, José de Valdivielso (d. 1638), explained to contemporary readers that Miguel de Cervantes Saavedra was involved in a programme of purification, of generic cleansing: 'he aims to expel the Books of Chivalry ('pretende la expulsión de los libros de caballerías'). In the same 'Aprobación' and in the same breath, the censor announced that Cervantes, in fact, had already 'cleansed these realms of their contagious disease' ('limpiado de su contagiosa dolencia a estos reinos'). Diagnosing the specific pathology of the Books of Chivalry, a task avoided even by Cervantes's censor, is more complicated than documenting the cultural nostalgia they spread. For Don Quixote—whose complacent and vainglorious chivalric pretensions are systematically eroded across Part 2—cultural nostalgia costs not less than everything. The text that contains this endearing failure to revive the past, however, also examines chivalry within a dynamic present, an age of American colonization that coincided with Cervantes's life. Writing during a period of tremendous social upheaval in Philip II's Spain, with its rise of a bureaucratic absolutism that extended from a centralized state across two oceans, Cervantes turned to parody, a vehicle of satire, to hold a mirror up to empire. The satire in *Don Quixote* is aimed not at medieval chivalry—such a retrograde target *would* be quixotic—but at its early modern revivals, at the mimicry of chivalry displayed by both Don Quixote and the conquistadores.

Before his visit to the Cave of Montesinos, Don Quixote had regarded chivalry as an institution that had to be protected from the kind of blasphemies ('tantas blasfemias') uttered by the Canon of Toledo, who had dared to dismiss as apocryphal such figures as Amadís, Tristan and Iseult, King Arthur, Lancelot and

Guinevere (1. 49). When Don Quixote encounters the super-annuated chivalric figures in the Cave of Montesinos, however, he discovers that chivalry is embodied in Durandarte, a literally heartless and mummified figure, who enjoins him to have patience and shuffle the cards ('Paciencia y barajar', 2. 23). Durandarte's oracular expression estranges readers from the world of high chivalry to that of low cardsharks. Enchanted for centuries, the erstwhile heroic figures in the Cave of Montesinos suffer financial hardships, rotten teeth, and menopause, all the coarse realities of life designed to jolt Don Quixote out of his adopted chivalric identity (2. 22–3). What Don Quixote witnesses in the Cave, as Helena Percas de Ponseti persuasively argues, is 'his own spiritual death' (1981: 986).[12] With the Cave of Montesinos, Cervantes constructs a literary sepulchre for Don Quixote's chivalric persona, which will systematically unravel across the rest of Part 2. Only people who live in language, as Don Quixote does, can fantasize that kind of sepulchral dwelling. In response to a youthful reading of Cervantes's novel, Freud claimed that 'we are all noble knights passing through the world caught in a dream' (Jones 1953: i. 191). In the Cave of Montesinos, however, Don Quixote is a noble knight caught in a dream that simultaneously explodes the ideals of noble knights.

Because Cervantes so pointedly ironized the values propounded by the Books of Chivalry, a number of European readers, taking their cue from the intentionalist passages in *Don Quixote*, were quick to pronounce its role in the demolition of chivalry and even the ruin of the monarchy that had sustained it. In England in 1690, for example, Sir William Temple declared that 'the History of Don *Quixot* had ruined the *Spanish* Monarchy; For before that time, Love and Valour, were all Romance among them, every young Cavalier that entred the Scene, Dedicated the Services of his Life, to his Honor first, and then to his Mistress. They Lived and Dyed in this Romantick Vein' (1690: 73). Close to a century later in Scotland in 1783, James Beattie, a Professor of Moral Philosophy at the University of Aberdeen, claimed that the publication of *Don Quixote* had caused chivalry to vanish 'as snow melts before the sun' (1970: 317). Cervantes's novel, Professor Beattie

---

[12] On the dream in the Cave of Montesinos, see also Johnson (1983: 154–68) and Wilson (1993: 59–80).

concluded, formed 'an important era in the history of mankind' and 'a great revolution in the manners and literature of Europe,' by effecting 'the final extirpation of chivalry and all its chimeras' (1970: 317–18). Cervantes managed to weaken, if not entirely to extirpate, the closed, monolithic, and aristocratic narrative forms of chivalry. The genre did not experience a sudden death but, to use Daniel Eisenberg's simile, lingered on 'like an aged person . . . gradually failing for years' (1982: 53). Although by the eighteenth century the genre would display what Bakhtin calls 'a hardened and no longer flexible skeleton' (1981: 3), that generic skeleton has been pressed into service again and again. It has enjoyed various literary curtain calls in the Anglo-American world, nostalgic revivals and generic transformations that have sometimes propped up aristocratic ideologies (as in Tennyson's *Idylls of the King*), and sometimes torn them down (as in Twain's *Connecticut Yankee in King Arthur's Court*). The American writer Walker Percy was still exploiting Arthurian discourses in his 1981 portrait of a modern-day Lancelot. But although versions of Camelot continue to surface in popular books or films, none of these isolated resurgences can be compared to the discursive practices of chivalry that were embedded in the social and political institutions of imperial Spain, that were codified into the dominant literary genre of the age, and that accompanied the conquistadores into the New World.

The belated nature of Cervantes's campaign against the Books of Chivalry surfaces periodically. Scholars will note that he was 'flogging a horse that was already dead' (Russell 1985: 25), or that his attack had all the hallmarks of an 'afterthought' (Flores 1982: 3), claims partly called into question by the continued circulation of these books in the late sixteenth and early seventeenth centuries (Eisenberg 1982: 51). A far more contentious issue, however, is the repeatedly advertised intention of *Don Quixote* —an intention that cannot be purged, banished, or bracketed, even though readers are neither persuaded to adopt it nor urged to regard it as a standard for evaluating the rest of the novel. The astoundingly popular manifesto on 'The Intentional Fallacy', co-authored by W. K. Wimsatt and M. C. Beardsley in 1946, granted critics custody of intention while declaring fallacious whatever an author intended. Since that time, the relations between authorial intention and critical interpretation have remained vexed. After a fifty-year controversy that has granted

increasing prestige to anti-intentionalism, however, the author
and his or her intention are making a comeback. Claiming that
intentionalists understand only one of two kinds of intention,
Bakhtin asks readers to look at the author's 'other intention'—
which is to make his work rich in potentials: 'To put the point
paradoxically but precisely, authors intend their works to mean
more than their intended meanings' (Morson and Emerson
1990: 286–7). No matter what kind of authorial intentions, if
any, twenty-first-century scholars may wish to entertain for *Don
Quixote*, the text will continue to present itself as a reproval of
the Books of Chivalry—of the genre that sustained, distributed,
and exported aristocratic and imperial values. Intended meanings abound: the reproval may be read as Cervantes's intention
to dismantle the outdated artistic forms of medieval chivalry, as
his intention to destroy the chivalric props of his age's waning
imperialist culture, as his intention to ridicule the institutional
remnants of chivalry both at home and abroad in the Indies,
or as all or none of the above. To read Cervantes's texts, in sum,
is to discern and attribute intention simultaneously.

   We are left with the reproval of a genre whose seductive
potential is vividly acknowledged. Edward Friedman wisely
explains that 'the destruction of chivalric romance is what *Don
Quijote* is about, if one understands the attempted erasure as a
symbolic gesture' (1994: 41). The gesture is both symbolic and
comic. The same literature that had helped to galvanize the conquistadores into performing acts of 'ocean chivalry' is put on trial
early in *Don Quixote*, during which selected books are 'purged',
'flogged', 'excommunicated', or given an 'overseas sentence'
(1. 6). But even as Cervantes stages an 'inquisition' for a whole
genre, showing its power to convert a bored country hidalgo
into a manic would-be conqueror, he intends his novel 'to mean
more' than its avowed intentions to destroy the genre. Lord
Byron—whose rich appetite for hyperbole should not signal
an impoverished understanding of intention—tried to sum up
Cervantes's accomplishment in a memorable canto of *Don Juan*:

> Cervantes smiled Spain's chivalry away;
> > A single laugh demolished the right arm
> Of his own country;—seldom since that day
> > Has Spain had heroes.
>
> > > > (13. 11)

Henry Thomas provides a check to such Byronic extravagance: if Cervantes did not extinguish a moribund genre with one blow, 'he at least had the satisfaction of saving us from a possible renaissance' ('tuvo al menos la satisfacción de salvarnos de un posible renacimiento') (1952: 136). Neither assessment is wholly accurate. The chivalric genre has had its renaissances and Spain has had its heroes. What we can safely conclude, however, is that Cervantes, like his great admirer Byron, was 'No Childe of Chivalry'.

6

Islands in the Mind: Utopography

THIS chapter, which takes as its point of departure the 'utopi-
anization' of Cervantes, focuses on the New World aspects of
that utopian strain. Early modern writings in the utopian genre
are best approached from a transnational perspective. Given that
the inaugural text of the genre, Thomas More's *Utopia* (1516),
was written in England; that it narrated, in learned Latin, the
voyage of a Greek-speaking Portuguese explorer; and that it
featured a voyage to an ultramarine 'no-place' in South America,
the codes of the genre invite a comparative, even a transatlantic,
approach. The Spanish historian who pioneered the utopian
reading of *Don Quixote*, however, rarely glances across the Atlantic.
José Antonio Maravall—whose monumental contributions to
Spanish historiography have been jointly and elegantly assessed
by Nicholas Spadaccini and Wlad Godzich—seeks to account,
through a *mentalités* approach, for the lived historical experience
of the Spanish peoples. Because Maravall has struggled to rethink
Spanish history from within Spain instead of, like Américo Castro,
from exile, his readings of *Don Quixote* are informed by a fundamentally peninsular and estatist structure. Where Maravall sees
Spain's domestic and metropolitan preoccupations as shaping
the utopian elements in *Don Quixote*, I see the Spanish colonial
achievement as an equally impressive model and point of reference for Cervantes's utopian conceptualization of space. Where
Maravall displays an intransigence about moving beyond the
binary dialectic advertised in the title of his book—*Utopia and
Counterutopia in the 'Quixote'*[1]—I see Cervantes's transactions with
space as less Manichaean, his locations of culture as less European, and his political or moral biases as less transparent.

[1] Although published in 1976 as *Utopía y contrautopía en el 'Quijote'*, and translated into English in 1991, Maravall's book is actually a re-elaboration dating back
to 1948. English citations from Maravall in this chapter are from the 1991 Felkel
translation. All citations from this text will give pages from the English translation
followed by pages from the original Spanish.

That the conquest and colonization of America opened the doors of Utopia—More's doors—is well known, acknowledged even by Maravall (1991: 30–31; 1976: 26). If we are agreed, then, that More's *Utopia*—a text that feigns Iberian encounters in South America—influenced Spanish utopian thinking, why does Maravall posit a Cervantes who caricatures utopian thinking but ignores the New World encounters that subtend it? Why does America merit only some half-dozen passing references in Maravall's study of utopias? Why do his insular reflections remain, in sum, so *peninsular*? As early as 1964, J. H. Elliott recognized that 'no serious historian of Spain could afford to exclude from the reckoning the transatlantic dimension of the Spanish past' (1995: 391). It is time to rethink the wages of Maravall's exclusion. The reasons for it are now clear. As Walter Mignolo reminds us in a different context, Maravall was mainly involved in 'charting the distinctive Spanish contribution to the European (mainly Italian) Renaissance', a contribution downplayed 'in the scholarly tradition of Renaissance studies' (1995: 324). In his specific contribution to Cervantine studies, on the other hand, Maravall was involved in charting the dangers of utopian thinking, which he repeatedly debunks under the rubric of 'utopian attitudes', 'utopian philosophy', or 'utopian political thought'. The present chapter calls into question some of Maravall's uses of utopias, whose chief characteristic he considers to be a 'denial of reality' ('negación de la realidad') (1991: 178; 1976: 237). The stress on this privative quality leads him to read *Don Quixote* as both a reflection and a critique of utopianism, which he regards as 'false' and 'escapist'. This censorious attitude seems oddly affiliated with the stance on utopias taken by the English poet and Puritan John Milton, whose *Areopagitica* assailed any notions of escapism from the 'world of evil' into which God had placed us unavoidably: 'to sequester out of the world into Atlantic and Utopian polities, which never can be drawn into use, will not mend our condition' (1957: 732–3). Although I agree with Maravall that the enterprise inspiring *Don Quixote* is 'clearly political' ('netamente política') (1991: 157; 1976: 203), I am less persuaded by his portrait of Cervantes as a mature writer condemning utopias because they are escapist. As I see it, Cervantes uses utopias to condemn—or, rather, to benevolently satirize—imperial, ducal, or gubernatorial corruption, both at home and abroad.

1. UTOPIAS, EUTOPIAS, DYSTOPIAS, HETEROTOPIAS

A few words about utopias and their subgenres may be in order at this point. In a challenging essay on 'Mapping Utopias', Steven Hutchinson rightly points out that eutopias and dystopias differ from utopias 'only in the degree to which the criteria of good/bad and desirable/undesirable predominate. Otherwise the same kinds of imaginative processes are involved in making them and the same kinds of interpretative processes are involved in understanding them' (1987: 179). Critics have found utopias, anti-utopias, counter-utopias, eutopias, heterotopias, and dystopias in Cervantes's novels. In a vivid reading by Julio Baena, for example, the entire *Persiles* has been categorized as a utopia: a baroque 'utopia of the novelist' (1988: 125–40). But the *Persiles* also contains within itself eutopias, as in Periandro's island paradise, a bejewelled dream landscape undisturbed by the seasons (bk. 2, ch. 15), and dystopias, as in the Barbaric Island narrative that opens the novel (bk. 1, chs. 1–6). *Don Quixote*, on the other hand, has been classified as both an anti-utopia (Morson 1981) and a counter-utopia (Maravall 1991). One could also argue for the presence of 'heterotopias' in Cervantes's two novels, not only in the Foucauldian sense of real world 'other places' like mirrors or prisons or psychiatric hospitals (Foucault 1986: 24–6), but also as communities based on the inclusion of differences (Siebers 1994: 20). Although the Cervantine 'no-place' visited in this chapter has the heterotopic element of a prison, it more handily qualifies as a dystopia or 'bad place', a termed coined in the 1950s (Negley and Patrick 1952: 298). Because various sections of the book in hand discuss the dystopia that opens the *Persiles*—an Americanized island where 'barbarians' every bit as savvy as Europeans are plotting to conquer the world—the present chapter focuses only on the dystopia of *Don Quixote*: the *ínsula* Barataria where Sancho is installed as governor.

The insularity of Barataria bears stressing. Although utopias may be situated 'on some distant island, valley, or mountain-top, in the Amazon basin, the Far East, Ethiopia, or the other side of the world, on the moon or other celestial bodies, inside the earth or a sea monster, or in the remote past or future' (Hutchinson 1987: 172), a distant and politically charged island remains the most visible sign of Cervantes's generic contact with

Thomas More's pioneering *Utopia*. Although the century-long itinerary from More's *Utopia* to Cervantes's experiments in utopography is a jagged one, various strong affinities exist between the two writers. The *Utopia*, for example, would seem to anticipate *Don Quixote* in being 'centrally concerned with the nature of literature and, especially, of fictionality' (Morson 1981: 168). But More and Cervantes display other commonalities as well. In addition to the legendary sense of irony that, as serio-comic writers, they both cultivate, their insular no-places share some peculiarly New World features.

Because Thomas More's title gave the Greek word *utopia* (Latin, *nusquama*) to literature, his 1516 work is considered by all accounts the foundational generic text. Although no Spanish translations of More's *Utopia* were published until Gerónimo de Medinilla's Castilian edition surfaced in 1637, the original Latin version of 1516 was widely disseminated among Spanish humanists until its appearance in the 1583 Index of the Inquisition. Trying to explain the derivation of utopian attitudes in England, Francisco de Quevedo would later write, in a prologue to a Spanish translation of *Utopia*, that More lived in a time and place where, 'in order to reprove the oppressive government' ('para reprender el gobierno que padecía'), he was obliged to imagine a suitable one.[2] Quevedo's interpretation of political reproval as the origins of English utopography is suggestive. One would wish for as clear a remark in some prologue of Cervantes. We can speculate on his approach to utopias, however, from at least two angles: from More's utopography or from his own. Although More's writings triggered the Spanish 'utopian' thinking that entered the discourses of Cervantes's age, the term *utopía* was not recorded by Covarrubias in his influential *Tesoro de la lengua castellana o española* (1611). Nor did Spain itself produce any systematic utopian text during its so-called Golden Age: the first Spanish literary blueprint for a model society emerged *c.*1682, when the anonymous *Descripción de la Sinapia, península en la tierra austral* was written.[3] This belated

---

[2] This passage from Quevedo's 'Noticia, juicio y recomendación de la *Utopía* de Tomás Moro' is cited in Maravall (1976: 245; 1991: 184).

[3] Cro discovered, edited, and published the anonymous edition of *Sinapia*. See Cro's splendid essays on 'New World in Spanish Utopianism' (1979) and 'Classical Antiquity, America, and the Myth of the Noble Savage' (1994).

utopian text raises its own set of questions, about why Spain produced neither a fictional utopia nor even an entry in the nation's first dictionary during the early modern period, but these belong to a different study. What Spain did produce, however, were social organizations in America based on utopian reformist ideas.

2. COLONIAL UTOPIAS

The utopian 'boom' in the Hispanic New World was influenced by More's *Utopia*, which, as Maravall notes, was read, quoted, and even applied ('leída, citada, aplicada') to real-life institutions in the Indies, both by governors and evangelizers [1991: 179; 1976: 239]. Sixteenth-century utopian experiments on the American mainland included, for example, the Erasmian labours of the Franciscan friar Juan de Zumárraga, who set out for Mexico in the vanguard of evangelizers to defend the Indians 'against the greed of the colonizers' ('contra la codicia de los colonizadores') (Bataillon 1950: 819). More well known than Zumárraga's utopian enterprise—although often dismissed as fiascos or failures—are the Lascasian communities of Cumaná in today's Venezuela (1520–21) and Vera Paz in Guatemala (1545–60). Vasco de Quiroga's mid-sixteenth-century experimental American townships have also been catalogued among these New World utopias (Zavala 1965). As the humane bishop of Michoacán and founder of the pueblo-hospitals of Santa Fe—evangelical townships for the Indians of Mexico and Michoacán—Vasco de Quiroga not only translated More's *Utopia*, but also tried to put into practice some of its regulations for his Indian colonies. Not unlike More's fictional utopian community, the pueblo-hospitals of Santa Fe were based on an agricultural economy with a six-hour workday and much leisure for religious development. In a passage from his *Información en derecho* that uncannily anticipates Don Quixote's famous speech to the goatherds (1. 11), Vasco de Quiroga perceives the New World inhabitants as living in a Golden Age, even as the inhabitants of Europe had fallen from it, having coming 'to a halt in this age of iron' ('a parar en esta edad de hierro') (Bataillon 1950: 820). Along similarly utopian lines may be counted the Jesuit missions in South America referred to as *reducciones*,[4] which were founded in 1610, squarely between the writings of Part 1 and Part 2 of *Don Quixote*. These 'reductions' —scattered through the territories of present-day Paraguay, Uruguay, Brazil, and Argentina, with two missionaries serving up to some 6,000 Indians—are generally regarded as the most successful of the experimental utopias attempted in the New World. Foucault, for one, who classifies 'those extraordinary Jesuit colonies' founded in South America as 'an extreme type of heterotopia', describes the colonies in Paraguay as well-regulated places 'in which human perfection was effectively achieved' (1986: 27). The heroic attempts on the part of such pioneering religious figures as Zumárraga, Las Casas, Vasco de Quiroga, or the South American Jesuits to try to organize different economies in the New World, in short, must be factored into the Spanish utopian thinking that Cervantes would absorb.

But religious communities founded by Spaniards are not the whole story. Reports from the New World, as J. H. Elliott explains—'whether of Indians living as innocent beings in a state of nature or as members of ordered polities like Inca Peru with its network of paved highways and its impressive stone buildings'—disclosed to the European imagination a new and heady spatial vision: 'America had given Europe space, in the widest sense of that word—space to dominate, space in which to experiment, and space to transform according to its wishes' (1995: 394, 406). These reports also generated or revived expectations among Sephardic Jews that tended to express themselves in utopian experiments. Attempts to organize real-world utopias by the oppressed peoples of the Old World are sometimes regarded benignly, as in this passage by Harry Levin: 'America, the land of Europe's futurity, provided a fertile soil for the largest number of earnest endeavors to put utopian theory into practice' (1972: 190). Maravall, however, considers such endeavours as less earnest than irrational. And he wants Cervantes to regard it that way too. Let's look at Maravall's arguments in the light of his hostile attitudes toward utopianism.

[1] Kupperman reminds us that the original meaning of 'to reduce', obsolete after the 17th cent., was 'to restore, especially to a belief, and it carried the implication of bringing back from error' (1995: 10).

3. UTOPIANISM ON TRIAL

Although the youthful Cervantes had participated in the utopianism that had distinguished the reign of Charles V, Maravall insists that these utopian ideas soon 'fell apart on him' ('se le vinieron abajo') (1991: 147; 1976: 189). Political utopianism —especially as manifested during the Caroline imperial phase by certain Spanish thinkers opposed to the new precapitalist spirit—offered the mature Cervantes, in Maravall's view, a position he could demolish in his writings. Maravall regards *Don Quixote* not only as 'the first great novel of the modern world' ('la primera gran novela del mundo moderno') (1991: 18; 1976: 11), but also as a text that, if read properly, can acquire 'a transparent and total meaning' ('un sentido transparente y total') (1991: 26; 1976: 21). Although I question these totalizing accounts, as well as the notion that Cervantes deploys an activist hero to ridicule utopian visions, I admire Maravall's attempt to enlighten the mentality of Cervantes's age through a rich culture of citation. The more programmatic aspects of Maravall's reading (aspects scarcely avoided by my own) may be fuelled by his chosen historical approach. Godzich and Spadaccini point to the 'fuzzy notion' of the French term *mentalités* (1994: 60). J. H. Elliott similarly warns readers that among the inherent problems in the history of *mentalités* is that 'it tends to take for granted the existence of an intellectual or cultural coherence which is rarely to be found' (1995: 401). Taken for granted in Maravall's study is a coherence of the class values of Spain's lower nobility, supposedly bound by a false utopianism that screams for caricature. Such a coherence, which presupposes a monolithic culture, is actually called into question by Cervantes's novels. The class values of the self-exiled Antonio in the *Persiles*, for example, who comes from a long line of hidalgos by the name of Villaseñor, are a far cry from those of Don Antonio Moreno in *Don Quixote*, the owner of an Enchanted Head and excessive amounts of leisure time, although both characters belong to the same stratum of Spanish society.

Maravall never wavers on his interpretation of intentionality. That Cervantes intended to debunk utopianism is shown by Don Quixote's rejection of three entities: administrative bureaucracies, early modern methods of warfare, and the new monetary economies. Even granting that Don Quixote rejects the idea of money, however, his anachronistic attitudes to it are not strictly utopian. Or at least they are much funnier, less social, and less moral than the attitudes remarked in such strictly literary utopias as More's and Campanella's, which ritually inveigh against greed—against the European *aurea fames*. Don Quixote's monetary attitudes seem to me more nostalgic than utopian: he refuses to give his consent of attention to the new mobile wealth because it has replaced the traditional feudal rewards of land or kingdoms—now called 'real estate'. The issue of Don Quixote's rejection of modern methods of warfare, of standing armies and gunpowder—*armas de fuego*—is more complex. Cervantes's hero makes very clear his retrograde attitudes toward gunpowder during his well-known speech on arms versus learning, where he looks back, with characteristic yearning, to warfare as practised in the classical Golden Age: 'Those were indeed blessed times which knew nothing of the frightful fury of those demonic instruments of artillery, whose inventor must be in Hell, receiving his due reward for so diabolical an invention' ('Bien hayan aquellos benditos siglos que carecieron de la espantable furia de aquestos endemoniados instrumentos de la artillería, a cuyo inventor tengo para mi que en el infierno se le está dando el premio du su diabólica invención', 1. 38). Not all readers, however, consider Don Quixote ridiculous for deploring the gunpowder that, according to Maravall, served as 'an instrument of Providence' ('un instrumento de la Providencia') for the conquest and colonization of America (1991: 109; 1976: 136). Don Quixote's rejection of firearms for their technical and 'diabolical' superiority could also be read as Cervantes's covert rejection of the providentialist view of the Spanish conquest of America, whose native populations were decisively overwhelmed by what Don Quixote calls the 'fiendish' invention of the cannon. In his heated rejection of firearms, Don Quixote would seem to be tilting toward Erasmian pacifism. Whether or not the famous humanist trio of Erasmus, Vives, and More incorrectly understood the basic premises of the state system, as Maravall claims (1991: 55; 1976: 73–5), their writings helped European humanism to develop an expansive conscience for social reform. Cervantes's affinity for the radical humanism founded by Erasmus, and continued by his like-minded contemporaries More and Vives, has been well documented by Alban K. Forcione, who magisterially articulates Cervantes's 'humanist vision' (1982), and by Javier Herrero, who staunchly defends it (1983: 22–33).

As manifested in More's *Utopia*, humanism included a new method of looking at the condition of, and reasons for, homelessness. Raphael Hythlodaeus's famous attack on enclosure and its dire social consequences in England sympathetically portrays the legions of homeless: 'Whichever way it's done, out the poor creatures have to go, men and women, husbands and wives, widows and orphans, mothers and tiny children. . . . Out they have to go from the homes that they know so well, and they can't find anywhere else to live' (More 1992: 47). Finding a *place* to live, in other words, even an imaginary place, is one of the staples of utopian discourse. The humanist method was not only hospitable to utopias but also, as More's text documents, to a dialogic exchange on the earthly value of such imaginal sites. Like More, Cervantes manifests the kind of dialogic imagination that engenders utopias as well as novels. Also like More, Cervantes maintains a sense of play, humour, wit, and whimsy throughout his utopian writings. Integral to the meaning of the utopias of both writers is a fierce irony, premised on an audience of elite readers who understand that 'no-places', like the city of Amaurotum in More's *Utopia*, are always 'dark or dimly seen'. In order to debunk these visionary 'no-places', however, Maravall posits a reactionary Cervantes, a writer who aimed to halt the diffusion of a kind of utopian thought that had come to signify, for a large sector of Spanish society, 'an escapist refuge' ('un refugio de escape') (1991: 19; 1976: 11). I find it difficult to believe that Cervantes created the 'inadequate and ridiculous figure of Don Quixote, hero of all failures' ('la figura inadecuada y ridícula de Don Quijote, héroe de todos los fracasos') (1991: 63; 1976: 71) in order to ridicule the idea of escapism. Don Quixote remains for many readers a lovable and sympathetic figure, partly because his will for remaking the world—and even for conquering and colonizing it if necessary—is sifted through the firm belief that each person is the child of his or her own deeds ('cada uno es hijo de sus obras'), a novel ideology of merit over blood (1. 4). This kind of prescient thinking may have itself seemed utopian to many of Cervantes's contemporaries.

We can safely say, then, that Maravall uses the term *utopian* to label projects regarded not merely as unfeasible but also as

undesirable. We can also say—and Maravall himself *does* say it—
that his notion of utopia is used loosely, that it has no strict
generic value. Don Quixote is 'not a utopia strictly speaking'
('no es propiamente una utopía'), but the idea of a utopia is
developed across the entire narrative 'in order to discredit those
who cling to such a concept' ('para descrédito de los que a ella
se aferraban') (1991: 17; 1976: 10). Who are these clingers who
need discrediting? They include men like Antonio de Guevara,
Vasco de Quiroga, and Bartolomé de las Casas—all architects
of the humanist currents of social reform articulated during the
reign of Charles V. As one of Charles V's Spanish collaborators,
Guevara had been appointed 'King's Chronicler' ('cronista del
rey') in 1526. As the bishop of Mondoñedo, he makes a brief
but memorable appearance in the Prologue to *Don Quixote*,
Part 1, where he is cited as an authority on prostitutes, a topic
invoked in his *Epístolas familiares*, 58 (1539). It is well known
that Guevara, a humanist scholar whose political philosophy
was deeply subversive and widely disseminated, shared the
same antipathy to the Books of Chivalry reiterated across *Don
Quixote*. I believe that Guevara and Cervantes also shared an
antipathy to Messianic imperialism. Guevara's condemnation
of the forces of conquest—an anti-imperialist stance he takes
in *El villano del Danubio* (*The Peasant of the Danube*)—may itself
qualify as utopian thinking. The reference in that text to
'the unfathomable ocean' ('la mar . . . en sus abismos') that
supposedly protected the Danube peasants from Roman imperialism makes it clear, as Américo Castro explains, that Guevara
was thinking of American Indians rather than German peasants
(1945: p. xxiii). In any case, Maravall regards *Don Quixote* as
'a genuine anti-Guevara treatise' ('verdadero anti-Guevara')
(1991: 18; 1976: 10). In similar fashion, he portrays Bartolomé
de Las Casas as yet another collaborator of Charles V and, as
such, a typical representative of the hated utopian ideology. Las
Casas's 'utopias of reconstruction', as Maravall puts it, would
give way to the pathetic 'utopias of evasion' that Cervantes
supposedly aimed to discredit (1991: 31; 1976: 27).[5]

To sum up Maravall's argument, then, Cervantes is not a bona
fide utopist but only a conceiver of utopias: 'While Las Casas
crossed the Atlantic to discover new men, Cervantes sought

---

[5] See also Maravall (1974).

them in literary creation, and by conceiving a utopia he also created a new literary genre, the modern novel' ('Si un Las Casas había ido al otro lado del Atlántico a buscar unos hombres nuevos, Cervantes los busca en la creación literaria, y al concebir así una utopía crea un género literario también nuevo: la novela moderna') (1991: 182; 1976: 242). The theoretical confusion here is compounded by Maravall's earlier claim that Cervantes had conceived a 'novel-utopia' ('novela-utopía') (1991: 161; 1976: 209), a hybrid entity that recalls Menéndez y Pelayo's classification of Thomas More's text as 'a utopian novel' ('una novela utópica') (1905–15: i. 392). The problem may lie in Maravall's discourse of conceptions and creations. It may be less confusing to say that *Don Quixote* includes utopian, dystopian, and heterotopian episodes that invite closer scrutiny. That kind of scrutiny might begin with a closer look at the English literary utopias that frame *Don Quixote*.

4. ENGLISHED IBERIAN EXPLORERS

As we noted in Chapter 5, islands feature as a feudal gift exchange in chivalric literature (as in *Ínsula Triste, Ínsula Sagitaria*, or *Ínsula Fuerte*). But they also operate as a characteristic device of closure and stasis in utopian literature. Via the medium of an island, Cervantes swerves from chivalric literature, which he parodies, to utopian literature, which he contacts generically. The writers of Renaissance utopias generally gravitated toward islands, which permitted them, as Hans Freyer long ago explained in *Die politische Insel*, to create ideal societies that were, to a greater or lesser degree, closed and static and difficult of access, with systems of control that strongly discourage the entry of foreigners (1936: 185). As what follows will show, however, the idea of an island operates not only as a bridge between genres in Cervantes, but also between continents. While testing the waters around these ideal islands, Cervantes would surely have remembered that in More's *Utopia*—the paradigmatic Latin text that so notably influenced sixteenth-century Spanish thinking—the island in question is 'discovered' by Iberian explorers. The main protagonist of More's text, the Portuguese mariner Raphael Hythlodaeus, explicitly sails to South America with Amerigo Vespucci on the last three of his four voyages to a 'nowhere' located 'somewhere south of the Equator'. The first two of Vespucci's voyages were under the Spanish flag, the last two under the Portuguese. As More writes:

Being eager to see the world, [Raphael] left to his brothers the patrimony to which he was entitled at home (he is a native of Portugal), and took service with Amerigo Vespucci. He accompanied Vespucci on the last three of his four voyages, accounts of which are now common reading everywhere; but on the last voyage, he did not return home with the commander. After much persuasion and expostulation he got Amerigo's permission to be one of the twenty-four men who were left in a fort at the farthest point of the last voyage. (More 1992: 5)

Although employed by the Spanish monarchy for his first two voyages, Amerigo Vespucci had made his last two voyages for the King of Portugal, so that Thomas More's choice of a Portuguese nationality for Raphael Hythlodaeus was reasonable. Vespucci had referred to his four voyages to America (1497, 1499, 1501, and 1503) in a letter—written in Lisbon in 1504 and addressed to Piero Soderini—whose authenticity has been long debated. Printed in Florence in 1505, this *Lettera di Amerigo Vespucci delle isole nuovamente trovate in cuatro suoi viaggi* was translated into French and then retranslated into Latin, in which form it began circulating throughout Europe, where it became available to More and his circle as part of the *Cosmographiae Introductio* (St Dié, 1507). More fictionalizes Raphael Hythlodaeus as sailing on the third voyage of 1501, a voyage also described in Vespucci's famous 'Mundus Novus' letter (1505), responsible for the heated polemics over the priorities of discovery. Neither the fact that America would be named after Amerigo Vespucci, nor that the site of More's fictional 'fort' would be later identified as the real-world Cape Frio ('Cabo Frío') in Brazil, concerns us here. What does inform our argument is More's choice of the New World as the site for a utopia that would reprove European politics, generate much discussion in Spain, and motivate many tractarian utopias in the New World.[6]

    In the later English utopia that More's *Utopia* seeded—Bacon's *New Atlantis* (1624)—the group of explorers who sail

[6] For details on Vespucci's voyages, including the polemics over the 'Mundus Novus' letter, see Vespucci's letters and Levillier's commentary in Vespucci (1951). See also the discussion of Vespucci's letters by Mignolo, who classifies them, despite their Italian origins, as 'cartas' or letters about the discovery (1982: 63–5).

into the Pacific from Peru all speak 'in the Spanish tongue' (1981: 211). After many hardships, they finally arrive at an island populated by tetralingual humanists, who supposedly use Spanish to describe to the narrator the workings of their whole technological utopia. Although written in English, the fiction of Bacon's *New Atlantis*, in short, is that everyone is speaking in Spanish. For all its scientific mechanicalism, the *New Atlantis* may be read as a posthumanist English parody of the Spanish *Chronicles of the Indies*. Published in 1623, about a century after the high age of discovery, Bacon does not influence—he reflects—Spanish utopian thinking. Although Cervantes never lived long enough to read the *New Atlantis*, published seven years after his death, he was certainly familiar with the Chronicles of the Indies that Bacon chose to parody in his utopian text. Indeed, Cervantes was himself parodying, as I argue in this book, selected incidents from the historiography of the conquest of America. Although Maravall specifically links the existence of knights errant in Don Quixote's imagination with the 'residents' ('pobladores') of both More's *Utopia* and Bacon's *New Atlantis* (1991: 62; 1976: 69), these 'residents' remain stubbornly peninsular, a far cry from the highly developed 'natives' inhabiting the famous islands that More and Bacon conceived as discursive sites. These literary islands are located somewhere (and therefore 'nowhere') in the Atlantic and the Pacific Oceans respectively. Cervantes's familiarity with this kind of ultramarine utopia may be detected even in his construction of Barataria.

5. THE BARATARIAN DYSTOPIA

Imagined islands abound in *Don Quixote*, which refers to *ínsulas* over sixty times. The novel also depicts, in the very heart of Aragon, the 'ínsula de Barataria', a name that would centuries later be borrowed, by the first settlers of Louisiana, to christen a swamp forest across the Mississippi from New Orleans (Grummond 1961: 3). In Americanist circles, the toponym 'Barataria' recalls numerous legends of physical force and economic power: 'In the stories told of Jean Lafitte, Barataria— the Gulf area which includes Grande Terre, Grand Isle, and Chênière Caminada—is the home and safehouse where pirated/ privateered gold, jewels and human beings who will be sold as slaves are secured' (Wolf, forthcoming). The links between a fictional Barataria as the contrivance of a cruel Spanish aristocracy and the real-world Barataria as the stronghold of American piracy invite further comparative study. To posit a Barataria that demonstrates, as Maravall claims, 'the dramatic inadequacy of the knight as social model' (1991: 189; 1976: 252) is a refeudalization that seems strangely inert to twenty-first-century readers. Although Barataria does indeed set the stage for cruel and even sadistic humour, this Cervantine dystopia discloses, to my mind, far more than the social inadequacies of the knighthood of yesteryear.

Let's look more closely at Barataria, an ironically landlocked insular 'nowhere'. The novel's first allusion to it occurs together with its first invocation of Sancho, that 'poor villager' ('pobre villano') seduced into Don Quixote's service by the knight's promise to win 'some island and leave him there as its governor' ('alguna ínsula y le dejase a él por gobernador della', 1. 7). Sancho's desire for an island increases as Don Quixote reiterates his desire to gain 'perpetual name and fame in all the discovered countries of the earth' ('perpetuo nombre y fama en todo lo descubierto de la tierra', 1. 25). He is in a position to make such a grandiose promise to Sancho because, even before he takes to the road, Don Quixote's mind is filled with imperial longings. As noted earlier, the promise itself functions as a parody of a feudal topos found in the Books of Chivalry: in *Amadís*, for example, the protagonist had made his squire count of Ínsula Firme. But the island over which Sancho, as the dupe of the dukes, is finally installed as governor is a far more complex space. The whole sham is first introduced by the Duke, who offers to make Sancho the governour of an island— and 'by no means a small one' ('de no pequeña calidad')—that happens to be available (2. 32). The island itself will be successively characterized in a series of chapters across Part 2 of *Don Quixote* (2. 45, 47, 49, 51, 53). Although the rich humour surrounding Sancho's administration of this island tends to occult the issues of fraud subtending it, Henry W. Sullivan correctly reminds us that Barataria is part of the ducal theatre of sadism, that the torments inflicted by the Dukes on Sancho, including his appointment as governor, are 'measured out with a certain semicriminal intelligence' (1996: 56–60). Although misread by both Don Quixote and Sancho, that kind of intelligence on the part of Spain's aristocratic classes may not have been misread in Cervantes's day and can scarcely be misread today.

As Joseph R. Jones rightly notes, however, 'modern readers need a compass to help them navigate the treacherous waters' around the events of Barataria (1999: 146). In an indispensable study titled 'The Baratarian Archipelago', Jones provides that compass. After rehearsing the large family of obsolete words related to *baratar*, the majority of which contain some notion of fraud, especially judicial fraud, Jones concludes that 'Cervantes is saying something about the venality or the arbitrary nature of justice circa 1600'. To be able to hear these fraudulent undertones, however, readers must understand that the term *gobierno* includes civil, judicial, and even military functions that only roughly translate into Anglo-American notions of the term 'governor' (1999: 142). Jones follows this caveat with a reminder of the abusive 'semifeudal' powers of the landholding nobility over their vassals (1999: 143). The numberless migrations produced by these abuses—migrations from seigniorial lands into cities—were not unlike those described in More's *Utopia* a century earlier. These abusive 'semifeudal' powers were also well known, however, to the 'vassals' who worked the mines, sugar cane mills, and plantations of the New World. The Cervantine parody of insular doles from the Books of Chivalry, in sum, operates as the vehicle for a satire of *all* appointed governors of islands within the Spanish empire. That would include islands in the Mediterranean such as Sicily, Sardinia, Corsica, Cyprus, Crete, Malta, Rhodes, and Cyprus, as well as islands in the Caribbean. Samsón Carrasco's remark on Spanish islands—that 'all or at least most of them' ('todas o las más que hay') are to be found in His Majesty's Mediterranean—allows for a vague percentage of islands that are *not* found there (2. 50). Although I acknowledge the various layers of colonial ideology in this Cervantine parody, the present argument addresses only those islands located in His Majesty's New World territories.

6. ISLANDS IN THE SUN

Three of the five articles in the Capitulations ('Capitulaciones de Santa Fé')—the charter of Christopher Columbus adopted by the Catholic Kings on 17 April 1492—repeatedly mention islands. In this legal document, Columbus wishes to be made 'Governor General' ('governador general') over these still undiscovered islands: 'todas aquellas yslas', 'todas las dichas tyerras firmes e yslas', 'las dichas yslas' (Columbus 1989*b*: 423–4).[7] It is a wish that Sancho will mimic just over a century later. Columbus's own gift of the island of 'La Bella Saonese' to Michele da Cuneo—which anticipated innumerable other American gifts of this territorial kind—is as operative in *Don Quixote* as Amadís's gift of 'Ínsula Firme' to his squire. In a letter written in 15 October 1495 to Jeronimo Annari, who wanted to know in more detail about this second voyage of Columbus, Cuneo himself describes the gift, shedding light on the legalities of the Spanish ceremony of possession (*toma de posesión*). 'In deference to me', Cuneo writes,

the Admiral named it the Bella Saonese and gave it to me as a gift. And under the accustomed modes and forms, I took possession of it just as the Admiral did with the other islands in the name of his Majesty the King. That is, according to the document of a notary public concerning the island, I tore up some grass, cut down some trees, planted the cross, erected a scaffold, and in the name of God I baptized the island the Bella Saonese.

el señor Almirante le puso el nombre de la Bella Saonese y me la dio en presente. Y bajo los modos y formas convenientes tomé posesión de ella como hacía el dicho señor Almirante de las demás en nobre de la Majestad del Rey. *A saber*, en virtud de un documento de notario público sobre la dicha isla arranqué yerba y corté árboles y planté la cruz y también la horca, y en nombre de Dios la bauticé con el nombre de la Bella Saonese. (Cuneo 1984: 256)

The *ínsula* that Columbus, with aristocratic largesse, gave to Cuneo was populated 'with 30,000 souls' ('con XXX mil almas') and is today called *Saona* (*Adamaney* by the indigenes). Like Cervantes's Dukes, Columbus was evidently fond of doling out islands and governorships. Even after returning from his fourth transatlantic voyage (1502–4), he managed, shortly before his death, to secure the governorship of the island of Hispaniola for his son Diego.

Through the dystopia of Barataria, Cervantes takes some ironical jabs at frivolous and abusive institutions of government, both at home and abroad. But Sancho's upwardly mobile

---

[7] I thank Michael E. Gerli for calling my attention to the Capitulations.

aspirations, his desire for social status and money, must also be factored into Barataria. Setting out for his governorship, Sancho, unlike Don Quixote, does not scorn the profit motive, as his letter to Teresa shows: '*I go with a great desire to make money, which they tell me is the case with all new governors*' ('*voy con grandísimo deseo de hacer dineros porque me han dicho que todos los gobernadores nuevos van con este mesmo deseo*', 2. 36). Although Teresa repeatedly counters her husband's desires for status, she is not averse to his making money. Nor is she shy about asking Sancho to send her some 'strings of pearls' ('sartas de perlas') from Barataria, 'if there be any on that isle' ('si se usan en esa ínsula', 2. 52). As was well known to Cervantes's age, bureaucrats in the Indies occasionally enriched themselves or their ladies with pearls from the 'Ocean Sea', sometimes of a legendary size.

But pearls like these were the exception. Most governors who went off to the Indies would express dismay at the astonishing cost, both physical and psychic, of situations reputed to be enriching. Even before Sancho finally gets the island he wants, his friend and neighbour Tomás Cecial, masquerading as the Knight of the Wood's squire, tries to warn him about the perils of his gubernatorial desires,

because governorships of islands aren't always what they're cracked up to be. Some of them are twisted out of shape, some are just downright poor, some are melancholy, and, to sum it all up, the ones that stand tallest and look best bring with them a heavy load of problems and discomforts, and the wretch unlucky enough to bear them on his shoulders gets beaten down.

a causa que los gobiernos insulanos no son todos de buena data. Algunos hay torcidos, algunos pobres, algunos malencónicos, y, finalmente, el más erguido y buen dispuesto trae consigo una pesada carga de pensamientos y de incomodidades, que pone sobre sus hombros el desdichado que le cupo en suerte.   (2. 13)

This colourful personification of twisted and impoverished insular governorships is a prescient description of Sancho's brief governorship of Barataria, a bogus career that references, among other things, the many discomforts and 'melancholies' experienced by countless governors in Spain's New World colonies. The rhetoric of prosopopoeia in Tomás Cecial's monitory passage allegorizes, for example, the 'twisted' governorship of Columbus who, while governor of the island of Hispaniola, faced enormous difficulties in the settlements of

Navidad and Isabela. Some six years after these wretched experiences, in July of 1498, Columbus would reach the island of Trinidad, the site of some really desperate New World gubernatorial experiences.

In *The Loss of El Dorado*, a gripping history constructed from both Spanish and English chronicles, V. S. Naipaul singles out Trinidad to discuss the hardships of Governor Diego de Escobar with hostile natives, sickness, and hunger. Writing to the metropolis for help, Escobar claimed that his governorship had become 'like a joke', that nobody in the world had ever had to endure 'such hard luck or such labours': 'I haven't been paid my salary. The enemy have robbed me four times since I have been here. I walk about barefooted and virtually naked. The whole thing is incredible' (Naipaul 1969: 115). During his stint as governor of Barataria, as Sancho later tells the Moor Ricote, he discovered that 'governors of islands get to eat very little' ('en las ínsulas deben de comer poco los gobernadores', 2. 54). This surprising state of gubernatorial emaciation gestures to the New World, where governors of islands were, indeed, often obliged to suffer hunger, and sometimes even reduced to eating grass. As Naipaul documents it in his transnational history of Trinidad's colonial past, 'the time came when no one wanted to be governor': candidates who were nominated by the Council of the Indies would regularly excuse themselves (1973: 115–16). In the light of these 'real-world' governors of Spain's overseas colonies, in short, Sancho's defection seems normative. It also seems satirical. Unlike the enchanted island in Shakespeare's *Tempest*, Cervantes's island of Barataria can never be read for its complicity with colonialism. As noted in Chapter 5, the passages in *Don Quixote* on *ínsulas*—promised, desired, granted, and renounced—reprove the medieval institution of chivalry codified in the Books of Chivalry. But these passages also reprove Spain's semi-feudal and pseudo-chivalric institutions of governance, including gubernatorial politics in the New World.

7. 'OLD AND MAIMED SOLDIERS'

As codified by Thomas More's *Utopia*, the utopian genre began, at the start of the sixteenth century, as an Englishman's literary response, in learned Latin, to the promise of Iberian overseas discoveries. Despairing of the corruption of Europe, More looked to the New World, presumably uncorrupted by European vices, to situate his Utopia. By the end of the same century, Cervantes would see the New World, through a more jaundiced eye, as a model for his dystopias. Through these 'bad places' he could satirize institutions instead of persons. He could avoid naming Philip II even as he caricatured the king's imperial overreaching and its tragic national consequences.

Let's consider a few of these satirical exercises. In a sonnet titled 'To the Entry of the Duke of Medina into Cádiz' ('A la entrada del Duque de Medina en Cádiz')—an occasional poem responding to the English Sack of Cádiz in 1596—Cervantes satirized what Adrienne Laskier Martín justly calls 'one of the darker moments in the history of Philip II's twilight reign' (1991: 93). Although the ostensible object of satire was the inept Duke of Medina Sidonia, who had already shown his inadequacies as a military leader of the Armada, Cervantes's criticism, Martín argues, was 'directed toward the king who had reduced Spain from a world empire to a nation economically and spiritually bankrupt' (1991: 102). This imperial bankruptcy was, of course, closely connected to the enterprise of the Indies. After Philip II's death, Cervantes composed a funeral eulogy in which the speaker 'justifies' his king's financial reverses. These sarcastic *quintillas* directly address Cervantes's dead monarch: the fact that your chests of gold are empty, the speaker observes, shows us that 'you were concealing [your treasure] in Heaven' ('en el cielo lo escondías').[8] Finally, when the Town Council of Seville constructed the most opulent and inaffordable of monuments for its dead king—a grandiose building project with farcical consequences wittily recounted by Martín (1991: 102–14)— Cervantes responded with his most celebrated sonnet, 'On the Tomb of Philip II' ('Al túmulo del rey Felipe II en Sevilla'). Pointing to the role of Seville as 'the paradoxically bankrupt conduit for Spain's importation of New World metals and artifacts', E. C. Graf describes this sonnet, in a scatalogical reading, as a poem that 'befouls a king' (1999: 77, 67). One need not share this strong reading, however, to see the poem as a caricature of Spain's corrupt institutions as a decaying imperial power. Insofar as this burlesque sonnet debunks all the funerary

---

[8] On these *quintillas*, see Castro (1974: 83–5).

pieties, it invites comparison with Robert Browning's 'The Archbishop Orders His Tomb at Saint Praxed's', a similarly devastating critique—if in a different language, poetic form, and linguistic register—of ostentatious Renaissance entombment. But the difference in Cervantes's poem is that an unnamed soldier functions as the main speaker of the critique. This 'señor soldado'—who imagines the spirit of the dead king ('la ánima del muerto') returning to earth to witness all the ostentation of his funeral (1991*a*: i. 53)—is a poetic persona very close to the author, himself a veteran of Philip II's Mediterranean wars.

Cervantes's plight as a veteran was adumbrated over sixty years earlier in Thomas More's *Utopia*. Although Cervantes was returning, after five years as a prisoner of war in Algiers, to a nation that ignored the needs of even its most heroic veterans, Spain was not unlike England in this inhumane policy. When Don Quixote meets up with a young man off to the wars and, once again, privileges the profession of arms over letters, he formulates the hope, popular with all the humanists, that 'old and maimed soldiers' ('los soldados viejos y estropeados') would be helped by the state,

because it's wrong to treat them the way some people do who liberate their black slaves when they're old and too enfeebled to work, driving them from home under the guise of freedom to enslave them to hunger, a master from whom only death can liberate them.

porque no es bien que se haga con ellos lo que suelen hacer los que ahorran y dan libertad a sus negros cuando ya son viejos y no pueden servir, y echándolos de casa con título de libres los hacen esclavos de la hambre, de quien no piensan ahorrarse sino con la muerte.   (2. 24)

With the addition of old soldiers and black slaves, the above Cervantine passage echoes Raphael Hythlodaeus's sentiments, cited earlier in this chapter, on sacking old retainers and sending them off to the cities to starve: 'Whichever way it's done, out the poor creatures have to go' (More 1992: 47). Hythlodaeus had, in fact, invoked the case of disabled old soldiers in an earlier context, when he sarcastically countered the stance of a smug English lawyer at Cardinal Morton's dinner party:

We may disregard for the moment the cripples who come home from foreign and civil wars, as lately from the Cornish battle and before that from your wars with France. These men, wounded in the service of king and country, are too badly crippled to follow their old trades,

and too old to learn new ones. But since wars occur only from time
to time, let us, I say, disregard these men. (More 1992: 10)

The crippled Cervantes was, fortunately, not too old to learn a
new trade. Also wounded in the service of a king and country
that did little for its veterans (for the English wars with France
we may substitute the Spanish wars with the Turk), Cervantes
would have surely sympathized with those multiple sixteenth-
century utopian visionaries who had tried to force Europe to
remodel, both at home and abroad, its corrupt political institutions. Shards of that remodelling project reappear in various
Cervantine dystopias, in geographies of the mind that gesture
—sometimes comically, often violently, always ironically—
toward the New World.

7

Jewels in the Crown:
The Colonial War Epic

DURING their scrutiny of Don Quixote's library, the priest and barber encounter Alonso de Ercilla's *La Araucana*, a long narrative poem about Spain's conquest of Chile (1569–89). Having earlier subjected some twenty-seven books of chivalry to a vivid bout of quality control, they cap that critical exercise with a scrutiny of Cervantes's *Galatea* (1585). In their role as inquisitors, these characters defer judgement on their own author's unfinished pastoral novel, a text that, as the priest would have it, 'proposes something, and concludes nothing' ('propone algo, y no concluye nada', 1. 6). On the heels of that self-referential passage, Ercilla's poem, the first of a trio of Spanish epics, surfaces in the inquisition of the books and, unlike Cervantes's writing, receives only superlatives. Regarded as too precious to be consigned to the bonfire, the *Araucana* is sentenced to be preserved as one of 'the richest jewels of poetry that Spain possesses' ('las más ricas prendas de poesía que tiene España', 1. 6). Why is the *Araucana* considered a 'jewel'? Why does a poem dedicated to Philip II avoid the fate of, say, the *Carolea*, a poem about Charles V that 'accidently' ends up in the bonfire of Don Quixote's books (1. 7)? This chapter aims to advance the question of Cervantes's readings of Alonso de Ercilla y Zúñiga (b.1533–d.1594)—the Spanish bard who spent almost eight years in the New World, fighting and writing the premier colonial war epic about conquest in America.

1. STRANGE ENCOUNTERS

The biographical question of an historical encounter between Ercilla and Cervantes, which has been addressed by a distinguished series of scholars, ranges from the possible to the certain.[1] Whether Ercilla and Cervantes ever met, either in person or in Portugal, concerns me less, however, than that they met in Don Quixote's library. Ercilla's distinguished niche there constitutes Cervantes's finest homage to his precursor. Reckoning the accounts of this homage, however, requires the kind of mantic globe featured in the *Araucana*: an American crystal ball that would not only magically mirror the battle of Lepanto, as Ercilla's globe does in canto 24, but also document Cervantes's response to the so-called 'Chilean *Aeneid*'.

Some two decades before the Spanish reading public would share in the scrutiny of Don Quixote's library, Cervantes had already mounted a tribute to Ercilla that opened with two oddly defensive disclaimers. In the 'Song of Caliope' ('Canto de Calíope'), interpolated in Book 6 of *La Galatea* (1585), Cervantes arranges for the Muse of Epic Poetry to celebrate Ercilla's poetic gifts: 'neither his voice nor his accent was raucous, | but each in turn possessed a strange grace . . .' ('no fue su voz, no fue su accento rauco, | que uno y otro fue de gracia estraña . . .'). For these qualities, Cervantes's Muse continues, Ercilla merits 'an eternal and sacred monument' ('merece eterno y sacro monumento') (1968: ii. 191). That Ercilla's voice is 'estraña'—*extraño* signifying 'strange', 'rare', 'foreign', 'outlandish'—and that it is not 'rauco', with its possible pun on *Arauco*, both point to the alien matter of America. In addition to his presence in the Muse's remarks, Ercilla may be 'personified' in the *Galatea* as the pastoral character of Lauso, a warrior and courtier who had visited Europe and Asia (Corominas, Juan, 1980: 14). Elsewhere in this same text, Cervantes places Ercilla second in a gallery of some hundred illustrious Spanish poets, sixteen of them residing not in Spain but in 'the faraway Indies subject to her' ('en las apartadas Indias a ella sujetas') (1968: ii. 189). Eleven of these sixteen transatlantic bards were apparently known to Cervantes.

---

[1] Miró Quesada Sosa writes of 'the possibility' ('la posibilidad') of Cervantes's friendship with Ercilla (1947: 62). Toribio Medina claims that the two writers 'must have encountered' ('se debieron encontrar') each other for the first time in Lisbon, during the campaign of Portugal (cited by Corominas, Juan, 1980: 12). Marcos A. Morínigo writes that Ercilla 'would have known Cervantes' ('hubo de conocer a Cervantes') in Lisbon in 1582 (1979: 13–14). Ofelia Garza de del Castillo claims that it was in Portugal where Ercilla met Cervantes, who would later praise Ercilla to the skies ('con much elogio') (1986: p. xviii).

A few years after Cervantes publishes his *Galatea*, with its ros-
ter of living American poets, Ercilla publishes some of his dark-
est poetry, summed up in the bitter closing stanzas of his third
and last book. In circulation by 1589, a year after the destruction of the Spanish Armada, Book 3 of the *Araucana* both absorbs
and reflects the increasing imperial disillusionment of the age.
The kind of Iberian triumphalism instanced at mid-century by,
say, Fernández de Oviedo, is clearly on the wane in the closing
years of Philip II's reign, when the great drain on the Spanish
crown of the imperial wars in America is common knowledge.
Year after year under Philip II, money had to be found to finance
the war in Chile against the Araucans. As early as 1603, when
Cervantes was well into his manuscript of *Don Quixote*, Part 1,
the Flemish humanist Justus Lipsius wrote to a friend in Spain
of his nation's imperial *contrapasso*: 'Conquered by you, the
New World has conquered you in turn, and has weakened and
exhausted your ancient vigor' (Elliott 1989: 24–5). That Spain's
American territories were becoming more of a liability than
a benefit was understood by all thinking Spaniards. How was
this imperial exhaustion absorbed into Cervantes's novels? What
ideological and narratival stances would Ercilla's American epic
have offered Cervantes?

2. 'THE CHILEAN *AENEID*'

Although Ercilla 'sings' the history of Spanish imperialism in
Chile—operating throughout some thirty-seven cantos as narrator, protagonist, and eyewitness—the degree to which he participates in its dominant ideology remains arguable. 'The poet
is as involved in the colonial machinery as the chronicler', claims
Beatriz Pastor, who reads the *Araucana* as the justifying epic of
a 'well-intentioned colonizer', indeed, of 'a narrator split by the
colonial situation' (1989: 154–8). Criticism on this issue seems
to be as split as Pastor's Ercilla, with fissures of opinion running
across the scholarly literature on the *Araucana*. One critic, for
example, claims to see Ercilla's epic 'for what it is', not as a
defence of the Amerindians but as 'a Spanish poem of the
European Renaissance' (Cevallos 1989: 17). Along the same lines,
another critic categorizes the poem as part of 'an officially
sanctioned literary culture' that 'interprets Spanish history in

harmony with contemporary ideals' (Hampton 1990: 239).
At the other pole, however, a critic rightly anxious to contest
Sarmiento's infamous judgement of Ercilla's heroes as 'filthy
Indians' ('indios asquerosos'), sees Ercilla as 'the tormented conscience of a Lascasian Christian' ('una conciencia atormentada
de cristiano lascasiano') (Delogu 1992: 82). A more generically
minded critic regards Ercilla's *Araucana* as an 'anti-epic work'
because it emphasizes 'the high cost of war and depicts Christian
Imperialism as barbaric' (Simerka 1998: 47).

If such extremes of interpretive judgement disclose a strong
conceptual ambivalence—a text torn between justification and
rejection of Spain's American wars in Chile—Ercilla's narrator,
regarded by most scholars as the main protagonist of the *Araucana*, seems well aware of it. The narrator's periodic eruptions
of selfhood are remarkably confessional. On the eve of the
capture of Caupolicán, for example, he describes himself as
'assaulted by joined contraries' ('[de] juntos contrarios com-
batido', 31. 50):

I don't know with what words, nor what pleasure I could narrate this
bloody and crude assault, nor with what just pity and just hatred, since
both concur at once.

> No sé con qué palabras, con qué gusto
> este sangriento y crudo asalto cuente,
> y la lástima justa y odio justo,
> que ambas cosas concurren juntamente.
>
> (31. 49)[2]

Another conscience-stricken passage stands between the above
verses and the narrator's striking confession: 'I condemn and
regard as evil what I do' ('condeno y doy por malo lo que hago',
31. 49). What the disillusioned narrator 'does' is what all Spanish
military were sent to Chile to do—to 'pacify' and, in turn,
Christianize the Araucanian Indians. The text seems to distribute
itself among a number of ideological options, from identification with the natives to identification with the absent Crown
against both the natives and the Chilean colonists oppressing

---

[2] Citations from Ercilla's *Araucana*, taken from the Morínigo and Lerner edition (1979), are by canto and stanza numbers and will be parenthetically documented in my text. Prose translations of Ercilla's poetry—which precede the
original and aim only to be as literal as possible—are my own.

them: 'since where the king is missing, grievances abound' ('que adonde falta el rey sobran agravios', 4. 5). At times Ercilla appears to be in complicity with the colonial project, as when he talks of 'uncultured barbarians' ('incultos bárbaros', 2. 30), or the 'inhuman barbarian' ('bárbaro inhumano', 6. 19), or 'the barbaric rabble' ('la bárbara canalla', 11. 166). More often, however, Ercilla is defending 'bárbaros', as he himself announces in the Prologue to the first part of his epic. Sometimes he is obliquely lamenting their abuse, as when he speaks of the growth of malicious interests 'at the cost of the sweat and ruin of the other' ('a costa del sudor y daño ajeno', 1. 68). Sometimes he is portraying the 'barbarians' as 'ethical, humanized individuals' (Gerli 1986: 85, 89). At other times he is idealizing them as chivalric heroes. Since this last idealization must have caught the attention of Cervantes, given his own involvement in the Books of Chivalry, Ercilla's chivalric discourse bears a closer look.

One editor of the *Araucana* sees Ercilla's Indians as invested with the 'primary virile virtues, always admired in the chivalric world' ('primarias virtudes viriles, admiradas siempre en el mundo caballeresco') (Morínigo 1979: i. 37). Another editor reminds us that Ercilla lived 'not only his age but also his epoch, that of the chivalry of knights errant' ('no sólo su edad sino su época, la de la caballería andante') (Garza de del Castillo 1986: p. xi). Ercilla's description of many events in this colonial war do indeed bear strong ideological imprints from the discourses of chivalry. The stanzas in which the handsome young barbarian ('el gallardo bárbaro') Gracolano catapults himself over a moat to storm the fort at Penco (19: 5–8) recall many a European chivalric scenario. The chivalric discourses that informed the enterprise of the conquistadores on the historical plane are, in this epic, projected over the enterprise of both the conquerors and the conquered. When the Araucans are not being 'uncultured barbarians', in short, they are being chivalric heroes.

Ercilla sings of arms and the Spaniards by the same ambivalent token, sometimes celebrating his valiant countrymen, sometimes excoriating them. His writing on the early Spanish colonists is characterized by repeated attacks on their 'insatiable greed' ('insaciable codicia', 3. 1)—echoing the ubiquitous lamentations of, among others, Las Casas. Ercilla's documented

return to Valladolid in 1551, after a three-year European trip
as a page in the retinue of Prince Philip, would have located
him in that city just a few months after it hosted the legendary
debates between Las Casas and Sepúlveda on whether or not
Spain was conducting a 'just war' against the New World
peoples. Although Las Casas's *Historia* remained unpublished
throughout the sixteenth century, his attitude had been manifested orally in the Great Debate and passionately in the
Brevísima relación (1552), in print while Ercilla was writing.[3] Almost
two decades later Ercilla would open his epic by mordantly
satirizing the greediness of the first wave of Spanish colonists
in Chile (3. 1). The conviction in this sustained attack on greed
easily outdoes Edmund Spenser's wooden stanza on the 'Gulfe
of Greedinesse' in the *Faerie Queene* (2. 12. 3)—that unabashedly
imperialistic and nearly contemporaneous English epic. Ercilla
incisively commands readers to look at Valdivia ('A Valdivia
mirad'), who rose to power from a poor infantryman to become
the leader of 50,000 vassals, Indians who offered him twelve
marks ('marcos') of gold a day. This, and much more—Ercilla
continues his mordant indictment—was still not enough to
satisfy Valdivia's 'hunger' ('la hambre') for gold. 'Greed', Ercilla
concludes, was the occasion for the incessant warfare and 'the
total perdition of this land' ('Codicia fue ocasión de tanta guerra
| y perdición total de aquesta tierra', 3. 3). Some thirty-one can-
tos later, in a decidedly Lascasian moment, Ercilla is still indict-
ing his fellow countrymen: 'they have thus exceeded, through
an inhuman mode, the laws and terms of warfare, performing
in their invasions and conquests enormous and heretofore
unseen cruelties' ('pues con modo inhumano han excedido |
de las leyes y términos de guerra, | haciendo en las entradas y
conquistas | crueldades inormes nunca vistas', 32. 4). After a
disastrous attempt at some new 'entradas' into the South of
Chile—during which the Spaniards, including Ercilla himself,
get lost in the icy cordilleras near the Straits of Magellan—the
narrator vividly compares the survivors, gorging on mazard
berries, to a 'swarm of locusts sent sometime to plague the human
race' ('banda de langostas enviadas | por plaga a veces del linaje
humano', 35. 45). Although this grim simile belongs to a cluster

---

[3] On the Las Casas connection, see Morínigo (1979: 8 n.). See also Pérez
Bustamante for Lascasian sentiments in *La Araucana* (1952: 157–68).

of some 832 verses posthumously added to the 1597 edition of the *Araucana*, it testifies that the Spanish conquerors can scarcely claim this poem—especially its bitterly ambivalent Part 3—as their epic.

The internal contradictions in the *Araucana* (many more than those cited above) disturb critics who, counting on reliability in their narrators, tend to regard Ercilla as defective. E. Anderson Imbert, for one, considers him 'an unreliable chronicler because he is in conflict with himself' ('un cronista poco confiable porque está en conflicto consigo mismo'):

> He is certain that his countrymen are valiant, and yet he paints them in black and realistic ink. With the same inconsistency, he desires the destruction of the Araucans, and yet he idealizes them with prodigious attributes.
>
> (Le consta que sus compatriotas son valientes, y sin embargo los retrata con tintas negras y realistas. Con igual inconsecuencia desea la destrucción de los araucanos, y sin embargo los idealiza con atributos prodigiosos). (1988: 38)

To demand reliability from a chronicler—to ask that he remain in one unconflicted subject position—may be asking too much. The charge of unreliability, in any event, stems from older, positivist notions of 'objectivity', the approved pole of a dualism in which subjectivity is regarded as something fundamentally mistaken, as the source of error or bias. Such epistemological issues as whether or not a narrator is reliable have been much cherished by traditional critics of *Don Quixote*, perhaps because the novel repeatedly invokes the binary of illusion/reality, a major epistemological doubt. Our own age, on the other hand, must take into account the defences of 'rigorous unreliability' that, as an ethical current, have been gaining momentum since the late 1980s.[4]

Ercilla's anguished negotiations with questions of truth—his confessed state of being 'assaulted by contraries'—seems very postmodern. The multiple and conflicting subjectivities in the *Araucana* anticipate the condition of fracturedness that Cervantes's novels would internalize and that our own era—with its understanding of the subjective component of human

---

[4] Buell's 'In Pursuit of Ethics', the introductory essay to a 1999 issue of *PMLA* whose Special Topic is ethics, cites Barbara Johnson and J. Hillis Miller as proponents of this current of thought.

knowledge as unavoidable—takes for granted. A rich variety of contradictory discourses is part and parcel of the project of colonialism, moreover, a project that demands, as Rolena Adorno notes, 'a simultaneity of various subject positions' ('una simultaneidad de varias posiciones del sujeto') (1988*b*: 14). The simultaneity of subject positions in Cervantes's own unreliably narrated texts—what we have begun to see as their discursive compatibility—has a retrievable relation to Ercilla's colonial epic, whose own proliferation of meaning opens it to a dialogic practice. The rise of the unreliable narrator, in sum, is theatricalized in both the *Araucana* and *Don Quixote*—the second book both containing and proclaiming the first as a national treasure.

3. QUESTIONS OF TRUTH

The relation of writing to truth-telling is a dense issue in Ercilla, and it will become denser in Cervantes. In one of his many negotiations with questions of truth, Ercilla's narrator declares that 'the truth goes shorn of artifice' ('va la verdad desnuda de artificio', 12. 73). By way of a sop to the Cerberus of this 'truth', Ercilla eliminates the artifice of supernatural Virgilian machinery, the goddess Bellona remaining the sole exception to his 'natural' representations of the supernatural. Although he tirelessly declares that his poem is a 'true story' ('historia verdadera')—in the tradition of sixteenth-century historiography and in anticipation of Cide Hamete's similar truth-telling claims—Ercilla estranges himself from the role of truth-teller by owning up to the dilemma of his writer's craft. The *Araucana* is a historical poem interpenetrated by both the true and the fictive. Both Marcos Morínigo (1979: 38) and Walter Mignolo (1982: 99) consider Ercilla's epic, despite its documentary value, to have more poetry than history in it. If we take into account that all writing from history is ideologically marked, however, with episodes everywhere erased or enhanced, Ercilla is not betraying history. The idea that the historiographer performs a poetic act even as he or she explains historical events—an idea most forcefully articulated for our generation by Hayden White—was foreshadowed by Sir Philip Sidney, who claimed in his 1595 *Defence of Poetry* that historiography had to take 'the great passport of Poetry', or to borrow Sidney's own word, that it had to include 'feigning' (1966: 20).[5]

Beyond using 'truth' to explain his flights from artifice, Ercilla's unreliable chronicler also uses it to justify the sterility of his narrative. His quest for verisimilitude ('por ir a la verdad tan arrimado') is linked to the monotony of his discourse, he laments, to his 'having to deal always with one thing' ('haber de tratar siempre de una cosa', 15. 4). Some of the ironic remarks to the reader ('Al Letor') that preface the second instalment of Ercilla's *Araucana* (1578) will be echoed by Cide Hamete Benengeli, the Arab historian who narrates *Don Quixote*. Ercilla enjoins the reader to take into account the harsh and mono-lithic material with which he is forced to work:

although this Second Part of the *Araucana* does not reveal the labour it costs me, whoever reads it might yet consider what has been endured in writing two books of such harsh material and of such little variety, since from beginning to end it contains nothing but the same thing.

aunque esta Segunda Parte de la *Araucana* no muestre el trabajo que me cuesta, todavía quien la leyere podrá considerar el que se habrá pasado en escribir dos libros de materia tan áspera y de poca variedad, pues desde el principio hasta el fin no contiene sino una misma cosa. (1987: ii. 9)

Ercilla's complaint, here again, is in 'having always to walk through the rigour of one truth and on a road so sterile and deserted' ('haber de caminar siempre por el rigor de una ver-dad y camino tan desierto y estéril'), even while having 'a thou-sand times desired to mix in some diverse things' ('mil veces mezclar algunas cosas diferentes', 1987: ii. 9).

Cervantes's narrator Cide Hamete levels a parallel, and sim-ilarly ironic, complaint against himself,

for having taken up so dry and so limited a history as this one of Don Quixote, for it seemed to him that he always had to be talking about him and Sancho, without daring to extend himself to other more seri-ous and more entertaining digressions and episodes.

---

[5] Between 1596 and 1616, Sidney's *Defense* was anonymously translated into the Spanish *Deffensa de la Poesía* and is available in the Brancaforte edition. On history as a narrative prose discourse ordered for readers through multiple modes of argu-ment, emplotment, and ideological implication, see White (1973).

un modo de queja que tuvo el moro de sí mismo, por haber tomado entre manos una historia tan seca y tan limitada como esta de don Quijote, por parecerle que siempre había de hablar dél y de Sancho, sin osar estenderse a otras digresiones y episodios más graves y más entretenidos. (2. 44)

Like Cervantes, Ercilla has often been accused of structural dissidence, of using episodes either 'inexplicable' ('inexplicables') or 'alien to his theme' ('ajenos al tema') (Morínigo 1979: i. 77–8). What David Quint describes as 'the loser's epic'—a subgenre that embraces the *Araucana* and, more broadly and prosaically conceived, *Don Quixote*—may deliberately trigger the formal shortcomings of 'episodicity and sprawling misshapenness' (1993: 11).

Moving beyond Ercilla's unreliable narrators and unjustified episodes, practices that may or may not have exerted pressure on Cervantes, we must account for the recurrent appearances of this American epic in his writings. Cervantes's citations from and allusions to the *Araucana* provide an anatomy of various sixteenth-century malaises attendant upon New World conquest and colonization. It is difficult, as James Nicolopulos argues, not to acknowledge 'the truly colonial nature of the *Araucana*' (forthcoming). To read this poem is to attend not only to the temporal gulf between Ercilla and his ancient models, but also to the spatial gulf between him and his contemporary readers. How does Cervantes negotiate the gulf between the peninsular scene of his own writing and the transatlantic matter of America in Ercilla? Testifying to the novelist's 'undeniable reading' ('lectura innegable') of the *Araucana*, Jorge Campos adds that Spain's ultramarine world was 'always present' ('siempre presente') in Cervantes (1947: 371–404). As a model, then, the *Araucana* communicated to Cervantes—and not only to Cervantes[6]—a world in the outposts of the Spanish empire where some very strange cultural realities had to be negotiated. The complex negotiations of mimesis with imperialism in the *Araucana* lead Barbara Fuchs to argue that the poem registers,

---

[6] Frank Pierce notes how *La Araucana* set the vogue for a series of 'American' poems: by Laso de Vega (1588, 1594), Pedro de Oña (*Arauco domado*: 1586 or 1596?), Castellanos (1589), Santisteban Osorio (1597), Saavedra Guzmán (1599), Barco Centenera (1602), Villagrá (1610), and others (1982: 230). In addition to these epics, there is both a *comedia* (1620) and an *auto sacramental* (1630) by Lope de Vega on the Araucanian Indians, as well as a *comedia* by Ricardo de Turia on Doña Mencía de Nidos (1616), the only Spanish heroine in *La Araucana*.

through its ideological confusion, the incommensurability of epic convention with first-hand knowledge of the American experience. Noting that 'the mimetic conventions of epic do not travel well to the New World', Fuchs concludes that epic, in fact, 'might be a dead end where America is concerned' (forthcoming). Cervantes's unorthodox uses of the *Araucana*—his repeated ironizing of the literary conventions of epic—suggest that he is aware of this 'dead end'. Never an acquiescent imitator, Cervantes engages Ercilla's New World epic in multiple and diverse ways. He may even have engaged it for the story of Dorotea's seduction in *Don Quixote* (1. 28), which, as one critic has shown, parallels the theme, sequence of narration, and many linguistic terms from—'by a strange coincidence'—canto 28 of the *Araucana* (Calhoun 1971: 331). But I am less concerned with peninsular seduction here than with colonial citation. Beginning with a discussion of Sansón Carrasco's discrete lexical borrowings from the *Araucana*, then, I shall move on to the field of shared topoi and, from there, to allegory.

4. SANSÓN'S CITATIONS

Placing a book in a library—either one's own or that of one's characters—does not always *guarantee* its having been read. Should hard evidence be required that Cervantes was reading Ercilla, evidence beyond the presence of the *Araucana* in Don Quixote's library, Sansón Carrasco, the newly minted Bachelor of Arts from Salamanca, will adduce some lexical points of contact to document that reading. In one of his more flamboyant remarks, Sansón cites ostentatiously from the *Araucana*. Murillo's edition of *Don Quixote* footnotes Sansón's invitation to a duel as follows: 'Verses, not cited literally, of Alonso de Ercilla' ('Versos, no citados literalmente, de Alonso de Ercilla') (1978: ii. 135 n.). Rico's edition concurs: although modified for the occasion, 'these are verses from Ercilla's *Araucana*' ('son versos de *La Araucana* de Ercilla') (1998: ii. 735 n.). Let's contextualize the episode in order to see how Cervantes parades his Chilean subtext.

When Sansón first turns up in the guise of the Knight of the Woods ('Caballero del Bosque'), he greets Don Quixote with an allusion to Garcilaso de la Vega (2. 14). This 'muffled echo' haunts what Robert ter Horst calls the 'ridiculous contest' between 'the dwarf giant' Sansón Carrasco and Don Quixote (1992: 42). Inarguably a giant in La Mancha's culture of citation, Sansón displays, throughout *Don Quixote*, Part 2, a multigeneric literary repertoire. In this episode, we note, he reaches beyond the lyric genre of his greeting and the chivalric mode of his costume to tap into the apparatus of epic. Before challenging the hoodwinked Don Quixote to a duel, Sansón lapses into a convention that looks back to Virgil's *Aeneid*, in which the victor strategically builds up his foe in order to glorify his own victory. To this end, Sansón explains how Don Quixote's defeat will cause whatever glory, fame, and honour he possesses to be automatically transferred to Sansón's own person. Aiming to give authority to this anticipated transfer of power, Sansón recites a couplet that loudly advertises its derivation from the opening stanzas of the *Araucana*, where Ercilla remarks on the equation of esteem between antagonists in a colonial war: 'the victor is not esteemed a degree more than the reputation of the vanquished' ('pues no es el vencedor más estimado | de aquello en que el vencido es reputado', 1. 2). Slightly recasting the syntax of Ercilla's couplet, Sansón reminds Don Quixote that the esteem of the victor actually hangs on the reputation of the vanquished: 'The victor is honoured by as much as the vanquished is esteemed' ('Y tanto el vencedor es más honrado, | cuanto más el vencido es reputado', 2. 14). Bending Ercilla's lines to his own purposes, Sansón ironizes what David Quint calls the 'aestheticization of warfare', a phenomenon he instances by a line from the *Iliad* about the flight of Hector from Achilles: 'it was a great man who fled, but far better he who pursued him' (1993: 3). This kind of classical aestheticization, however, is mockingly unsettled through the devious and envious Sansón Carrasco, a sham imitation knight challenging his model, a mad imitation knight, to a chivalric duel.

Although duels were a standard feature of the Books of Chivalry, they were the object of repeated prohibitions, under threat of excommunication, by the Council of Trent (1545–63). Cervantes shows a keen knowledge of these bans when the Duke reminds Don Quixote, prior to his duel with the lackey Tosilos, that his furnishing the battlefield for such an event goes counter to the decree of the 'sacred Council' ('santo Concilio', 2. 56). Sansón Carrasco distances his own challenge from these peninsular prohibitions by citing from a colonial war epic. His silly conditional games, however, align him with Cervantes's many other caricatures of university-trained bureacrats, whose pedantries seem to increase in proportion to their powerlessness. In every sense a loser, Sansón plays at being a winner, aligning himself with the Spanish ideology of superiority that Erasmus, a committed pacifist, had earlier debunked. 'The Spaniards', Erasmus had written in his *Encomium moriae*, 'yield to none in military prowess' (1989: 45), a judgement that, joined with his other liberal opinions, may have helped to consign *The Praise of Folly*, along with the rest of his other productions 'en romance', to the *Index Librorum Prohibitorum* of 1559. Depicting the figure of Sansón as 'one of Don Quixote's most devoted (and hence most destructive) followers', George Mariscal pointedly articulates the 'contradictory desires' of this rascally academic—one of Don Quixote's first readers—who publicizes, participates in, and ultimately destroys the hero's project (1991: 179). Explaining how Sansón actually covets Don Quixote's individuality, and how 'the transference of cultural power to an individual produces both the disciple and its opposite', Mariscal concludes by branding Sansón Carrasco as 'one of the first assassins in literature' (1991: 185). This strong reading compellingly stresses the hunger for cultural power that moves Carrasco to a literary rivalry and, ultimately, to a wish for personal vengeance. I would like to remit this rivalry, however, to where Sansón's own citation directs it: to its colonial subtext. By referencing Ercilla (rather than, say, Homer or Virgil) at the critical juncture of inviting his rival to a duel, Sansón is aestheticizing not just warfare in general but, specifically, Spain's colonial wars in Chile. The couplet he cites from the *Araucana* serves to identify him with the Spanish *vencedores* in Chile, whose project of domination—not unlike Sansón's own project of dominating (and even 'assassinating') Don Quixote—met with great resistance and required repeated encounters.

Also in the mode of the colonial enterprise, Sansón's project is hypocritically cloaked over with a salvific, almost benevolent, intent to rescue Don Quixote from his mad project of freedom. Newly graduated during an era of traumatic underemployment —this 'aggressive, moon-faced youth' has been linked to Spain's overproduction of *letrados* (Cruz 1993: 102–8)—Sansón uses his enforced leisure to protect Don Quixote from himself. Sansón's 'protectionism' is, of course, a standard trope of colonial writing. And Don Quixote's resistance to it tends to provoke, like the resistance of the beseiged Araucans, readerly sympathy. The idea of toppling the high and mighty ('los soberbios levantados') and raising the downtrodden ('los humildes abatidos')—as Camacha's prophecy in *The Colloquy of the Dogs* (*El coloquio de los perros*) puts it (1975*b*: ii. 310)—appeals not only to witches and talking dogs.

David Quint has usefully classified the *Araucana* as an 'epic of the defeated', locating it within a long anti-Virgilian tradition that looks backwards to Lucan's *Pharsalia* and forwards to D'Aubigné's *Les Tragiques,* a poem of Huguenot resistance. Insofar as *Don Quixote* sympathetically renders a chastized and ultimately defeated hero, Cervantes's novel may also be slotted —if only as 'an ugly child' ('un hijo feo')—into the tradition of 'epics of the vanquished'. From start to finish *Don Quixote* thematizes resistance to and freedom from captivity: from erotic bondage (as in Marcela's tale), from physical imprisonment (as in the Captive's tale), and from aristocratic encagement (as in the episodes with the Duke and Duchess). Having sprung himself from this last season in captivity, Don Quixote reminds Sancho, in a celebrated paean, that freedom—'La libertad'— 'is one of the most precious gifts that the heavens gave to mankind' ('es uno de los más preciosos dones que a los hombres dieron los cielos', 2. 58). In a moving adaptation of one of Malraux's insights, Ian Watt casts *Don Quixote* as one of a trinity of books—the other two being *Robinson Crusoe* and *The Idiot* —that retained their truth for people who had known prisons and concentration camps (1962: 133).

5. SHARED TOPOI

Unlike speculations driven by citations, the inferences or conclusions that may be drawn from topoi can scarcely be called definitive. One need not appeal to intertextuality to explain topoi—learnt stereotypes or commonplaces that, as Thomas Greene notes, repetition has removed from the domain of any one writer or historical period. Because the etiological itinerary of a topos 'is far more jagged and less than fully knowable', the reader should recognize its conventionality rather than know its history (1982: 50). But because topoi invoke whole traditions behind them, they often provide a generative field for inter-pretation. Ercilla and Cervantes share numberless topoi, begin-ning with the book-as-progeny topos that opens the respective prologues of the *Araucana* and *Don Quixote*, Part 1, with Ercilla's book represented as a child reared in 'poor swaddling clothes' ('pobres pañales') and Cervantes's as 'an ugly child with no graces whatsoever' ('Un hijo feo y sin gracia alguna'). With these poor and ugly children in tow, Ercilla and Cervantes join the legions of literati who represent themselves as fathers or stepfathers. Another commonplace shared by Ercilla and Cervantes is the ancient topos of epic prophecy to legitimate empire building. Whereas Ercilla's American sorcerer Fitón prophesizes, via his crystal ball, the triumphant battle of Lepanto under 'CARLOS QUINTO' (the king is capitalized in the text) (393), by the time Cervantes renders this same epic topos, a mere generation later, prophecy no longer seems reliable. It is disclosed as a sham in *Don Quixote*, when Merlin's prophecy of Dulcinea's dis-enchantment, written in gold letters on parchment, suddenly materializes as a postscript to the Clavileño episode hatched by the Duke and Duchess (2. 41). Not only is epic prophecy a 'prime target of Cervantes's parody' in *Don Quixote*, as Eric MacPhail argues (1994: 62), but it continues to invite mockery in the *Persiles*. When Soldino—a judicial astrologer who soldiered for many years under Charles V—turns to prophecy, he foresees not a glorious battle but an ordinary kitchen fire (3. 18).

Unlike the above episodes, however, which circulate around authorial or regal exploits, the 'frozen duel topos' that surfaces early in *Don Quixote* strenuously invites a New World reading. As what follows will show, Cervantes specifically recycles Ercilla's 'frozen duels' to interrupt a passage to the Indies. Let's look again at the two duels in *La Araucana*—one of them frozen for over a decade between the publications of Parts 2 and 3. Toward the end of canto 14 of the *Araucana*, Ercilla describes a furious encounter between Rengo, a mace-wielding 'bárbaro' with special killer talents—'he caves in brains, grinds up nerves, flesh and hard bones' ('rompe sesos, | muele los nervios, carne y duros huesos', 14. 42)—and Andrea, an Italian whose 'humble origins' ('estirpe humilde') from Genoa recall those of Colum-bus (14. 46). Andrea certainly matches his opponent in his fondness for wholesale carnage—'he quarters, dismembers, and disfigures' ('descuartiza, desmiembra y desfigura', 14. 45). The formal aspect of all this violence is perhaps most arresting because it is suddenly arrested: the semi-chivalric battle between these warriors is suspended between cantos, dropped in the fourteenth, by design, to be resumed in the fifteenth: 'But I wish the combat to be deferred until the other canto' ('Pero el combate | quiero que al otro canto se dilate', 14. 51). Ercilla was evidently fond of this freezing technique: with the change of one protagonist, a similar duel is replayed—and refrozen— at the close of Part 2 of the *Araucana*. The same brainbashing *bárbaro*, Rengo, returns to battle, not with a European opponent this round but with an Araucanian rival called Tucapel (29. 53), whose sword remains in mid-air for over a decade between the publications of Part 2 (1578) and Part 3 (1589).

A version of these freezing scenes is replayed in chapter 8 of *Don Quixote*, Part 1, when the hero meets a Basque lady ('vizcaína') en route to Seville. She is travelling to join her husband, 'who was about to embark for the Indies where a lofty position awaited him' ('que pasaba a las Indias con un muy honroso cargo')—perhaps another projection of Cervantes himself, twice denied a longed-for position in the Indies. In return for having saved the lady from the 'lying rabble' ('fementida canalla') of two friars on mules, Don Quixote requests that she make the obligatory trip to Toboso and testify to Dulcinea of his heroics. This change of itinerary is hotly contested by the lady's squire, Don Sancho de Azpeitia, a Basque whose broken Castilian—itself a literary topos of the sixteenth and seventeenth centuries—links him, via the trope of *barbarismos*, to the New World peoples. This is not a novel link. In the *Naufragios* (1542), for example, Cabeza de Vaca had already compared the 'primahaitu', a language group he had encountered in Northern Mexico, to the Basques ('[los] primahaitu . . . que es como decir vascongados') (1989: 205–6). Don Quixote and the Basque squire—aided only by a pillow serving him as a shield—begin their hostilities, fighting furiously until the narrator stops them in the famously open-ended closure to chapter 8: 'at this point and closure the author of this history leaves this battle dangling, with the excuse that he found nothing else written' ('en este punto y término deja pendiente el autor desta historia esta batalla, disculpándose que no halló más escrito'). In the following chapter, the narrator reminds readers that he'd left

the Basque and Don Quixote with their drawn swords lifted up,
ready to deliver 'two such furious slashing blows that, had they
landed squarely, they would have split and slashed the combatants
asunder from top to toe and opened them like a pomegranate'
('dos furibundos fendientes, tales, que si en lleno se acertaban,
por lo menos se dividirían y fenderían de arriba abajo y abrirían
como una granada'). It is at this suspenseful moment—as the
so-called 'second author' will explain to us—that the history of
Don Quixote remains curtailed. E. C. Riley's vivid description
of this moment, which he sees as an ironic 'piece of artistic exhibi-
tionism displaying the power of the writer', recalls the Ercilla
connection:

[Cervantes] abruptly stops the action as one might cut off a cine-
matograph projector. Everything is arrested at a dramatic moment when
Don Quixote and the Biscayan are engaged in mortal combat. They
are left frozen, with their swords raised, while Cervantes interposes
an account, several pages long, of how he discovered Benengeli's
manuscript. He often uses the device of interruption as a way of procuring suspense and variety, just as Ercilla and others had done, but
nowhere so graphically as here (1962: 41)

Let's recall exactly what Ercilla *had* done with the topos of
interruption. To begin with, he had overturned 'epic models
of closure', particularly Virgilian models that equate narrative
completion with definitive military victory (Quint 1993: 168).
Secondly, he had reached back to Ariosto, whose use of the interrupted duel in *Orlando Furioso* functions as a 'cantus interruptus'
(Javitch 1980: 66–80). Ercilla's use of the topos, however,
interrupts not merely a canto but Part 2 of his book, which closes
with the topos of a suspended duel to reopen with its Part 3
some eleven years later. Ercilla's structural novelty, in short, was
his use of the seminal Italian topos of hand-to-hand combat to
end a *parte*-division.

What does Cervantes do with the same topos? Should we
acknowledge Ercilla's twice-frozen duel as providing Cervantes's
'artificio', as Rodríguez Marín suggested?[7] Are we confronting,
in the duel between Don Quixote and his Basque antagonist,

---

[7] According to Murillo, Rodríguez Marín invoked only the *second* duel, the one
between Rengo and Tucapel, whereas Clemencín looked to the *Espejo de príncipes
y caballeros* as a possible source. In a note to Part 1 of his edition of *Don Quixote*,
Murillo claims that Cervantes could have remembered both (1973: 139 n.).

a topos or a novelty? I would suggest both. Cervantes's use of the interrupted duel is not only structurally novel, ending a chapter division and amputating a nascent narrative, but also thematically, generically, and narratologically 'new'. In the hands of Cervantes the same frozen-duel topos explodes into action— interrupting a journey to the New World, launching a new genre for early modern Europe, and introducing a new 'author'. A fictional 'Cervantes' or Second Author steps into the breach of this interruption to accomplish three distinctly literary tasks: to talk about his fondness for reading 'even the scraps of paper in the streets' ('aunque sean los papeles rotos de las calles', 2. 9); to purchase the Arabic original of the manuscript we are reading; and to search out a freelancing bilingual Moor who will translate that manuscript into Spanish. Cervantes's rendering of the 'frozen duel' topos addresses not only some violent swordplay but also the activities of reading, writing, and translation. After all the chivalric antics are over, a manuscript will be translated out of the Arabic, and a Basque couple translated into the New World. In the hands of Cervantes, in short, the 'frozen duel' topos qualifies as an 'outdoing' topos.

6. BRAVEHEARTS AND BARBARIANS

Ercilla lurks not only in *La Galatea* and *Don Quixote*, but also in two Cervantine *comedias*: *La Numancia* and *El gallardo español.* The title of this last play, in fact, derives from canto 2 of the *Araucana*. Ercilla's role in the *Persiles*, however, is especially vigorous. Less visible than either the lexical borrowings or gestural topoi discussed thus far, a different kind of intertextuality occurs between the *Araucana* and the *Persiles*. Both texts are codependent, spatially and allegorically, on New World 'barbarians'. As mentioned earlier, Cervantes's last novel opens with a sustained six-chapter parody whose object is the symbolic acts of a tribe of barbarians awaiting the birth of their Messiah, foreseen as a world conqueror. Because their discursive milieu is suggestively American, a long-standing hermeneutic problem is why Cervantes would represent Americanized barbarians —objects and not subjects of empire for the Spaniards—as empire builders.

Ercilla had earlier represented a similar American dream of world conquest. In canto 8 of the *Araucana*, he displays the imperial longings of 'bárbaros' during a council of war in the Valle de Arauco, a boastful powwow following a military victory. Although the council of war functions as a standard topos of the literary epic, this one is scarcely commonplace. All of the Araucans, from the 'General' down to the common people, are pictured as impersonating Spaniards:

All the celebrated captains dressed themselves up in the Spanish mode; the common people and the soldiers dress themselves from the spoils that they had taken; breeches, doublets, tattered leather were held in great esteem and at high price; whoever failed to dress up in Spanish spoils was regarded as useless and base.

> Todos los capitanes señalados
> a la española usanza se vestían;
> la gente del común y los soldados
> se visten del despojo que traían;
> calzas, jubones, cueros desgarrados,
> en gran estima y precio se tenían:
> por inútil y bajo se juzgaba
> el que español despojo no llevaba.

> (8. 14)

The cross-cultural transvestism taking place here may be enlightened by Barbara Fuchs's study of 'dressing up as a Moor' in *Don Quixote*, a kind of ethnic transvestism that evinces the porosity, even the fragility, of national boundaries (1996: 5). In his Araucanian council of war—with every Indian 'dressing up as a Spaniard'—Ercilla performs a similar kind of transformational magic. The fertile game of 'Who's who?' may be played out, of course, across any national boundaries. Othello's furious question to the wrangling Europeans is instructive here: 'Are we turned Turks, and to ourselves do that | Which heaven hath forbid the Ottomites?' (II. iii. 169–70). If, on the other hand, the conventionally vilified Turks were portrayed as having 'turned European', the scenario would parallel, in a Mediterranean key, Ercilla's strategy.

After the Araucanian warlords enjoy a celebratory bout of drinking, their leader Caupolicán—resplendent in the dead Valdivia's Spanish uniform (8. 13)—convenes 'the great Senate' ('el gran Senado'). There he proposes to all the assembled 'brave hearts' ('fuertes corazones') the invasion and conquest of Spain:

I consider it an easy thing to enter Spain and to subject the great Emperor, the unvanquished Charles, to the dominion of the Araucans.

> entrar la España pienso fácilmente
> y al gran Emperador, invicto Carlo,
> al dominio araucano sujetarlo.

(8. 16)

Ercilla allows Caupolicán to think big. Why stop with Spain? The Indians should engage, his harangue continues, in the more challenging campaign of world conquest ('y *conquistar del mundo la campaña*', 8. 16). This is precisely the kind of campaign featured in Cervantes's *Persiles*.

With their fantasies of plenitude and control, their ultramarine ambitions, and their dreams of world conquest, Ercilla's 'bárbaros' uncannily mimic—even dressing up for the part— the 'real-world' Spanish enterprise. What all of this suggests, of course, is that the Spaniards are themselves 'barbarians' in the New World. Or as David Quint notes in his fine discussion of this canto, 'the imperial ambitions of the Indians . . . parody the actions of their would-be Spanish masters' (1993: 17–18). We might add, on the historical front, a few other behaviours that 'parodied' the actions of the Spaniards. The Araucans of Southern Chile, who called themselves *mapuches*, adopted the Spanish pike, for example, the finest weapon for stopping charging horses, and used it to resist their invaders. The Mapuches were also 'the first South American Indians to adopt the Spaniards' horses, and they became brilliant horsemen' (Hemming 1970: 307, 461). What they did not choose to adopt, however, was the European fastidiousness about human remains. After 300 mounted Araucans annihilated an entire Spanish camp in a dawn attack in 1598, they 'continued for many decades to use the skull of Governor García de Loyola as a ceremonial drinking vessel' (Hemming 1970: 461).

I would argue that Ercilla's 'barbarians'—divested of their highflown Latinate rhetoric—resurface in the *Persiles*, where they embody a projection, in a Freudian but unclinical sense of that term. Understood by some theorists as a 'disowning' or defence mechanism—a method of throwing out what is either unrecognizable or unacceptable in the self—projection attributes taboo inner thoughts to an external object while, at the same time, displacing any guilt feelings for those thoughts. Although Freud saw projection as the leading characteristic of symptom-formation in cases of paranoia, he did not confine the mechanism to its appearance in psychological conditions (1959: 385–470). On the contrary, he claimed that projection had 'a regular share assigned to it in our attitude to the external world. For when we refer the causes of certain sensations to the external world, instead of looking for them (as we do in the case of others) inside ourselves, this normal proceeding also deserves to be called projection' (1959: 452). Cervantes represents this projection at the threshold of the *Persiles*, where the global ambitions of the Spanish conquerors are ironically displaced onto fictional 'barbarians'. Insofar as both the *Araucana* and the *Persiles* suggest the hidden relations between two apparently opposite cultures, European and American, they function as congeneric texts, each casting light on the dissimulative techniques of the other. Both texts operate through an ironically intended decoy message: that the barbarians are at the gate, that they are coming to devastate Europe.

This is ironic parody of great social significance, in that its object of criticism is the imperial attitude of a whole culture. Cervantes, I would conclude, does not seek to trump but rather to expand upon his precursor. Ercilla's one-canto powwow is expanded, in the *Persiles*, into a six-chapter parody of Iberian expansionist policies. Although often distinguished from satire by its targeting of a preformed language, parody is by no means indifferent to extra-literary norms, to the relationship between a text and its context. Cervantes's parody of the discourses of Iberian expansionism in the *Persiles* engages not only the texts, but also the authors and readers of the Chronicles of the Indies, disrupting some heavily providential modes of discourse and breaking up many long established schemata. For Cervantes's last word on imperialist expansion, then, we must turn to this posthumous novel, which opens with a violent representation of a culture of would-be world conquerors who manage to self-destruct.

Cervantes's barbarians pin their hopes on 'a king who would conquer and win over a great part of the world' ('un rey que conquiste y gane gran parte del mundo', 1. 2), a king who calls to mind Ercilla's 'invicto Carlo'. Earlier in this book we have noted Charles V's nomination, by conquistadores like Cortés, for the role of global monarch. In the Erasmian Spain of 1528, as J. H. Elliott explains, we find a nation 'under the leadership of men fired by ambitious ideas of universal empire' (1989: 28). Although shared by eminent figures in the imperial entourage, these ideas and aspirations did not go unquestioned. Elsewhere Elliott reminds us that Franciso de Vitoria devoted a whole section of *De Indis* (1. 2. 2) to refuting the thesis that Charles V could be 'lord or monarch of the whole world' ('señor o monarca del mundo entero') (1970: 84–5). This idea of global monarchy had a stubborn longevity. Long after the age of conquest, Inca Garcilaso de la Vega would recall Fray Vicente de Valverde's praise of Charles V, both for his potency in the arms race and for 'his diligence in sending out captains and soldiers to conquer the world' ('la diligencia que tenía de enviar capitanes y soldados para conquistar el mundo') (1960: 50). Given that the dream of world conquest motivates both the *Persiles* and Chapter 8 of this book—and that Inca Garcilaso plays a key role in both—let us now turn to Cervantes's negotiations with perhaps the most complex, and certainly the most devious, 'matter of America'.

8

Remembrance of Things Lost:
Ethnohistory

THE native American subject always stands 'at the heart' of
Spanish colonial writings, Rolena Adorno claims, 'even when not
explicitly mentioned' (1990: 181). Cervantes does not mention
native Americans in his last novel, *Persiles and Sigismunda* (1617),
but they stand at the heart of the colonial writing that opens
its narrative. Neither does he mention Inca Garcilaso de la Vega
(1539–1616), the Peruvian *mestizo* who lurks in the margins
of that same narrative. This chapter addresses both of these
unmentionables and aims, through their convergence, to draw
readerly interest back to the *Persiles*. Representing the discursive site of an encounter between Europeans and barbarians
sometime in the recognizable 1560s, the inaugural chapters
of the *Persiles* gesture to Inca Garcilaso's *Royal Commentaries*
(*Comentarios reales*) (1609), a remembrance of Peru's pre-
Hispanic past by an American royal subject. Having addressed
Cervantes's various negotiations with *La Araucana*, we closed
Chapter 7 with Ercilla as the model for a patently ironic scenario:
a narrative about American dreams of European and, in turn,
of world conquest. This chapter moves from Ercilla to Inca
Garcilaso as one of Cervantes's later models for the matter of
America. After glancing at the critical polemics over the question
of influence, as well as documenting some of the astonishing
parallels between these two writers, we shall focus on some
of the Inca's depictions of his vanished culture and, in turn,
Cervantes's uses of them.

The extent of the Inca's influence upon Cervantes is still
unknown. As what follows will show, some critics categorically
deny his influence, while others assertively, if briefly, identify

him as a model or source for Cervantes. Aligning myself with the latter, I see in Cervantes's last novel a conscious appropriation of fragments—of what Nicholas G. Round would call 'semantically productive' expressions (1994: 10–11)—from various ethnographic portions of the Inca's work. The main goal of this chapter is to consider how Cervantes recasts the writings of Inca Garcilaso, a contemporary American subject. In his last novel, Cervantes is engaged in a curious discursive struggle—not unlike the Inca's own—to accommodate American elements to European discourse. The opening chapters of the *Persiles* come to us advertising their derivation, in teasing bits and pieces, from an alien New World culture not unlike the one depicted in the *Commentaries*. But Cervantes's text also struggles to distance itself from the more providential aspects of that subtext. Cervantes's last novel, as I hope to show in what follows, is indebted to the signifying world of the *Commentaries* which it both reanimates and unsettles.

In his psychobiography of Inca Garcilaso, Max Hernández envisions the Inca as having proposed to himself both 'the task and the privilege of translating a world' ('la tarea y el privilegio de traducir un mundo') (n.d.: 27). The title of Hernández's book, *Memoria del bien perdido*, echoes a line by Inca Garcilaso concerning the laments of his mother's dispossessed family of Inca royals: 'and with the memory of good things lost, they always finished their conversation, in tears and moans, saying: "our sovereignty has been exchanged for vassalage" ' ('y con la memoria del bien perdido siempre acababan su conversación en lágrimas y llanto diciendo: "Trocósenos el reinar en vasallaje" ', 1. 1. 15).[1] That lost world was a new one for Europeans, and Cervantes was, I believe, an attentive reader of the Inca's 'translation' of it. Before we speculate on the nature and extent of that reading—which seems to have riveted itself on various ethnographic passages in the *Royal Commentaries*—let us consider what the critics say about the relationship between Cervantes and the Inca.

---

[1] All citations from the Inca's *Comentarios* are from the two-volume edition of Miró Quesada (1976), parenthetically cited in my text by volume, book, and chapter number; all English translations are my own.

1. QUESTIONS OF INFLUENCE

In the introduction to a new collection of essays on 'Garcilaso Inca de la Vega' that focuses on his role as 'an American humanist', José A. Rodríguez Garrido notes that the 'debates surrounding the work of the mestizo historian remain both open and in need of new critical approaches' (1998: 1). One of those debates involves the relationship between this American humanist historian and the novelist Cervantes, a relationship invoked only once in the above collection, in a comparison of the Inca's name change in 1563—from 'Gómez Suárez de Figueroa' to 'Garcilaso Inca de la Vega'—to a similar 'self-baptism' in Cervantes, from 'Alonso Quijano' to 'Don Quixote' (Avalle-Arce 1998: 42–5). Because records thus far disclose no definitive contact between Cervantes and the Inca, scholars remain divided on the issue of influence. Those who note the presence of the Inca in the threshold chapters of the *Persiles*, moreover, have not investigated it with any sustained rigour. On the strength of a number of spotty parallels, for example, Schevill and Bonilla claim in their early twentieth-century edition of the *Persiles* that Cervantes carefully read ('leyó con detenimiento') the *Royal Commentaries*, and that he began the *Persiles* only after its 1609 publication (1914: vol. i, p. ix). Inca Garcilaso, according to these editors, 'seems to have been the source most accessible to Cervantes and closest to the *Persiles*' ('parece haber sido la fuente más accesible a Cervantes y más cercana al *Persiles*') (1914: vol. i, p. xxvii n.). Jorge Campos moves beyond these speculations to assert Cervantes's 'undeniable reading' ('lectura innegable') of the *Commentaries*: in Cervantes, he claims, 'the Spanish world on the other side of the Ocean was always present' ('estaba presente siempre el mundo español del otro lado del Océano') (1947: 403). Situating the parallels more graphically, William Entwistle writes of Cervantes's depiction of a tribe of barbarians who 'practise the rites and wear the clothing of Garcilaso de la Vega el Inca's American aborigines' (1969: 164). Turning from rites and clothing to sexuality, John Grier Varner—whose biography of the Inca is rich in cultural data—sees Cervantes as having 'ostensibly utilized a description of the premarital sexual initiations found in Garcilaso's history of the Incas' (1968: 307). Varner's allusion here is to Cervantes's use of the *lex primae noctis* for his episode of Transila, a narrative about ritual defloration in the *Persiles* (108–21). The passage supposedly appropriated from the Inca's *Commentaries* reads: 'In other provinces, the groom's kinsmen and his best friends would corrupt the virgin who was about to be wed' ('En otras provincias corrompían la virgen que se había de casar los parientes más cercanos del novio y sus mayores amigos', 1. 1. 14). Along the same lines of source study, Alban Forcione mentions Inca Garcilaso as among 'the historians of the Indies [who] were a source of much of Cervantes's marvelous subject matter' (1972: 38 n.).

A few Cervantes scholars, on the other hand, dismiss the Inca's presence in Cervantes. Mack Singleton, who dates the composition of the *Persiles* back with *La Galatea* (1585), is forced to deny the Inca's 1609 text as an influence on Cervantes in order to maintain his theory. Juan Bautista Avalle-Arce, who correctly regards Singleton's early dating of the *Persiles* as a mere 'intuition', goes on to date the first half of the *Persiles* between 1599 and 1605—that is, also preceding the publication of Inca Garcilaso's *Commentaries*—and the second half between 1612 and 1616 (1969: 14–19). Avalle-Arce does not see the *Commentaries* as an irrefutable or infallible touchstone' ('piedra de toque irrefutable e infalible') for dating the *Persiles* (1969: 14 n. 5). Finally, Carlos Romero Muñoz, who has recently published a monumental edition of the *Persiles* (1997) with copious annotations, claims that it is 'excessive' ('excesivo') to think in terms of only *one* source ('*una* sola fuente') for the novel, and to locate that source, as did Schevill and Bonilla, in the Inca's *Royal Commentaries* (Cervantes 1997: 119 n. 9).

I do not claim the Inca's text as the *one* source for the *Persiles*. If I had to think in such exclusive terms, Heliodorus would qualify as the primary 'source', given that Cervantes himself cites his emulation of that Greek novelist. My wish here is only to foreground some passages in the *Persiles* that Cervantes seems to have appropriated from Inca Garcilaso. Anyone requiring bibliographical evidence that would *guarantee* Cervantes's reading of Inca Garcilaso will be disappointed: such evidence remains, as of this writing, teasingly circumstantial. In place of strictly bibliographical proof, however, there is an impressive quantity of historical and textual evidence that the two writers were in the same place—sometimes physically, often intellectually—at the same time. Some of this evidence lends vigorous support to the presence of the Inca in Cervantes's last novel.

2. SHARED HISTORIES

While questioning the 'romantic myth' of Cervantes's poverty, his purported inability to buy books for a personal library, Daniel Eisenberg catalogues in a footnote the 'extraordinary parallels' with Cervantes, beyond reputed economic hardships, of Inca Garcilaso's life:

A wheat merchant in Andalusia for a while, a man of letters who dreamed of military glory, interested in both true and false history, many years of reading disguised by affirmations of small learning, dead in 1616: that is, Gómez Suárez de Figueroa el Inca Garcilaso.

Durante un tiempo comerciante de trigo en Andalucía, hombre de letras que soñaba con la gloria militar, interesado por la historia verdadera y la falsa, muchos años de lectura disfrazados con afirmaciones de poca erudición, muerto en 1616: es decir, Gómez Suárez de Figueroa el Inca Garcilaso. (1991: 14–15 n. 11)

Let's open out and add to some of these parallels, beginning with the arms-and-letters affiliation. Both writers fought in Philip II's wars almost simultaneously, Inca Garcilaso in the Alpujarras, helping to quell the rebellion of the *moriscos* in response to Philip II's repressive legislation against their culture and language (1568–71), and Cervantes at Lepanto, helping to quell the repeated Turkish assaults on European Christendom (1571). Both the Inca and Cervantes soldiered under the same commander—Philip's illegitimate brother Don Juan de Austria, who moved from the Alpujarras to Lepanto—and both writers struggled with the lack of royal recognition for their soldiering.

   Putting aside their swords, both men took up their pens in mid-life, when each turned his attention to the same writer: the Portuguese Jewish Neoplatonist León Hebreo—born Judah Abrabanel into a family of Sephardic Jews and known in Italian, his adopted language in exile, as Leone Ebreo. Inca Garcilaso reached for León Hebreo's *Dialoghi d'amore* (1535) in order to translate it. In a 1590 publication designed to set an example ('dexar ejemplo') for New World peoples, as Philip II's prefatory notice to the Inca's *Traduzión* noted, Inca Garcilaso translated León Hebreo, the writer whom Cervantes would be citing, some fifteen years later, as the *sine qua non* for writing about love. Cervantes's plaudits occur in the Prologue to Part 1 of *Don Quixote*, where an invented 'amigo' reminds the apprehensive would-be novelist that there is only one authority for this kind of amorous writing: 'with two ounces of Tuscan, you can read Leon the Hebrew' ('con dos onzas que sepáis de la lengua toscana, toparéis con León Hebreo'). Although Cervantes may have consulted the Tuscan original, the third—and by all accounts the finest—of the Spanish translations of León Hebreo became available to him in 1590: Inca Garcilaso's *Traduzión*. The Italian text of a Portuguese Jew exiled from Spain had been reintegrated back into the Spanish language by an American Indian historian. The degree of transculturation attending this text is remarkable.

Although Inca Garcilaso proudly offered this translation, his first literary work, to Philip II, not everybody at the time celebrated this publishing event. Some readers regarded it as part of the deplorable insubordination of the colonized classes. The humanist Don Francisco Murillo, for example, fumed about the presumption of an 'Antarctic Indian', a man who lived below the equatorial line, to make himself an interpreter ('hacerse intérprete') between Italians and Spaniards. 'And since he had already presumed to do so', Murillo continued, 'why didn't he choose any other book instead of the one most esteemed by Italians and least known by Spaniards' ('y ya que presumió serlo por qué no tomó libro cualquiera y no el que los italianos más estimaban y los españoles menos conocían'). That the Inca himself cites this mean-spirited speech in the Prologue to his *Historia general del Perú* (1960: 14) suggests that Don Francisco Murillo's racist reception of his translation rankled for years.[2] One modern critic believes that the Inca's translation of León Hebreo was an attempt to identify himself —given his doubly anomalous situation of 'half-breed and bastard' ('mestizo y bastardo')—with an international intelligentsia, a fraternity of humanists (Avalle-Arce 1964: 11–12). Inca Garcilaso's translation of León Hebreo, traditionally read either as a kind of internship in his career of aspiring European humanist or as a model for his accounts of pre-Hispanic

---

[2] On Murillo's speech, see also Varner (1968: 300).

indigenous religions, has been generatively resituated by Roland Greene, who reads it as 'a sustained exploration of the extant discourses of romantic love and geopolitical conquest' (1992: 238). Noting the sixteenth century's renovation of Petrarchism into a colonial discourse—into a double-edged tool for both amatory and colonial desire—Greene argues that the Inca's translation of León Hebreo's dialogues represents 'indigenous American interests', that it allows itself 'to be read as an intervention in contemporary imperialist ideology with both personal and political stakes' (1992: 238). Although it is impossible to determine whether Cervantes read León Hebreo's Neoplatonic dialogues with an eye to indigenous Americans, we know that in the Prologue to his 1605 *Quixote* he explicitly recommends the *Dialoghi d'amore* (1535)—a text whose most recent translation into Spanish was by Inca Garcilaso—as a model for writing about love.

Not only did Cervantes and the Inca share a common literary passion in León Hebreo, but they also shared a publisher, a publication date, and a common attitude toward the Books of Chivalry. Portuguese inquisitors gave the Flemish printer Pedro Crasbeeck permission to print both *La Florida del Inca* and *Don Quixote de la Mancha* in March of 1605. *La Florida*—a seminal and elegantly written work on the Spanish conquest of Florida and its southern environs—may have influenced Cervantes's negative portrayal of that 'homicidal' Floridian territory in *The Fortunate Pimp* (*El rufián dichoso*), a religious play written sometime between 1596 and 1615 (1991*b*: 415). The simultaneous licensing of their texts in 1605 is neither the first nor the last in a series of uncanny correspondences between the Inca and Cervantes. The texts themselves express some strong opinions about, if not a shared hostility to, the Books of Chivalry (*libros de caballerías*). In words that recall *Don Quixote*'s avowed enmity to the Books of Chivalry, Inca Garcilaso roundly trumpets his distaste for chivalric fiction, an aversion he traces to his reading of Pedro Mejía's 1545 attack on the genre: 'All my life'—the Inca reminisces in *La Florida*—'I was an enemy to fictions, such as the Books of Chivalry and other similar works' ('Toda mi vida . . . fui enemigo de ficciones como son libros de cavallerías y otras semejantes') (1988: 200–21). The Inca's subject position on this genre resembles that of Cervantes's fictional figure of Don Diego de Miranda, the Man in Green ('el Caballero del

Verde Gabán') in *Don Quixote*. This character claims that no Books of Chivalry have been allowed to cross the threshold of his library, which extends to some six dozen historical and devotional books (2. 16). Inventories have shown that the Inca's own personal library, also rich in devotional and historical books, was surprisingly scarce in fiction. Although numerous books on the Indies were found among the Inca's holdings, 'there is not a single novel by Cervantes' ('no hay una sola novela de Cervantes') (Miró Quesada 1976: vol. i, p. xxxix).[3]

Another literary connection between Cervantes and two figures close to the Inca also bears noting here. Inca Garcilaso's godfather in Peru, Diego de Silva, was the son of Feliciano de Silva, a writer whom Cervantes would vividly memorialize. Don Quixote's fulsome praise for Feliciano de Silva—his favourite chivalric novelist and the author of those deathless lines on 'the reason of unreason' ('la razón de la sinrazón')—is well known to all *cervantistas* (1. 6). Just as the father of the Inca's god-father covertly finds his way into Don Quixote's library, the Inca's more famous ancestor and namesake, the lyric poet Garcilaso de la Vega, finds his way into Cervantes's library.[4] One thinks, for example, of the first exchange between the protagonists of the *Persiles*, when the hero whispers to the heroine a garbled version of Garcilaso's famous Sonnet 10: 'O Jewel, found for —I scarcely know which to say—my good or ill fortune' ('o prenda, que no sé si diga por mi bien o por mi mal hallada', 67). In a later episode, the hero of the *Persiles* returns to Garcilaso's same sonnet, this time regarding the discovery of the 'sumptuous jewels' ('ricas prendas') as a good thing (278). Cervantes repeatedly shows and tells that he is a great admirer of Garcilaso's texts. When the pilgrims in the *Persiles* arrive at the Tagus river in Spain, where Periandro (the disguised Persiles) cites from Garcilaso's First Eclogue, the narrator mentions that the recently published works of the 'never sufficiently praised poet Garcilaso de la Vega' ('del jamás alabado, como se debe, poeta Garcilaso de la Vega') are much celebrated in Icelandic court circles (327).

---

[3] See also Durand (1948: 239–64).
[4] For the poet Garcilaso's influence on Cervantes, see Rivers (1983a: 565–70). See also Rivers's classic edition of Garcilaso's *Obras completas* (Rivers 1974). 'For major studies of Petrarchism, see Cruz (1988) and Greene (1998)'.

To summon literary figures—León Hebreo, Feliciano de Silva, Garcilaso de la Vega—as links between Cervantes and the Inca is perhaps not as fruitful as summoning up geographical sites. The most fertile of historical correspondences between Cervantes and the Inca have to do with geography—with such sites as Montilla, Córdoba, and Trujillo. While narrating his life story, Berganza, the canine hero of Cervantes's *Colloquy of the Dogs* (*El coloquio de los perros*), recalls how one of his many masters, a constable ('alguacil'), showed three sword sheaths to the Lieutenant Governor ('Asistente') of Seville. The man who held this office at the time, as the dog smartly recalls, was the licenciate Sarmiento de Valladares, a real-life functionary who served between 1589 and 1590 (1982: iii. 281 n.). This episode shows the political alertness of Cervantes's talking dog to people in office or in power. It is soon after that episode that Berganza arrives in the village of Montilla near Córdoba, a specially vivid site for Cervantine prosaics. Not only was Montilla the home of the famous sorceress who plays a lead role in Cervantes's *Colloquy*—Leonor Rodríguez, also known as La Camacha—but it was also the home of Inca Garcilaso for over twenty-five years. It was the home, as well, of the Marquis of Priego, who was 'related to Garcilaso' (Anadón 1998: 154). The Inca participated in the Battle of Alpujarras under the protection of this Marquis, with whom he would eventually quarrel. That Cervantes knew about this Marquis is documented in his *Colloquy*, when the talking dog Berganza describes Montilla as the site of the 'famous and great Christian Marquis of Priego' ('famoso y gran cristiano Marqués de Priego') (1982: iii. 288).

Still on the Montilla front, we should take into account the professional connections between Cervantes in his official role as royal purveyor at Écija and the Inca in the role of tax suppliant for the neighbouring village of Montilla. As preparations for the Armada were taking place, the villages of Spain were forced to contribute food, horses, and men for the King's offensive against the English heretics. These conscriptions were loudly protested by the village of Montilla, with Inca Garcilaso as their spokesman. On 19 July 1587, the Council of Montilla testily protested the entry of any commissaries 'into this said town to boast or brag or make any displays' ('a esta dicha villa a hazer alardes') (Porras Barrenechea 1955: 237–9). Cervantes may have heard not only *about* the Inca but also *from* the Inca, in a collective if not personal communication, when he invited the neighbouring villages of Écija and Castro del Río to join Montilla in its plea for tax relief.[5] A few years after the disaster of the Armada, Cervantes and Inca Garcilaso narrowly miss a personal encounter in Montilla. Documents show that the Inca leaves Montilla in November of 1591, when he sells his house and moves to Córdoba. The very next month Cervantes arrives in Montilla, as a tax-collector, remaining there from early December of 1591 until mid-1592. The Inca continues to hold property in Montilla, however, where documents show him listed as a resident in 1591, 1592, and 1593 (Porras Barrenechea 1955: 237–9). It seems unlikely that a tax collector and a property owner in the same small village would remain strangers.

Moving from Andalusia to Extremadura, we find yet another historical link between the Inca and Cervantes in the Pizarros of Trujillo. The reference to 'don Francisco Pizarro' in the long interpolated story of Feliciana de la Voz in the *Persiles* (bk. 3, chs. 2–5) involves the descendants of Francisco Pizarro, the conqueror of Peru. Cervantes's kinship to the Pizarros of Trujillo is discussed under the Orellana connection in Chapter 5, above. Given the infamous exploits of their ancestor in Peru, these good citizens of Trujillo would certainly have known about Inca Garcilaso, whose mother's royal family had been conquered and colonized by Pizarro. Stelio Cro rightly notes that Cervantes's use of the 'Pizarro' and 'Orellana' surnames shows his familiarity with the matter of the Indies ('con las cosas de Indias') (1975: 8 n.). I would only add that these surnames show Cervantes's familiarity with the specific matter of the Inca empire, especially as chronicled by his contemporary Inca Garcilaso.

The above evidence, historical and circumstantial, leads me to consider Inca Garcilaso's *Royal Commentaries*, easily accessible to Cervantes, as an important subtext of the *Persiles*. I would argue that Cervantes quarried passages from the *Commentaries* in order to question, among other things, the providentialist perspective of the Spanish conquest. Inverting the long-standing tendency of imposing European models on American texts, then, I would impose—or, more modestly, propose—Inca Garcilaso's *Commentaries* as an American model for a European text. The first six chapters of the *Persiles* constitute, as what follows will

---

[5] On the Écija–Montilla connection, see Varner (1968: 293–5).

show, not only an absorption of but also a reply to Inca
Garcilaso's dense and complex *Commentaries*—a text composed
of the Inca's own vivid replies to many different Chronicles of
the Indies.

3. 'THE HERODOTUS OF THE INCAS'

The density and complexity of the *Commentaries* have helped to
complicate its generic classification, which has run the gamut
from history to autobiography to 'history as autobiography'
(Anadón 1998: 149–63). One hundred years of scholarship have
finally dislodged the text from Menéndez y Pelayo's classification of it as 'an utopian novel, like that of Thomas More'
('una novela utópica, como la de Tomás Moro') (1905: i. 392).
Classifying the text has been problematic, with some notable
efforts made to regard it as 'literature' rather than 'history'.
Building on the pathbreaking work of Enrique Pupo-Walker,
for example, who documented the influence of literary techniques
on Renaissance history, Margarita Zamora argues that the Inca's
intensely subjective narration, although mired for many years
in a 'history versus fiction' debate, is 'not a history' (1988: 5).
In a study of the *Commentaries* that aims for the text's cultural
reclassification—'its passage from the discipline of history to that
of literature' (1988: 6)—Zamora claims that Renaissance linguistic theories inform this 'rhetorical' work, whose strategies
were aimed at convincing an educated minority of European
readers of the justice of 'the Amerindian cause' (1988: 9).
Cervantes—whom Zamora incidentally mentions because his
'history' of Don Quixote parodied the ambivalence of history
and fiction (1988: 6)—may have been one of these readers.

Beyond the 'history versus fiction' debate, the *Royal Commentaries* seems to have prompted a variety of anthropological
generic labels for the text: Alberto Escobar, for example,
describes it as an ethnohistory ('etnohistoria') (1965: 18–20);
Elias Rivers calls it an 'ethnographic masterpiece' (1983*b*: 136);
and Julio Ortega celebrates it as a 'cultural text' ('texto de
cultura') (1992: 199–215). Shedding light on these categories
is Nicolás Wey-Gómez's depiction of the classical ethnographic
document as one that 'dramatises an intersubjective dialogue
between Self and cultural Other which in effect must have been

brought to an end before its "meaning" can be negotiated with one's peers' (forthcoming). Predictably, there is resistance to these modern and postmodern anthropological categories. Efraín Kristal, to cite one resistant reader, dismisses both the ethnographic value ('su valor etnográfico') and the literary invention ('su invención literaria') of Inca Garcilaso's myths. The significance of these myths, for Kristal, resides in their moral and theological intention ('su intención moral y teológica') (1993: 47–59). Aligning the classical and Neoplatonic myths in the *Commentaries* with the exegetical techniques used by the Renaissance to interpret myths, Kristal argues that it is necessary to understand Renaissance concepts about myths in general, and Spanish versions of these concepts in particular. Most useful to Inca Garcilaso, in Kristal's view, were strategies about veiling truths through allegory, concepts that the Inca would have found in the very book he translated: León Hebreo's *Dialogues of Love* (*Dialoghi d'amore*), published in Italian in 1535 (1993: 47–59). Although I have elsewhere argued that León Hebreo did indeed write some masterfully devious allegories, and that his work motivated Cervantes as well as the Inca (Wilson 1991: 93–105), I see no need to separate ethnography from allegory. Nor, for that matter, from history. One wonders what generic or discursive laws can be invoked to dismiss the 'ethnographic value' of Inca Garcilaso's writing or to cordon off ethnohistory from the so-called 'standard categories' of the historiography of the Indies. We might consider that the division between the two domains here in question—ethnography and history—tends to be reinforced, as Katie Trumpener argues in a memorable defence of gypsy culture, by 'the rhetoric of nationalism and the model of cultural legitimation' (1992: 884). Whatever genre wars may still be declared over the *Commentaries*, I would only maintain that the passages in this text to be discussed in what follows—the ones Cervantes appropriated—qualify as ethnohistory.

The ethnohistorical portions of the *Royal Commentaries* that find their way into Cervantes's last novel specifically engage the customs of the pre-Incas or rival tribes of the Incas. These passages belong to the kind of writing that earned Inca Garcilaso the epithet of 'Herodotus of the Incas'.[6] The flattering editorial

---

[6] 'El Heródoto de los Incas' is Pedro Henríquez Ureña's phrase for Inca Garcilaso. See the back cover of Miró Quesada Sosa (1976: vol. i).

antonomasia used to describe the Inca as a latter-day 'Herodotus' could scarcely have been intended to reference the Greek historian's unfortunate reputation, throughout antiquity, as both 'the father of history and a liar' ('fabulosus'). Regarded as excessively pro-Barbarian (*philo-barbaros*) by Plutarch, among others, Herodotus was translated in the fifteenth century by the humanist Lorenzo Valla, and vindicated in the sixteenth by, among others, Henricus Stephanus (*Apologia pro Herodoto*, 1566). Only after his methods and reliability had been subjected to an animated debate, did Herodotus begin to be celebrated for his writing method. Apart from serving as an honorific for the Inca, however, his epithet reminds us that the ancient Greek historian Herodotus was rescued for posterity *because of* the Indies. Herodotus was finally vindicated, as Arnaldo Momigliano explains, by the 'comparative method of ethnography' emerging from the '*relaciones*' of Spanish missionaries and Italian diplomats in America (1958: 10). We need not assume that these New World writers were specifically inspired by Herodotus, Momigliano continues: 'what matters to us is that they vindicated Herodotus, because they showed that one could travel abroad, tell strange stories, enquire into past events, without necessarily being a liar' (1958: 10). Although neither a missionary nor a diplomat, a New World writer like Inca Garcilaso not only told but also inspired 'strange stories'—such as the ones in the *Persiles*. It is 'a strange truth', as Momigliano puts it, 'that Herodotus has really become the father of history only in modern times' (1958: 13). Like that of his namesake Herodotus, the Inca's reliability has been subjected to heated debate, doubtless aggravated by the puritanical evaluation of him as a self-centred gossip by, among others, the unreliable American historian William H. Prescott. Echoing the question of reliability but superbly unaware of chronology, one critic actually traced Cervantes's desire to settle in one of the newly established cities of that 'semifabulous and recently discovered New World' ('mundo semifabuloso recién descubierto') to Inca Garcilaso's fantasies:

It is pleasant to imagine the good Mr. Cervantes, in his last years of life as the great patriarch of letters, . . . reading the *Comentarios reales*, more accurately called the 'ideal' commentaries, of Inca Garcilaso de la Vega, in whose remarks there is more flight of fantasy than historical veracity.

Place imaginarse al buen señor de Cervantes, en su postrimerías de gran patriarca de las letras, . . . leyendo los *Comentarios reales,* que mejor diríamos ideales, del inca Garcilaso de la Vega, en cuyas noticias hay más vuelo de fantasía que veracidad de historia.   (Mesa 1948: 435)

Flights of fancy may be found, of course, in the work of any historiographer. Thanks in part to the recuperative work of such scholars as Raúl Porras Barrenechea, Aurelio Miró Quesada, José Durand, and the contributors to the recent 'Tribute to José Durand' edited by José Anadón, we have moved beyond the tiresome polemics over Inca Garcilaso's accuracy and credibility as a historian. In their place we might consider, among other things, his impact on the novel.

4. 'TRANSLATING' TAHUANTINSUYU

The Inca's *Comentarios* furnished Cervantes, and not only Cervantes, a moving recollection of the rites, customs, ceremonies of Tahuantinsuyu and its vanquished peoples. The Quechua word for the Inca empire, *Tahuantinsuyu,* means, as the Inca himself explains, 'the four parts of the world' ('las cuatro partes del mundo', 1. 1. 5). He often describes this vanished culture from a European subject position, as a humanist whose learning precludes a full identification with his American origins. At the beginning of the *Comentarios,* for example, he writes that the New World has been lately discovered 'for us' ('para nosotros', 1. 1. 1). A chapter later, however, he distances himself from that European 'us': 'They called it the New World with good reason, because it is so in all things' ('con razón le llamaron Nuevo Mundo, porque lo es en toda cosa', 1. 1. 2). As an American humanist using a European classical heritage, then, Inca Garcilaso sets out to describe, to 'translate' for his readers, the lost Inca empire of Tahuantinsuyu.

For this task, he borrows not only from a great variety of discursive models, including 'biblical hermeneutics, forensics, utopian discourse, philology, [and] theology', but also 'from the chronicles and missionary narratives describing the newly discovered peoples' (Zamora 1988: 8). The result is a text that provides readers with some vivid descriptions of the customs, institutions, and even anxieties of the Incas: how they built a suspension bridge ('puente de mimbre') over the Apurímac

(1. 3. 7), or how they operated the House of Virgins in Cuzco (1. 4. 1–4), or how they imagined that rainbows caused tooth decay (1. 3. 21). But remembrance of things past sometimes gives way to resentment of things present: how Spaniards categorize *criollos*, *cholos*, and *mestizos* (2. 9. 31), or how cocaine contracts enrich Spaniards (2. 8. 15). Inca customs, fears, and grudges are all strategically interpolated into a history of wars and conquests (1. 2. 20). The Incas were conquerors just before they were conquered. As compellingly documented in the *Commentaries*, they were forced into whole lifetimes of militaristic expansion by a royal ancestor cult that promoted 'split inheritance': whereas one principal heir would receive the position, rights, and duties, of the deceased Inca, the other descendants or 'trustees' would be assigned, corporately, his personal possessions and sources of income. Denied his predecessor's inheritance, a new ruler was forced to undertake conquests as a way of accumulating his own wealth (Conrad and Demarest 1984: 91–4). The Inca cult of the royal mummies, then, demanded the growth of empire. Such a dynamics explains why a certain phrase in the *Commentaries*—'The Inca thus moving forward in his conquest' ('Pasando, pues, el Inca en su conquista', 1. 3. 2)—virtually becomes a refrain. That refrain may have played again in Cervantes's head as he lifted his quill to represent a tribe of barbarians moving forward in their world conquest.

To further thicken the intertextuality between Cervantes and Inca Garcilaso, the *Comentarios* is a cannibalizing text, one that incorporates the writing of multiple peninsular chroniclers. To read the Inca is to entertain his own wide reading of texts that span the sixteenth century, taking us back to Thomas More and forwards to José de Acosta. The *Commentaries* includes over eighty references to such noted chroniclers as Pedro Cieza de León, Agustín de Zárate, José de Acosta, and Franciso López de Gómara.[7] Inca Garcilaso's sense of injured merit, his strong indignation toward this last figure is well known. The Inca's marginal notes to an edition of Gómara's *Historia* (in the Biblioteca Nacional in Lima) include a personal defence of his father's tarnished military reputation at the Battle of Huarina. These notes challenge Gómara's claim that Captain Garcilaso de la Vega had given a horse to the rebel Gonzalo Pizarro

---

[7] For the classic study of the Inca's library, see Durand (1948: 239–64).

in the heat of the battle: that lie, wrote Inca Garcilaso, 'has cost me my bread' ('Esta mentira me ha quitado el comer'). Earlier we mentioned López de Gómara's dissemination of the rumoured lifestyle of Indians in the province of Esmeraldas —who 'live like sodomites, speak like Moors, and look like Jews' ('viven como sodomitas, hablan como moros y parecen judíos'). Noting the 'error' of these similes, the Inca felt compelled to defend and differentiate Amerindians from Spain's other vilified peoples. 'They are neither Jews nor Moors but Gentiles' ('pues ni son judíos ni moros sino gentiles'), the Inca wrote in the margins of his edition of Gómara's text. Although at least one editor considers the Inca's annotations to López de Gómara's text as 'the germ' ('el germen') of the *Commentaries* (Miró Quesada, 1976: vol. i, p. xxi), the Inca himself may have reserved this distinction for Padre Blas Valera (1545–98), a Jesuit and a fellow *mestizo* who left behind the 'tattered papers' of an unfinished history of Peru written 'in the most elegant Latin' ('en elegantísimo latín', 1. 1. 6). Inca Garcilaso explains how Padre Blas Valera's 'torn papers' ('papeles rotos')—harmed during the 1596 Sack of Cádiz by the Count of Essex—found their way, thanks to another Jesuit named Maldonado de Saavedra, into his hands (1. 1. 11 and 6). These tattered papers provided the Inca with a treasury of citations from the Jesuit's own extensive reading, which included, among many other chroniclers of the Indies, the epic poet Alonso de Ercilla.[8]

The uses of these multiple borrowings are complicated by the Inca's cautious strategies of representation and by his eloquent silences (Durand 1966: 66–72). As we noted earlier, he takes up various—often simultaneous—subject positions: as an Inca, he reproduces the imperial ideology of the Incas; as a Christian, he reproduces the providentialist ideology of the Spaniards; as a *mestizo*, he regularly subverts both. His fluidity of identity is remarkable: not only is he an Indian among Spaniards and a Spaniard among Indians (Avalle-Arce 1964: 9–12), but he is sometimes a Tuscan among Indians, as when he describes the Petrarchan songs composed by the Colla tribes: 'songs . . . of amorous passions, now of pleasure, now of pain, of favours or disfavours of the lady' ('cantares . . .

---

[8] Inca Garcilaso was unjustly accused of plagiarism of Blas Valera, an accusation definitively refuted (see Miró Quesada 1976: vol i, pp. xx–xxx).

de pasiones amorosas, ya de placer, ya de pesar, de favores o disfavores de la dama', 1. 2. 26). The text of the *Commentaries*, one sees, is the product of a colonized subject and a cultural go-between: it is a construction as richly mixed as the Inca himself, with a variety of contradictory discourses. The Inca's text, in short, is part of a colonial literary production that was constituted, as Rolena Adorno argues, by some 'subtle, complex, and contradictory maneuvers—both internal and external to discourse itself—whose full understanding lies yet before us' (1986: 19).

Inca Garcilaso's contradictory approach to the authorities bears mention here in that, like Cervantes, he seems to have little use for them. Cervantes's attitude may be summed up in the Prologue to *Don Quixote*, Part 1: 'I can say [it] better . . . without authorities' ('podré decir mejor . . . sin autoridades'). Where Cervantes *excludes* authorities, however, Inca Garcilaso *outdoes* them. He aims to supplement, as well as to rectify, the peninsular historians of Peru, whose representations, he claims, have distorted its language and culture: 'as a native son, I shall be able to speak better than one who is not' ('como propio hijo, podré decir mejor que otro que no lo sea'), he writes in the 1586 Dedication to his translation of León Hebreo's *Dialoghi d'amore*. When a politically touchy subject comes up, however, the Inca, aiming for gravity and veracity, does not hesitate to call in the authorities. He invokes a prior textual tradition when discussing, for instance, the Inca resurrection of the body, 'because a thing so alien to gentiles . . . would seem an invention of mine, its not having been written by some Spaniard' ('porque cosa tan ajena de gentiles . . . parecía invención mía, no habiéndola escrito algún español', 1. 2. 7). This kind of deference gives way to an authoritative tone, however, when the Inca takes up the subject of cannibalism.

As models of Amerindians who practised cannibalism, Inca Garcilaso offered Cervantes a portrait of the pre-Incas, to whose horrific lifestyle he dedicated no fewer than six chapters. As the Inca depicts them, these pre-Incas were 'super-barbarians out of all imagining' ('Barbarísimos fuera de todo encarecimento', 1. 1. 14). This vivid superlative is specifically directed at tribes who, like Cervantes's barbarians, 'made some very barbarous sacrifices' ('hacían sacrificios muy bárbaros', 1. 1. 20). Like Cervantes, Inca Garcilaso uses—perhaps even abuses—the word vain ('vanos') throughout his description of these sacrifices, directly linked to dietary habits. The pre-Incas, according to Inca Garcilaso, were 'extremely fond of human flesh' ('amicícimos de carne humana', 1. 1. 12), and some of them, again like Cervantes's barbarians, had a special predilection for organ meats: 'they used to burn . . . the heart and lungs until they could consume them' ('quemaban . . . el corazón y los pulmones hasta consumirlos', 1. 1. 11). The Inca's descriptions recall Aristotle's Anthropophagi, those Black Sea tribes of the Achaeans and Heniochi, who were said to 'delight in human flesh' (*Politics*, 1338^{b}19). The search for any 'objective' formulation of the truth of human sacrifice among the pre-Incas seems fruitless to our argument here. Although Garcilaso leaves us the impression that, before the messianic eruption of Manco Cápac into the pre-Incan dark ages, the whole Andean world lived in a dire state of savagery, recent studies in archaeology and ethnohistory regard this debasement of the pre-Incas as part of 'Cuzco's imperial propaganda', as well as 'the most flagrant fiction' (Conrad and Demarest 1984: 86). Along the same lines, Roberto González Echevarría suggests that Inca Garcilaso's own personal recognition and enfranchisement depended on his establishing the nobility of the Incas which, in turn, depended on documenting the corresponding 'barbarism' of earlier cultures (1987). This chapter, in any case, is not the place to question the motives that may have impelled Inca Garcilaso to accuse the pre-Incas of cannibalism. What most concerns our enquiry here is the portrait of pre-Incaic barbarism that Inca Garcilaso made available to Cervantes, whose own barbarians are ritual heart-consumers. In Chapter 3, above, we discussed cannibalism in the context of Cervantes and Defoe. Let us now revive the topic, recontextualizing it with various other ethnographic passages from the posthumous *Persiles* (1617), in order to reflect on Cervantes's retrievable relationship to the Inca's *Commentaries*, published some eight years earlier (1609).

5. CERVANTES'S 'SAVAGE PAGE'

Although the *Persiles* covers an astonishing territorial range—a pan-European novel avowedly written to compete with a Greek novel set in Ethiopia—the text itself opens, *in media res*, on a suggestively American island. Because this site is presented to readers at the threshold of the book, the New World allegory takes on a disproportional weight. Almost three decades ago, Stelio Cro rightly noted that American materials, from both poetry and chronicles, 'were deviously incorporated into the *Persiles*, wrapped in the cultured and baroque garb of the byzantine novel' ('fueron incorporados al *Persiles* disimulada-mente, envueltos en el ropaje culto y barroco de la novela bizantina') (1975: 25). This American matter is not wholly occulted, however, by what the sixteenth century called the 'devious trope' of allegory. Taking a 'savage page' out of Michel de Certeau—who, like Cervantes himself, so often posits the convergence of fiction and historiography—let us look more closely at these American materials.

The space 'over there' that readers encounter at the begin-ning of Cervantes's last book is an all-male fantasy island that strongly invites a gender analysis.[9] The inaugural presence on the Barbaric Isle has, in fact, been astutely identified, in a strong psychoanalytic reading, as that of the 'macho' (González 1985: 126). But one can take that reading a few steps further by locating this fictional island at the intersection of gender and colonial studies. Envisioned as a 'contact zone'—a space 'where disparate cultures meet, clash, and grapple with each other, often in highly asymmetrical relations of domination and subordination' (Pratt 1992: 4)—Cervantes's island provides the location for two disparate cultures, European and 'barbar-ian', to meet and clash. The relations between the two seem, at first glance, pointedly asymmetrical. Whereas the Europeans entertain some notably Petrarchan ideas of women, for exam-ple, the barbarians simply purchase them 'at inflated prices, paid for in chunks of unminted gold and in extremely precious pearls' ('a subidísimos precios, que los pagan en pedazos de oro sin cuño y en preciosísimas perlas', 57). In an essay on the Roman and British empires, Laura Brown argues that the cluster of dis-courses representing 'the initiation, consolidation, celebration, defense, and even the critique of imperialism' is intimately tied to the representation of women (1994: 121). The merchandizing of women practised on Cervantes's Barbaric Isle is specifically tied to the 'initiation' of empire. The practice is uncannily

---

[9] See *Allegories of Love* (Wilson 1991: 109–29).

reminiscent of some of Spain's foundational moments in the New World. En route home as a prisoner after his third voyage, for example, Columbus describes, in the year 1500, the traffic in women on the island of Hispaniola (Española):

> For one woman moreover a hundred castellanos are given, as if for a farm, and this is very common, and there are now many merchants who go seeking for girls; nine or ten are now for sale; for women of all ages, there is a good price to be had.

> por una muger tanbién se falla cient castellanos como por una labranca; y es mucho en uso, y ay fartos mercaderes que andan buscando muchachas; de nueve á diez son agora en precio: de todas hedades ha de tener un bueno.   (1988: ii. 60–1)

Although merchants 'go seeking for girls' as early as the Greek novels, the enslaved and colonized bodies of women depicted by both Columbus and Cervantes belong to what de Certeau calls 'a new function of writing in the West'—to a '*writing that conquers*'. It is the kind of writing, as de Certeau puts it, that 'will use the New World as if it were a blank, 'savage' page on which Western desire will be written' (1988: p. xxv). Cervantes opens his last novel with precisely that kind of writing.

What do we find on Cervantes's 'savage' page? Readers may not be surprised to discover that writing about Western desire in the *Persiles* embraces such *domestica* as food and drink. Where *Don Quixote* opens with its hero's weekly Manchegan menu— hash ('salpicón') on most nights, lentils ('lantejas') on Fridays, a pigeon ('palomino') to grace the table on Sunday (1. 1)— the *Persiles* introduces its European pilgrims to a New World cuisine, including the wheatless bread ('pan . . . que no era de trigo', 80) mentioned earlier in this book. The allusion here is to cazabi bread, an 'easily digested' American bread, as Peter Martyr informed Europe, and perhaps also Cervantes. After extracting the poisonous juice of the yuca, the earliest islanders 'made from the cooked flour cazabi, *a bread better suited to human stomachs than wheat bread*' (1912: i. 384). Like Cervantes's European pilgrims, Montaigne had also tasted that wheatless wonderbread: 'In place of bread they use a certain white substance like preserved coriander. I have tried it; it tastes sweet and a little flat' (1957: 154). But the inhabitants of Cervantes's discursive island do not live by bread alone: they also eat shellfish ('conchas . . . y marisco', 80) and dried fruits ('frutas secas', 65), and they drink water in vessels made from tree bark ('cortezas de árboles', 71).

Ethnocentric details mark every page of Cervantes's Barbaric Isle narrative, which assembles in a six-chapter miniature the main themes of the novel. The barbarians—who dress in animal hides ('con pieles de animales, no cosidos', 94)—sail about in visibly American rafts or 'balsas', of the kind used by the Andean Indians. Inca Garcilaso's description of these rafts —'big and small ones, of five or seven long logs, each tied to the other' ('grandes y chicas, de cinco o de siete palos largos, atados unos con otros', 1. 3. 16)—could be a model for the fictional rafts in Cervantes.

Along similar American lines, Cervantes's barbarians use hemp ('cuerdas de cáñamo') for lifting objects (52); small flutes or 'chirimías' for making music (61); and bows and flintstone-headed arrows ('de pedernal') for making war (53). As ancillary weapons, they carry stone daggers ('puñal[es] . . . de piedra', 68). In trading with Europeans, the barbarians use gold and pearls ('oro y perlas', 85). For these transactions the Europeans are obliged to communicate with the barbarians by signs ('por señas', 53)—in the mode inaugurated by Columbus with the Arawaks. But because linguistic confusion reigns supreme on this island, sometimes the barbarians use an 'intérprete', a kidnapped translator whose role is examined in the Conclusion of this book. The most American custom on Cervantes's 'savage page', however, is the institutionalized practice of eating hearts. As in Inca Garcilaso, the practice is linked to some curious facial tics.

Believing that their tribe is destined to produce a world conqueror, in order to identify this Messiah's father, Cervantes's barbarians have devised a foolproof test: the pulverized hearts of sacrificed males must be swallowed, by all potential fathers, without wincing or twisting their faces ('sin torcer el rostro', 57). The pre-Incas, we read in the *Comentarios*, had devised a similar facial test, for hardihood rather than fatherhood. All potential victims would be cannibalized if, while being tortured, they made any 'sign of response with their faces' ('señal de sentimiento con el rostro', 1. 1. 11). Cervantes's 'powdered drink' ('bebida de polvos') has points of contact not with pre-Inca sadists but with Inca mummies. The 'cult of the royal mummies' involved a certain idol in Cuzco, a statue of the sun god whose hollow stomach was filled with a mixture of gold dust and the powdered ashes of the hearts of Inca kings. Father Bernabé Cobo, a Jesuit who arrived in Lima in 1600, would use Inca Garcilaso as a source for his story of this idol (1890–5: iii. 325).

The practice of cardiophagy has also been noted in other New World chronicles—as, for example, in the graphic descriptions by Fray Toribio de Benavente (also known as 'Motolinía') of human sacrifice in New Spain, where the victims' hearts were sometimes eaten by the elder ministers ('Los corazones a las veces los comían los ministros viejos') (D'Olwer 1981: 221). But the origins of the ritual in Cervantes show some striking verbal parallels with a passage in the *Commentaries* that describes a rival tribe of the Incas, the Chancas. This tribe had been 'persuaded by demons, their gods' ('persuadidos de los demonios, sus dioses', 1. 4. 15) to practise human sacrifice, much as Cervantes's barbarians have themselves been 'persuaded, perhaps by a demon, perhaps by an old magician' ('persuadidos, o ya del demonio, o ya de un antiguo hechicero', 57)—to adopt the same practice. Human sacrifice has evidently soured the Chancas, who feel 'rancour in their hearts' ('el rencor del corazon', 1. 4. 15), a quality that Cervantes's barbarians also entertain, their own hearts being filled 'with anger and vengeance' ('con la ira y la venganza', 69). The rancorous Chancas live in the 'septentrional' part of Cuzco ('el *septentrión* del Cuzco', 1. 4. 15), a site that may have inspired the subtitle of the *Persiles*: 'Historia Setentrional' (35). An earlier passage in the *Commentaries* explicitly notes that the septentrional regions of the New World 'correspond to the septentrional regions of the Old World' ('corresponden a las regiones septentrionales del mundo viejo', 1. 2. 6). Inca Garcilaso's correspondence between Old and New World northern regions, in short, may have provided the germ for the setting—and not only the setting—of the narrative that opens the *Persiles*, Cervantes's own 'septentrional' story.

6. 'NON SUFFICIT ORBIS'

Neither Inca Garcilaso's Chancas nor Cervantes's barbarians can be affiliated with the sentimentally appealing 'noble savage' we find in Montaigne. Where Montaigne memorably recasts the pieties of a Spanish historiographical tradition, as María Antonia Garcés persuasively argues (1992: 155–83), Cervantes fashions a cultural critique dependent not upon an inversion but a subversion of the civilization–barbary opposition. The macabre narrative that opens the *Persiles* enacts the prehistory of the birth of a world conqueror—of *any* world conqueror—as a form of savagery. The Barbaric Isle narrative neither aligns itself with facile condemnations of the European conquest, nor celebrates that conquest as providential. Famously deploring writers who whitewash American cultures of their vices and rob them of their human complexities, Simon Schama describes the Spanish encounter with the Aztec empire in bluntly egalitarian terms: 'one bellicose and sacrificial culture faced another, one despotism of tribute and service was annihilated by another' (1992: 32). Cervantes does not whitewash his Americanized barbarians of their own human complexity in order to deplore the barbarity of the Spanish conquest. Rather than take sides in the debate between New and Old World imperialists, his text raises it to a new level.

Cervantes's representation of what constitutes barbaric behaviour may be usefully filtered through Bartolomé de Las Casas's well-known division of the term *barbarian* into four different categories: those who behave, in great fits of passion, worse than brutes; those who lack letters or speak a different language; those who do not profess Christianity, no matter how civilized they are; and those who lack laws and marriage contracts (1992: 1576–86).[10] Although Cervantes's barbarians fit most of these categories, they are not lawless—at least they obey a 'Barbaric Law' (Ley Bárbara)—and they treat imported women well, the only quality, for Cervantes, in which they are not barbarians ('que sólo en esto muestran no ser bárbaros', 57). But these barbarians are not 'good' objects of knowledge: they are depicted, in fact, as cruel empire builders, sharing attributes of both Old *and* New World imperialists. It bears remembering that Las Casas, in his 1550 arguments against Sepúlveda, had called the Spanish colonists in America 'barbarísimos' for their cruel treatment of the natives (1992: 1578). Shards of this Lascasian

---

[10] The *Apólogetica* (1559) is divided into three books and an epilogue, this last containing four meanings of the term *barbarism*. The text, written *c.*1555, was not published in its entirety until the 19th cent. See Rabasa (1989) on the 'Utopian Ethnology' in Las Casas.

nomenclature may have found their way into Cervantes's last novel. Inca Garcilaso reiterates this accusation, albeit in a more linguistic key, when he suggests that certain non-Inca tribes were 'barbarous in their language like the Castilians' ('bárbaros en la lengua como los castellanos', 1. 5. 21).[11] The contemporary Peruvian historian Jorge Basadre launches into a less temperate accusation of Castilian 'barbarity': 'For their destruction of walkways, highways, terraces, temples, cities, granaries, and tributes; for their rape, their cruelty, their lust, and even their military superiority, the Spaniards appeared *as barbarians to the Indians*' (Por su destrucción de andenes, caminos, terrazas, templos, ciudades, graneros y tributos; por su rapiña, su crueldad, su lascivia y hasta su superioridad guerrera, los españoles aparecieron *como bárbaros entre los indios*, 1984: 13; emphasis added). The idea that the conquistadores would become what they thought they were conquering would have appealed to any moral ironist.

Cervantes's discursive strategy suggests that all empires will have their barbarians, their fair share of atrocities, their sacrificial rituals, their pious rationales for conquest. Old and New World imperialist practices during Cervantes's age, the *Persiles* implies, were disturbingly similar. The echoes, affinities, and uncanny structural parallels between the Incas and the Spaniards who supplanted them were not lost on Cervantes, who perceived the hidden network of resemblances between their ostensibly opposite cultures. Cervantes seems to have read Inca Garcilaso's heroic past of the vanquished Incas—those master empire builders of the New World—as a laundered version of the Spanish imperial present. Both cultures share a radical identity in their territorial appetitite, their desire to be 'spacious in the possession of dirt', to use Hamlet's derisive phrase (v. ii. 89). For Cervantes, this kind of thinking, whether underwritten by Providence or by Viracocha, turns men into 'barbarians'.

The complex dream of Spanish political and religious hegemony described throughout this book was, in fact, a providential kind of imperialism. It emerged in the 1520s, when many Castilians, looking to the Roman empire as a model, began to see themselves as a chosen, and therefore a superior, people,

---

[11] For an exploration of the conquest of the Incas as a conflict of discourses, see Garcés (1991).

entrusted with a divine mission which looked towards universal empire as its goal (Elliott 1989: 8–9). But although many Europeans, and even some anti-imperialist Castilians, were alarmed at the spectre of an Iberian hegemony, Spain's Messianic imperialism continued well into the reign of Philip II, whose monarchy was regarded by many of his subjects in global terms. Geoffrey Parker discusses a medal of Philip II struck in 1580 that showed the king with the Latin inscription 'PHILIPP II HISP ET NOVI ORBIS REX' ('Philip II, king of Spain and of the New World') on one side and, on the other, the legend 'NON SUFFICIT ORBIS' ('The World is Not Enough') circling a terrestrial globe. During their raid on the Spanish Caribbean in 1585–6, Parker adds, Drake's men found an escutcheon in Santo Domingo with the very same legend, which they regarded as 'a very notable marke and token of the vnsatiable ambition of the Spanish King and his nation' (1995: 254).

What the English saw as 'unsatiable', many Spaniards saw as providential. Inca Garcilaso seems to have shared this providentialist view of the Spanish conquest—a Christian, progressive interpretation of history that justified Spanish imperial expansion as a divine mission. The Inca's theory of Messianic providentialism, as Juan Bautista Avalle-Arce explains, converts imperialism and providentialism 'into two sides of the same coin' ('en las dos caras de la medalla') (1964: 17). This is not a coin used by Cervantes, who seems to ridicule *all* imperialist policies tied to providentialist schemes—whether by the expansionist Incas or by the expansionist Spaniards who thoroughly consumed their cities. Six short chapters of the *Persiles* thematize all the barbaric realities of universal empire. Where the chronicles so often posit difference between European and American cultures, Cervantes intuits points of deep resemblance. This intuition leads him to create a new kind of geopolitical formation: an imperial barbary. The trademarks of the 'barbaric' for Cervantes—inventoried at the opening of his last novel and at the close of his life—were unambiguous: Messianic prophecies, providentialist schemes, militant aggressivity, vanity, vengeful anger, and dreams of a global empire.

Cervantes moves into apocalyptic discourse when the island of the barbarians burns down in a holocaust. This occurs before their imperial dreams are realized but not before one female native has surreptitiously mixed her blood with that of a European. Perhaps rewriting the tragic history of Inca Garcilaso's own parents—a Spanish officer and an Inca royal princess or *palla*—Cervantes marries off a 'civilized' male Spaniard to a 'barbaric' female. George Mariscal has written presciently about the importance of this marriage and its 'mestizo' progeny (1998). Cervantes even gives his mixed couple translation lessons, during which each learns the language of the other: 'He has taught me his language and I have taught him mine' ('Háme enseñado su lengua y yo a él la mía', 82). This practice of translation—between two vastly different languages, cultures, and continents—may be the richest of Inca Garcilaso's American legacies to Cervantes.

Conclusion
Transila and La Malinche:
Women in Translation

THE astonishing cluster of virilized women in Cervantes's texts has been marked and remarked in the postmodern: mustachioed women, bearded women, pirate women, gun-toting women, cross-dressed pregnant women, and even a woman who yells and smells like a man, the 'hombruna' Aldonza Lorenzo, recycled into Don Quixote's supreme fiction, Dulcinea del Toboso. A few of these Cervantine women are fatal to men: in *Don Quixote*, the Catalonian maiden Claudia Jerónima precipitously guns down her fiancé with a musket and two pistols (2. 60); and in the *Persiles*, the Lithuanian widow Sulpicia hangs some forty would-be rapists from the tackle and yards of her ship (237). None of these women, however, approaches the New World dimensions of Transila, the kidnapped interpreter for an all-male culture of barbarians who are unable or unwilling to negotiate in languages other than their own.

Kidnapped for ideological purposes during the fictional 1570s, Transila first appears as a Polish-speaking Irishwoman on the 'Barbaric Isle', a signifying space that, as discussed in various earlier chapters, both opens the *Persiles* and haunts most of its narrative. As a polyglot in captivity, Transila precisely embodies what has been called, in another context, 'the polycultural and multilingual colonized subject as an author or agent of discourses'.[1] Before her kidnapping, she had been fleeing from her countrymen's torpid sexual custom of ritual defloration, a custom traced by various critics, as we noted in Chapter 8, to Inca Garcilaso de la Vega. A captive in 'Isla Bárbara', Transila may represent, *in nuce*, some of the traumas that Cervantes himself experienced during his five years as a captive in Barbary.

[1] My translation of a phrase from Adorno (1988*b*: 20).

Forced into becoming the resident translator for a culture with world-conquering pretensions, Transila shows translation to be a highly politicized process. In the text she functions both as a metaphor for oppression and for resistance to oppression—and her great weapon of resistance is her tongue. In an essay on 'The Translator as Hero', Jon Thiem discusses, as a postmodern development, 'the debut of the translator as literary character and representative figure', a phenomenon he sees funded by, among other things, the 'internationalization of literature' (1995: 208–9). An early modern kind of internationalization, both literary and non-literary, was also occurring, as I have argued in this book, across the sixteenth century with the conquest, exploration, and colonization of America. Cervantes's Transila may, in fact, provide the debut of the *kidnapped* translator as a representative literary figure. But before taking a closer look at Transila—including her possible affiliations with the New World's most notorious translator, Malintzîn Tenepal, also known as Doña Marina—let us glance at some of the other translators in Cervantes's two novels, as well as their ideas of translation.

The importance of translators to *Don Quixote* requires little glossing. The function of the translator as a cultural mediator or 'go-between' always intrigued Cervantes, who fictionalized the *morisco* translator of *Don Quixote* as a live-in guest of the reader-editor-narrator, requited for his translation labours with 'fifty pounds of raisins and two bushels of wheat' ('dos arrobas de pasas y dos fanegas de trigo', 1. 9). Hired to translate the Arabic notebooks of *Don Quixote* into a rigidly equivalent Castilian —'without removing nor adding anything' ('sin quitarles ni añadirles nada', 1. 9)—this nameless translator is shown to be cheating on his contract. After his first and only appearance in Part 1 of *Don Quixote*, where he is shown laughing at author Cide Hamete's marginalia, he reappears in Part 2 to criticize and demystify the book he has been translating, even raising questions about suspected apocrypha: for example, Sancho's conversation with his wife Teresa or Don Quixote's descent into the Cave of Montesinos (2. 5, 24, 27). Although 'truth' is this translator's avowed priority, fidelity to the original is not. On his own authority of what qualifies as trivia, for example, the *morisco* translator opts to suppress Cide Hamete's elaborate description of Don Diego's house:

the translator of this history decided to pass over these and other similar trifles in silence, since they don't tally well with the main intention of the story, the strength of which comes more from its truth than from any frigid digressions.

al traductor desta historia le pareció pasar estas y otras semejantes menudencias en silencio, porque no venían bien con el propósito principal de la historia; la cual más tiene su fuerza en la verdad que en las frías digresiones. (2. 18)

Measured against the old Italian proverb about all translators being traitors—*traduttore, traditore*[2]—the fictional *morisco* translator of *Don Quixote* qualifies as a deep-dyed *traditore*. His initial appearance as an attentive reader of marginal notes gives a clue to his own status as a marginal, eccentric, but self-authorizing translator. Since the putative author of the Arabic text he is translating is considered a 'liar', the very treachery of his translator may, indeed, locate its strength in the 'truth'. Evidently his labours are a thundering success, since Sansón Carrasco, in his very first speech in Part 2 of *Don Quixote*, blesses the translator of Part 1 more ardently than its author: 'Blessings on Cide Hamete Benengeli . . . and even more blessings on the inquiring spirit who took the care to translate them from Arabic into our native Castilian, for the universal entertainment of all peoples' ('y rebién haya el curioso que tuvo cuidado de hacerlas traducir de arábigo en nuestro vulgar castellano, para universal entretenimiento de las gentes', 2. 3). Not only have over 12,000 copies of that Spanish 'translation' been published in Portugal, Barcelona, Valencia, and even Antwerp, but also, Sansón claims—perhaps more accurately—'there will be no nation on earth, and no language spoken, into which it shall not be translated' ('no ha de haber nación ni lengua donde no se traduzga', 2. 3).

Besides the *morisco* translator, other translators in *Don Quixote* include the nameless Italian whom the hero meets in the Barcelona printing press, who translates words by their proper equivalents, and who wants to make money rather than a reputation (2. 62). In both his practice of literalism and his thirst for profit, the Italian affords a pointed contrast to the above *morisco* translator, who refuses word-by-word translation and who works for mere sustenance. Cervantes here thematizes translation as a game of compromise and of judging priorities:

[2] See Allen (1979*b*: 1–13) on translations of *Don Quixote* in English.

whatever passages the *morisco* regards as trivial or frigid in the original will not be allowed to survive in translation. By this standard, Cervantes's own novels—which are themselves presented as translations—become games of compromise. The rules of the game become clearer, however, when Don Quixote intones his famous, if quite unoriginal, theory of translation:

> It seems to me that translation from one language into another, save from Greek and Latin, the queens of languages, is like looking at the wrong side of Flemish tapestries, for though the figures are visible, they are full of threads that make them indistinct, and they don't appear with the smoothness and texture of the right side.

> me parece que el traducir de una lengua en otra, como no sea de las reinas de las lenguas, griega y latina, es como quien mira los tapices flamencos por el revés, que aunque se veen las figuras, son llenas de hilos que las escurecen, y no se veen con la lisura y tez de la haz. (2. 62)

This simile of translation as the underside of a tapestry, as editor Luis Murillo notes, may have been suggested to Cervantes by Luis Zapata (Cervantes 1978: ii. 519 n.). Wherever this simile originated, however, Don Quixote's use of it as an icon for untranslatability is distinctly ironic. Measured by Don Quixote's theory of translation, the very text in which he appears—*unless we are reading it in Arabic*—remains the dim and tangled underside of a Flemish tapestry. Only Cide Hamete's Arabic phantom 'original' would qualify as the bright, that is, the right, side of it. What all this suggests is that everything is *gained* in translation, even, or sometimes especially, in translations that 'betray' the original. Or put another way, nothing is lost in translation except ownership, a loss that Cervantes pre-empts by renouncing it, by refusing authorship to himself, by presenting *Don Quixote* as a translation. Cervantes, then, would seem to subscribe to translation, in the Bakhtinian sense, as 'the most fundamental of human acts' (Emerson 1984: p. xxxi). Or as Daniel O. Mosquera elegantly puts it, translation is the most *natural* of human acts: 'having survived Babel, translation not only becomes urgent and necessary but also natural, and such a recognition brings us to *Don Quijote* . . . or rather, *Don Quijote* brings us to such a recognition' (1994: 546).[3]

---

[3] Mosquera's is one of a cluster of excellent essays on Cervantes and translation. See also the essays by Allen (1979*b*), Moner (1990), and Percas de Ponseti (1991).

Such a recognition also brings us to the *Persiles*, a text extraordinarily on the cutting edge of translation, a text that obsessively thematizes the labours of interpreting, both between and within languages and cultures. Countless laborious remarks about translation appear in this novel, as, for example, 'He began to sing this in his own native Tuscan, which translated into Spanish said the following' ('en su propia lengua toscana, comenzó a cantar esto, que vuelto en lengua española, así decía', 132); or 'he began to sing in his own tongue what the barbarian Antonio would later say meant in Castilian' ('comenzó a cantar en su lengua lo que después dijo el bárbaro Antonio que en la castellana decía', 171). Such gouty passages appear in an exemplary relation to the whole text of the *Persiles*, which is itself presented to the surprised reader, in an abrupt aside well into the novel, as a translation: 'in this translation, which is just that' ('en esta tradución, que lo es', 159). This disclosure comes, almost as an afterthought, with less fanfare and more mystery than it does in *Don Quixote*: neither the author nor the language of the original *Persiles* is ever revealed.

Why does Cervantes choose to hide behind translators? Why would he wish to assert that neither of his novels is an original? There are, of course, no easy answers to these questions. Cervantes wrote under the heavy sixteenth-century humanist shadow of translators and translations. At the same time as Cervantes was writing, a massive New World translational phenomenon was taking place, alluded to at the famously amputated closure to chapter 8 of *Don Quixote*, Part 1, where a duel interrupts the journey of a Basque couple to the Indies. Legions of Spaniards were being 'translated' across the Ocean Sea to encounter, upon arrival, the need for translators. Indeed, the centrality of translators to the historiographical tradition of New World encounters scarcely needs commentary. As is well known, translators played a crucial role in the literature of American origins, especially after 1550, when they revived European interest in the New World. Across the space of a pan-European world and during a time of tremendous linguistic ferment, translations transmitted knowledge of voyages, explorations, and conquests in the New World. To cite only one instance of the relative speed and occasional euphoria of this transmission, the Sevillan doctor Nicolás Monardes's survey of American medicinal plants, *Historia medicinal de las Indias*, first published in Seville in 1565, appeared in 1577 in John Frampton's English translation *Joyfull Newes out of the Newe Founde World* (Elliott 1970: 37–8). Discussing a passage from Bernal Díaz's *True History . . .* (*Historia verdadera . . .*), where the old and the new have merged into a single image of Mexico City, Stephen Gilman claims that 'the New World must be given in translation', that the very act of translation recreates the old 'in such a way that it means more than it ever meant before. Language and tradition, both English and Spanish, are submitted in America to the proof of adventure' (1961: 111 n.). Translations, in other words, are recreations, adventurous and abusive transformations, permeated by what Mosquera compellingly calls 'quixotics' (1994: 547).

In Cervantes's last novel, these transformative labours of translation are assumed by Transila, an intrepid woman warrior in whom the ancient virago topos is recreated through lingual and genital metaphors. The discourse of discovery, as Louis Montrose has argued for English texts, was often 'grounded in a territorial conception of the female body' (1991: 13). Transila documents this grounding when she contests the land/woman trope so frequent in the discourses of conquest. Metaphorizing her own body as a country field, she accuses her would-be rapists of wishing 'to cultivate other people's fields without the license of their legitimate owners' ('cultivar los ajenos campos sin licencia de sus legítimos dueños', 113–14). In this particular episode, which readers hear about in a later flashback, Transila is describing the practice of ritual defloration—the *ius primae noctis* or Law of the First Night—a 'custom of the country' for which she is a candidate. Although the country in question is identified as Hibernia, the practice of ritual defloration was reported by a number of New World chronicles. Writing in *Hispania victrix*, for example, López de Gómara tied the practice to polygamy among the American Indians: 'they married many women, and the lords and captains "ruptured" the brides either for honour or for tyranny' ('Casaban con muchas mujeres, y los señores y capitanes rompían las novias por honra o por tiranía') (1858: i. 294). Ritual defloration is also discussed in Pedro Cieza de León's *La crónica del Perú nuevamente escrita* (1554), a text that may or may not have caught Cervantes's eye. Building on Pedro de Cieza's testimony, however, Inca Garcilaso also reported a version of the custom, practised by

Andean tribes other than the Incas. Inca Garcilaso's version of ritual defloration most closely tallies with Cervantes's text, especially in its use of the phrase 'the nearest kinsmen' ('los parientes más cercanos'): 'In other provinces, the groom's nearest kinsmen and his best friends would corrupt the virgin who was to be married, and under these conditions they settled the marriage' ('En otras provincias corrompían la virgen que se había de casar los parientes más cercanos del novio y sus mayores amigos, y con esta condición concertaban el casamiento', 1. 1. 14).

All this talk of sexually 'corrupted' women leads us to the links between Transila and Doña Marina or La Malinche, a question that remains not only unanswered but unasked.[4] These concluding pages—the end of a study which, as Cervantes puts it in *The Fortunate Pimp* (*El rufián dichoso*), 'has joined Mexico and Seville' (1991*b*: i. 412)—do not, indeed, cannot answer that question. I must leave the relationship between Doña Marina and fictional translators to Chicana feminist literary scholars, currently retroping 'La Malinche at the Intersection'.[5] The various correspondences between the two sixteenth-century women discussed here—as translators, mediators, and sexual objects—may profit from closer scrutiny. Doña Marina, as is well known, was the translator famously attached to Cortés, whom Don Quixote mentions admiringly in a discussion of fame (2. 8). Cortés was given this woman, who could speak both Nahuatl and the Mayan tongue, in Tabasco, and she would serve him faithfully in her double role of mistress and interpreter.

Doña Marina has been persuasively juxtaposed to the 'barbarian' Ricla, yet another character in Cervantes's *Persiles*. George Mariscal sees the figure of Ricla—both as a Catholic convert and as the mother of a 'new mestizo family'—as 'a literary sister of Malintzîn Tenepal, La Malinche' (1998: 207). But Malintzîn-Marina, whose name has been widely circulating in Chicana feminist literary discourses since the 1970s, has not always fared so well. She has also been stigmatized as La Malinche, a traitor to the Mexican nation for having collaborated with the Spanish colonizers. As Cortés's concubine and the mother of

---

[4] I thank Anne J. Cruz for urging me to articulate the Transila-Malinche connection.
[5] The title of Sánchez's essay in the Jan. 1998 'Ethnicity' issue of *PMLA*.

their son, moreover, La Malinche is also regarded as La Chingada ('acted on'). This more recent term of violation, which may or may not be the sad legacy of Octavio Paz, is urgently being countered by Chicana feminists, who rightly aim to transform La Malinche 'from a figure of destructive social and sexual agency (a traitor and a whore) to one of affirmative agency (a cultural bridge and a translator)' (Sánchez 1998: 118).

More to our purposes, La Malinche is also known, to both Spanish and indigenous peoples, as La Lengua ('The Tongue'), a term that Cervantes uses in various discussions of Transila. He not only describes her tongue as prone to being disturbed ('tongue-tied') by rage ('lengua a quien suele turbar la cólera', 113), but he also depicts it as an effective instrument of persuasion: her listeners are left 'hanging onto the smoothness of her tongue' ('colgados de la suavidad de su lengua', 115). The tongue as a 'woman's weapon' is, of course, an ancient topos, but let us remember that Cervantes was quick to invoke his own tongue. In the 'Prologue to the Reader' of the *Novelas ejemplares*, for example, where he supplies a literary self-portrait for a friend who has left him 'blank and unillustrated' ('blanco y sin figura'), Cervantes describes himself in the same tongue-tied position as he describes Transila: 'I shall have to make do with my tongue, which, though tied, will be quick enough to tell home truths, which are wont to be understood even in the language of signs' ('será forzoso valerme por mi pico, que aunque tartamudo, no lo será para decir verdades, que, dichas por señas, suelen ser entendidas') (1992: i. 2–3). In Avellaneda's apocryphal sequel to *Don Quixote*, which includes an infamous *ad hominem* attack against Cervantes, the author accuses Cervantes, amidst a litany of virulent abuses, of having a monstrous number of tongues: 'As a soldier as old in years as he is youthful in courage, he has more tongue than hands' (1980: 3–5). Where Avellaneda sees his rival as old and multi-tongued, Cervantes sees himself as tongue-tied but capable of speaking in signs.

The tongue is also a programmatic feature of the *Persiles*, a text where tongues become as loose as thought (121) or as sharp as double-edged swords (120); where they stick to the roof of mouths (100), stammer in shame (113), or choose to play mute (94); where they are muzzled (135), tied by imprisonment (118), or pierced by arrows (68). In the light of all these lingual metaphors, how might the Malinche-as-Lengua trope illuminate

Transila, a polyglot captive also forced into mediating between Europeans and 'barbarians'? A colonized translator uneasy about 'collaborating'? A woman at the crossroads of gender who stoutly resists being 'chingada'? These two early modern women—one historical, the other fictional—lead us to pose, if not answer, one question: what is the task of the multilingual female translator caught up in, and exploited by, warring male worlds?

It is easy, perhaps too easy, to interpret Transila—a woman filled with 'manly spirit' ('varonil brío', 69)—in the light of the European virago tradition, aligning her with virile female characters from the Renaissance epic who had themselves been modelled on Graeco-Roman figures. Transila's epic antecedents may include Ariosto's Bradamante (also a precursor for Spenser's Britomart) or Tasso's Clorinda, behind which stand some hardy classical models: the Amazons Hippolyta and Penthesilea, or the Virgilian Camilla. But none of these women is represented as multilingual nor, in the manner of Transila, as 'sold' to a culture where she must work as a translator. And none of the Old World warrior women, at least to my knowledge, articulates the potential dangers of translating between men: 'These my masters', Transila explains to the castaway Europeans, 'become displeased when I dilate my speech in anything but what pertains to their business' ('estos mis amos no gustan que en otras pláticas me dilate, sino en aquellas que hacen al caso para su negocio', 62).

Glossing these dangers in the context of the Mexican Spanish language, Mary Louise Pratt reminds us that betrayal there is coded as *female*: 'to be a traitor is by implication to become female, while to be female is to be inherently a potential traitor' (1993: 860). In her attempts to gain and to maintain control of her own sexuality—*and* her own representation—Cervantes's Transila, not unlike Pratt's equations noted above, betrays the sexual customs of her countrymen. For the catalyzing power of her 'smooth' tongue, Transila is closer to Doña Marina than to Virgil's Camilla or Tasso's Clorinda. Intricately linked to the matter of America—a matter that must be given in translation— Transila allegorizes many of the problems of translation in the New World. She is presciently aware, for example, of the 'many harmful pens' ('muchas injuriosas plumas', 227) ready to rewrite her story, an awareness that uncannily anticipates the 'harmful pens' that would demean, through sexual metaphors, the 'real world' female translator La Malinche.

Like the *morisco* translator, Transila is a cultural outsider, even
an outlaw, less invested in literalism than in survival. Like the
Mexican translator Doña Marina, she is a colonized female
translating a putative 'barbarian' language for Europeans. But
Transila is also a figure for translation. The last, and the most
polyglot, of Cervantes's translators will escape from captivity
in a barbarian culture, just as she escaped from the abusive
sexual legislation in her native Hibernian culture. As she rows
herself out to sea, alone in a small boat, away from oppressive
laws and customs, Transila is also turning her back on the
exhausted literary forms of antiquity. Hers is a new and a New
World story. As María Menocal notes, 'in the New World, across
the sea, up the river, and deep in the jungle, the simple story
of following in the footsteps of the Greeks and then reinvent-
ing Rome could not be told anymore' (1994: 48). What would
be told instead—through translations real and fictional—is the
modern novel.

Bibliography

Acosta, Joseph de [José de] (1962), *Historia natural y moral de las Indias* (1590), ed. Edmundo O'Gorman (México: Fondo de Cultura Económica).

Acosta, Pedro (1993), 'La vigilia del Almirante', review of *El Quijote y el Almirante* by Roa Bastos, *El Tiempo*, section on 'Lecturas dominicales' (Bógota, 4 July 1993), 15.

Adorno, Rolena (1986), 'Literary Production and Suppression: Reading and Writing about Amerindians in Colonial Spanish America', *Dispositio*, 11/28–9: 1–25.

—— (1988*a*), 'Colonial Spanish American Literary Studies: 1982–1992', *Revista interamericana de Bibliografía*, 38: 167–176.

—— (1988*b*), 'Nuevas Perspectivas en los Estudios Literarios Coloniales Hispanoamericanos', *Revista de Crítica Literaria Latinoamericana*, 28: 11–27.

—— (1990), 'New Perspectives in Colonial Spanish-American Literary Studies', *Journal of the Southwest*, 32/2: 173–91.

—— (1992), Introduction to *Books of the Brave* by Irving A. Leonard (Berkeley and Los Angeles: University of California Press), pp. ix–xl.

Agulló y Cobo, Mercedes (1966), *Relaciones de sucesos*, i. *Años 1477–1619* (Madrid: CSIC).

Aladro Font, Jorge (1994), 'Don Quijote y Cristóbal Colón: o, la sinrazón de la realidad', *Lienzo*, 15 (June), 37–54.

Allen, John J. (1969 and 1979*a*), *Don Quixote: Hero or Fool?*, 2 vols. (Gainesville, Fla.: University Presses of Florida).

—— (1976), 'Autobiografía y ficción: El relato del Capitán cautivo (*Don Quijote* I. 39–41)', *Anales Cervantinos*, 15: 149–55.

—— (1977) (ed.), Miguel de Cervantes, *Don Quijote de La Mancha II* (Madrid: Ediciones Cátedra).

—— (1979*b*), 'Traduttori traditori: *Don Quixote* in English', *Crítica Hispánica*, 1: 1–13.

Alter, Robert B. (1981), 'The Mirror of Knighthood and the World of Mirrors', in Miguel de Cervantes, *Don Quixote*, ed. Joseph R. Jones and Kenneth Douglas (Norton Critical Edition; New York: W. W. Norton), 955–74.

Anadón, José (1998), 'History as Autobiography in Garcilaso Inca', in id. (ed.), *Garcilaso de la Vega: An American Humanist* (Notre Dame, Ind.: University of Notre Dame), 149–63.

Anderson Imbert, Enrique (1988), 'El punto de vista narrativo en "La Araucana" de Ercilla', *Boletín Academia Argentina de Letras*, 53: 71–90.

Apuleius (1965), *The Golden Ass: Being the Metamorphoses of Lucius Apuleius* (1566), trans. W. Adlington (Loeb Classical Library; London: William Heinemann).

Arciniegas, Germán (1965), 'Don Quijote y la conquista de América', *Revista Hispánica Moderna*, 31: 11–16.

—— (1998), 'El hijo de don Quesada', *Senderos* (Publicación Semestral de la Biblioteca Nacional de Colombia), 9/33: 1246–51.

Arens, William (1979), *The Man-Eating Myth: Anthropology and Anthropophagy* (New York: Oxford University Press).

Armas, Frederick A. de (1998), *Cervantes, Raphael and the Classics* (Cambridge: Cambridge University Press).

Arrabal, Fernando (1996), *Un esclavo llamado Cervantes* (Madrid: Espasa Calpa).

Astrana Marín, Luis (1948–58), *Vida ejemplar y heroica de Miguel de C. Saavedra*, 7 vols. (Madrid: Instituto Editorial Reus).

Auerbach, Erich (1953), 'The Enchanted Dulcinea', in *Mimesis: The Representation of Reality in Western Literature*, trans. Willard R. Trask (Princeton: Princeton University Press), 334–58.

Avalle-Arce, Juan Bautista (1964), *El Inca Garcilaso en sus 'Comentarios'* (Madrid: Gredos).

—— (1969) (ed.), 'Introducción' in *Los trabajos de Persiles y Sigismunda* (Madrid: Clásicos Castalia).

—— (1971), 'El poeta en su poema [El caso Ercilla]', *Revista de Occidente*, 132: 152–70.

—— (1982) (ed.), *Novelas ejemplares*, 3 vols. (Madrid: Clásicos Castalia).

—— (1998), 'The Self-Baptism of Garcilaso Inca', in José Anadón (ed.), *Garcilaso de la Vega: An American Humanist* (Notre Dame, Ind.: University of Notre Dame), 42–5.

Avellaneda, Alonso Fernández de (1980), *Don Quixote de La Mancha (Part II): Being the spurious continuation of Miguel de Cervantes's Part I*, trans. and ed. Alberta Wilson Server and John Esten Keller (Newark, Del.: Juan de la Cuesta).

Bacon, Francis (1981), *New Atlantis*, in Frederic R. White (ed.), *Famous Utopias of the Renaissance* (Putney, Vt.: Hendricks House).

Baena, Julio (1988), '*Los trabajos de Persiles y Sigismunda*: La utopía del novelista', *Cervantes*, 8/2 (Fall): 127–40.

—— (1996), *El círculo y la flecha: Principio y fin, triunfo y fracaso del 'Persiles'* (Chapel Hill, NC: University of North Carolina Press).

Bakewell, Peter (1995), 'Conquest after the Conquest: The Rise of Spanish Domination in America', in Richard L. Kagan and Geoffrey Parker (eds.), *Spain, Europe and the Atlantic World: Essays in honour of John H. Elliott* (Cambridge: Cambridge University Press), 296–315.

Bakhtin, M. M. (1981), *The Dialogic Imagination: Four Essays*, ed. Michael Holquist, trans. Caryl Emerson and Michael Holquist (Austin, Tex.: University of Texas Press).

—— (1984*a*), *Rabelais and His World*, trans. Hélène Iswolsky (Bloomington, Ind.: Indiana University Press).

—— (1984*b*), *Problems of Dostoevsky's Poetics*, ed. and trans. Caryl Emerson (Minneapolis: University of Minnesota Press).

Barthes, Roland (1979), 'From Work to Text', in José V. Harari (ed.), *Textual Strategies: Perspectives in Post-Structuralist Criticism* (Ithaca, NY: Cornell University Press), 73–81.

Basadre, Jorge (1984), *Perú: problema y posibilidad* (Lima: Cotesca).

Bataillon, Marcel (1950), *Erasmo y España: Estudios sobre la historia espiritual del siglo xvi*, trans. Antonio Alatorre (Mexico: Fondo de Cultura Económica).

Beattie, James (1970), 'From *On Fable and Romance*, 1783', in Ioan Williams (ed.), *Novel and Romance 1700–1800: A Documentary Record* (New York: Barnes & Noble), 309–27.

Benítez-Rojo, Antonio (1992), *The Repeating Island: The Caribbean and the Postmodern Perspective*, trans. James E. Maraniss (Durham, NC and London: Duke University Press).

Benjamin, Walter (1969), 'The Storyteller', in *Illuminations*, ed. Hannah Arendt (New York: Schocken Books).

Bertonio, P. Ludovico (1984), *Vocabulario de la Lengua Aymara* (1ˢᵗ pub. 1612) (Cochabamba, Bolivia: Centro de Estudios de la Realidad Económica y Social).

Bhabha, Homi K. (1983). 'Difference, Discrimination, and the Discourse of Colonialism', in Francis Barker et al. (eds.), *The Politics of Theory* (Colchester: University of Essex), 194–211.

—— (1990), 'DissemiNation: Time, Narrative, and the Margins of the Modern Nation', in id. (ed.), *Nation and Narration* (London and New York: Routledge), 291–322.

—— (1991). 'The Postcolonial Critic', *Arena*, 96: 61–3.

—— (1994*a*), 'How Newness enters the World: Postmodern Space, Postcolonial Times and the Trials of Cultural Translation', in *The Location of Culture* (London: Routledge), 212–35.

—— (1994*b*), 'Of Mimicry and Man: The Ambivalence of Colonial Discourse', in *The Location of Culture* (London: Routledge), 85–92.

—— (1994*c*), 'The Commitment to Theory', in *The Location of Culture* (London: Routledge), 19–39.

Bleiberg, Germán (1985), *El 'Informe secreto' de Mateo Alemán sobre el trabajo forzoso en las minas de Almadén* (London: Tamesis).

Bloom, Harold (1973), *The Anxiety of Influence: A Theory of Poetry* (New York: Oxford University Press).

—— (1994), *The Western Canon: The Books and School of the Ages* (New York: Harcourt Brace and Co.).

Bolaños, Álvaro Félix (1994), *Barbarie y canibalismo en la retórica colonial* (Bogotá: Cerec).

Borges, Jorge Luis (1960), 'Parábola de Cervantes y de Quijote', in *El hacedor* (Buenos Aires: Emecé), 38.

Brancaforte, Benito (1977) (ed.), *Deffensa de la Poesía: A 17ʰ-Century Anonymous Spanish Translation of Philip Sidney's 'Defence of Poesie',* transcription of Ms. 3908 in the Biblioteca Nacional, Madrid (Chapel Hill, NC: North Carolina Studies in the Romance Languages and Literatures).

Braudel, Fernand (1972), *The Mediterranean and the Mediterranean World in the Age of Philip II* (1ˢᵗ pub. 1949 and 1966), trans. Siân Reynolds, 2 vols. (New York: Harper & Row).

Brown, Homer Obed (1995–6), 'The Institution of the English Novel: Defoe's Contribution', *Novel,* 29: 299–318.

—— (1997), *Institutions of the English Novel: From Defoe to Scott* (Philadelphia: University of Pennsylvania Press).

Brown, Laura (1994), 'Amazons and Africans: Gender, Race, and Empire in Daniel Defoe', in Margo Hendricks and Patricia Parker, *Women, 'Race', and Writing in The Early Modern Period* (London: Routledge), 121.

Buell, Lawrence (1999), 'Introduction: In Pursuit of Ethics', *PMLA* 114/1 (Jan.): 7–19.

Bueno, Raúl (1996), 'Sobre la heterogeneidad literaria y cultural de América Latina', in José Antonio Mazzotti and U. Juan Zevallos Aguilar (eds.), *Asedios a la Heterogeneidad Cultural: Libro de homenaje a Antonio Cornejo Polar* (Philadelphia: International Association of Peruvianists), 21–36.

Caballero Calderón (1948) (ed.), *Cervantes en Colombia* (Madrid: Afrodisio Aguado).

Cabeza de Vaca, Alvar Núñez (1989), *Naufragios* (1ˢᵗ pub. 1542), ed. Juan Francisco Maura (Madrid: Cátedra).

Calhoun, Gloria D. (1971), 'Ercilla, A Possible Literary Source of Cervantes?', *Abside: Revista de Cultura Mejicana,* 35: 315–34.

Campos, Jorge (1947), 'Presencia de América en la obra de Cervantes', *Revista de Indias,* 8: 371–404.

Canavaggio, Jean (1977), *Cervantès Dramaturge: Un théâtre à naître* (Paris: Presses Universitaires de France).

—— (1990), *Cervantes,* trans. J. R. Jones (New York: W. W. Norton).

Cantor, Paul A. (1997), 'Tales of the Alhambra: Rushdie's Use of Spanish History in *The Moor's Last Sigh',* *Studies in the Novel,* 29/3: 323–41.

Carbaxal, Fr. Gaspar de (1992), *Relación del descubrimiento del famoso río grande que desde su nacimiento hasta el mar descubrió el Capitán Orellana en unión 56 hombres,* in *Vida Amazonas: Biblioteca Amazonas de la Historia,*

i. *Descubrimiento del Río de las Amazonas* (repr. of Seville 1894 edn.; Valencia: Estudios Ediciones y Medios), 211–84.

Carpentier, Alejo (1979), *The Lost Steps*, trans. Harriet de Onís (New York: Bard/Avon).

Carvajal, Gaspar de (1934), 'Carvajal's Account', in *The Discovery of the Amazon According to the Account of Friar Gaspar de Carvajal and Other Documents*, introd. José Toribio Medina, trans. Bertram T. Lee, ed. H. C. Heaton (New York: American Geographical Society), 167–242.

Cascardi, Anthony (1986), 'Genre Definition and Multiplicity in *Don Quixote*', *Cervantes*, 6/1: 39–49.

Castañeda de Nájera, Pedro de (1940), 'Castañeda's History of the Expedition', in George P. Hammond and Agapito Rey (eds.), *Narratives of the Coronado Expedition, 1540–1542*, ed. George P. Hammond and Agapito Rey, vol. ii. (Coronado Cuarto Centennial Publications, 1540–1940; Albuquerque, N. Mex.: University of New Mexico Press).

Castro, Américo (1945), Introduction to *El Villano del Danubio y Otros Fragmentos* by Antonio de Guevara (Princeton: Princeton University Press).

—— (1974), *Cervantes y los casticismos españoles* (Madrid: Alianza, 1974).

Cervantes Saavedra, Miguel de (1968), *La Galatea* (1ˢᵗ pub. 1585), ed. Juan Bautista Avalle-Arce, 2 vols. (Madrid: Espasa-Calpe).

—— (1969), *Los trabajos de Persiles y Sigismunda* (1ˢᵗ pub. 1617), ed. Juan Bautista Avalle-Arce (Madrid: Clásicos Castalia).

—— (1973 and 1978), *El ingenioso hidalgo Don Quijote de la Mancha* (1ˢᵗ pub. 1605 and 1615), ed. Luis Andrés Murillo, 2 vols. (Madrid: Clásicos Castalia).

—— (1975*a*), *La gitanilla*, in *Novelas ejemplares* (1ˢᵗ pub. 1613), ed. Francisco Rodríguez Marín, 2 vols. (Madrid: Espasa-Calpe), i. 1–130.

—— (1975*b*), *Novela y coloquio que pasó entre Cipión y Berganza*, in *Novelas ejemplares* (1ˢᵗ pub. 1613), ed. Francisco Rodríguez Marín. 2 vols. (Madrid: Espasa-Calpe), ii. 209–340.

—— (1982), *Novelas ejemplares* (1ˢᵗ pub. 1613), ed. Juan Bautista Avalle-Arce, 3 vols. (Madrid: Clásicos Castalia).

—— (1985), *Los trabajos de Persiles y Sigismunda* (Madrid: Espasa-Calpe).

—— (1991*a*), 'Al túmulo del Rey Felipe II en Sevilla', in *Obras completas*, ed. Ángel Valbuena Prat, 2 vols. (Mexico: Aguilar), i. 53.

—— (1991*b*), *El rufián dichoso*, in *Obras completas*, ed. Ángel Valbuena Prat, 2 vols. (Mexico: Aguilar), i. 389–437.

—— (1991*c*), *Viage del Parnaso. Poesías varias*, ed. Elías L. Rivers (Madrid: Espasa-Calpe).

—— (1991*d*), *Pedro de Urdemales*, in *Obras completas*, ed. Ángel Valbuena Prat, 2 vols. (Mexico: Aguilar), ii. 607–58.

Cervantes Saavedra, Miguel de (1992), *Exemplary Novels* (*Novelas ejemplares*), ed. B. W. Ife, with introductions, translations, and notes by Michael and Jonathan Thacker, 4 vols. (Warminster: Aris & Phillips Ltd).

—— (1995), *Don Quijote de la Mancha*, trans. Dong Yansheng (Zheijang: Artes y Letras).

—— (1997), *Los trabajos de Persiles y Sigismunda* (1ˢᵗ pub. 1616), ed. Carlos Romero Muñoz (Madrid: Cátedra).

—— (1998), *Don Quijote de la Mancha* (1ˢᵗ pub. 1605 and 1615), edition directed by Francisco Rico, with the collaboration of Joaquín Forradellas, and preliminary study by Fernando Lázaro Carreter, 2 vols. (Barcelona: Instituto Cervantes).

—— (1999), *The History of that Ingenious Gentleman Don Quijote de la Mancha*, trans. Burton Raffel, ed. Diana de Armas Wilson (Norton Critical Edition; New York: W. W. Norton).

Cevallos, Francisco Javier (1989), 'Don Alonso de Ercilla and the American Indian: History and Myth', *Revista de estudios hispánicos*, 23/3 (Oct.): 1–20.

Chanca, Diego Álvarez (1988), 'La Carta del Doctor Chanca, que escribió a la Ciudad de Sevilla', in Cecil Jane (ed.), *The Four Voyages of Columbus*, 2 vols. bound as 1 (New York: Dover), ii. 20–73.

Chevalier, Maxime (1976), *Lectura y lectores en la España del siglo XVI y XVII* (Madrid: Ediciones Turner).

Clamurro, William H. (1997), *Beneath the Fiction: The Contrary Worlds of Cervantes's 'Novelas ejemplares'* (New York: Peter Lang).

Clayton, Jay, and Rothstein, Eric (1991), 'Figures in the Corpus: Theories of Influence and Intertextuality', in eid (eds.), *Influence and Intertextuality in Literary History* (Madison: University of Wisconsin Press), 3–36.

Clemencín, Diego (1993), 'Comentario', in Miguel de Cervantes Saavedra, *El ingenioso hidalgo Don Quijote de la Mancha*, Edición IV Centenario (Valencia: Editorial Alfredo Ortells), 977–1936.

Close, Anthony (1977), *The Romantic Approach to 'Don Quixote': A Critical History of the Romantic Tradition in 'Quixotic' Criticism* (Cambridge: Cambridge University Press).

—— (1993), 'A Poet's Vanity: Thoughts on the Friendly Ethos of Cervantine Satire', *Cervantes*, 13/1: 31–63.

Cobo, Bernabé (1890–5), *Historia del Nuevo Mundo*, ed. Marcos Jiménez de la Espada, 4 vols. (Seville: Sociedad de Bibliófilos Andaluces).

Coetzee, J. M. (1988), 'Simple Language, Simple People: Smith, Paton, Mikro', in *White Writing: On the Culture of Letters in South Africa* (New Haven: Yale University Press), 115–35.

Cohen, Andrew (1975), *A Sociolinguistic Approach to Bilingual Education* (Rowley, Mass.: Newbury House Publisher).

Coleridge, Samuel Taylor (1936), 'Lecture VIII: Don Quixote, Cervantes', in *Coleridge's Miscellaneous Criticism*, ed. Thomas Middleton Raysor (London: Constable & Co.), 98–110.

Colón, Cristóbal (1988), *Textos y documentos completos: Relaciones de viajes, cartas y memoriales*, ed. Consuelo Varela (Madrid: Alianza Editorial, 1982).

Columbus, Christopher (1988), *The Four Voyages of Columbus*, trans. and ed. Cecil Jane, 2 vols. (New York: Dover Publications).

—— (1989*a*), *The 'Diario' of Christopher Columbus's First Voyage to America: 1492–1493*, abstracted by Fray Bartolomé de las Casas, ed. and trans. Oliver Dunn and James E. Kelley, Jr. (Norman, Okla.: University of Oklahoma Press).

—— (1989*b*), 'Capitulación del Almirante Colón, 1492', in René Jara and Nicholas Spadaccini (eds.), *1492–1992: Re/Discovering Colonial Writing* (Minneapolis: Prisma Institute), 423–5.

Congreve, William (1970), 'Preface to Incognita, 1691', in Ioan Williams (ed.), *Novel and Romance 1700–1800: A Documentary Record* (New York: Barnes & Noble), 27–8.

Conley, Tom (1988), Translator's Introduction de Certeau (1988).

—— (1996), *The Self-Made Map: Cartographic Writing in Early Modern France* (Minneapolis: University of Minnesota Press).

Conrad, Geoffrey W., and Demarest, Arthur A. (1984), *Religion and Empire: The Dynamics of Aztec and Inca Expansionism* (Cambridge: Cambridge University Press).

Cook, Noble David (1981), *Demographic Collapse: Indian Peru, 1520–1620* (Cambridge: Cambridge University Press).

Cornejo Polar, Antonio (1982), *Sobre literatura y crítica latinoamericanas* (Caracas: Universidad Central de Venezuela, 1982).

—— (1989), 'Actas del simposio "Latinoamérica: Nuevas direcciones en Teoría y crítica literarias"', *Revista de Crítica Literaria Latinoamericana*, 15/29: 19–58.

—— (1996), 'Mestizaje, Transculturación, Heterogeneidad', in *Asedios a la Heterogeneidad Cultural: Libro de homenaje a Antonio Cornejo Polar* (Philadelphia: International Association of Peruvianists), 54–6.

Corominas, Joan (1991), *Diccionario Crítico Etimológico Castellano e Hispánico*, with the collaboration of Juan de Pascual, 6 vols. (Madrid: Editorial Gredos).

Corominas, Juan M. (1980), 'Cervantes y Ercilla', in Michael D. McGaha (ed.), *Cervantes and the Renaissance* (Easton, Pa.: Juan de la Cuesta Press).

Correa-Díaz, Luis (1998), 'El Quijote Indiano / Caribeño: Novela de caballería y crónica de Indias', *Anales cervantinos*, 34 (1998), 85–123.

Cortés, Hernán (1986), *Letters from Mexico*, trans. and ed. Anthony Pagden, introd. J. E. Elliott (New Haven: Yale University Press).

Cortés López, José Luis (1990), 'Aproximación a la vida del esclavo negro en la España de los siglos XV y XVI', *Studia Africana*, 1: 39–48.

Covarrubias Orozco, Sebastián de (1994), *Tesoro de la lengua castellana o española*, ed. Felipe C. R. Maldonado (Madrid: Editorial Castalia).

Cro, Stelio (1975), 'Cervantes, el "Persiles" y la historiografía Indiana', *Anales de literatura hispanoamericana*, vol. iv (Madrid: Universidad Complutense), 5–25.

—— (1979), 'The New World in Spanish Utopianism', *Alternative Futures*, 2/3 (Summer 1979): 39–53.

—— (1994), 'Classical Antiquity, America, and the Myth of the Noble Savage', in Wolfgang Haase and Meyer Reinhold (eds.), *The Classical Tradition and the Americas*, vol. i, pt 1 (Berlin: Walter de Gruyter), 379–418.

Cruz, Anne J. (1988), *Imitación y transformación: El petrarquismo en la poesía de Boscán y Garcilaso de la Vega* (Amsterdam: Johns Benjamins).

—— (1993), 'Mirroring Others: A Lacanian Reading of the *Letrados* in *Don Quixote*', in Ruth Anthony El Saffar and Diana de Armas Wilson (eds.), *Quixotic Desire: Psychoanalytic Perspectives on Cervantes* (Ithaca, NY: Cornell University Press), 93–116.

—— (1999), *Discourses of Poverty: Social Reform and the Picaresque Novel in Early Modern Spain* (Toronto: University of Toronto Press).

—— and Johnson, Carroll B. (1998) (ed.), *Cervantes and his Postmodern Constituencies* (New York: Garland).

Cuneo, Miguel de (1984), *Cartas de particulares a Colón y Relaciones coetáneas*, ed. Juan Gil and Consuelo Varela (Madrid: Alianza Editorial), 235–60.

D'Olwer, Luis Nicolau (1981), *Cronistas de las culturas pre-colombinas* (Mexico: Fondo de Cultura Económica).

Dadson, Trevor (1998), *Libros, Lectores y Lecturas: Estudios sobre bibliotecas particulares españolas del Siglo de Oro* (Madrid: Arco/Libros).

Dampier, William (1994), *A New Voyage round the World . . .* (repr. of 5th edn., London, 1703), excerpt repr. in Defoe (1994a), 227–9.

Daniels, Marie Cort (1992), *The Function of Humor in the Spanish Romances of Chivalry* (New York: Garland).

Davis, Elizabeth B. (1989), ' "Conquistas de las Indias de Dios": Early Poetic Appropriations of the Indies by the Spanish Renaissance', *Hispanic Journal*, 11/45–54.

de Certeau, Michel (1986), 'Montaigne's "Of Cannibals": The Savage "I" ', in *Heterologies: Discourse of the Other* (Minneapolis: University of Minnesota Press).

—— (1988), *The Writing of History*, trans. Tom Conley (New York: Columbia University Press).

Defoe, Daniel (1985), *Robinson Crusoe*, ed. Angus Ross (London: Penguin Classics).

—— (1994*a*), *Robinson Crusoe*, ed. Michael Shinagel (Norton Critical Edition; 2nd Edn.; New York: W. W. Norton).

—— (1994*b*), 'Preface to Volume III of *Robinson Crusoe*', from *Serious Reflections during the Life and Surprising Adventures of Robinson Crusoe* (1st pub., London, 1720), repr. in Defoe (1994*a*), 240–1.

De Grandis, Rita (1997), 'Incursiones en torno a hibridación: Una propuesta para discusión. De la mediación lingüística de Bajtin a la mediación simbólica de Canclini', in *Memorias de JALLA Tucumán 1995*, vol. i (Tucumán, Argentina: Projecto 'Tucumán en los Andes'), 284–96.

Delbaere-Garant, Jeanne (1995), 'Psychic Realism, Mythic Realism, Grotesque Realism: Variations on Magic Realism in Contemporary Literature in English', in Lois Parkinson Zamora and Wendy B. Faris (eds.), *Magic Realism: Theory, History, Community* (Durham, NC: Duke University Press), 249–63.

Delogu, Ignazio (1992), 'Sobre una posible presencia de Calibán en *La Araucana* de Don Alonso de Ercilla y Zúñiga', *Nuevo Texto Crítico* 5/9–10: 73–84.

Deyermond, Alan (1971), *The Middle Ages: A Literary History of Spain* (New York: Barnes & Noble).

Díaz del Castillo, Bernal (1980), *Historia de la conquista de Nueva España*, ed. Joaquín Ramírez Cabañas (Mexico City: Editorial Porrúa).

Doody, Margaret Anne (1989), 'Heliodorus Rewritten: Samuel Richardson's *Clarissa* and Frances Burney's *The Wanderer*', paper delivered at the Second International Conference on the Ancient Novel, Dartmouth College, 24 July 1989.

—— (1996), *The True Story of the Novel* (New Brunswick, NJ: Rutgers University Press).

Downie, J. A. (1997*a*), 'The Making of the English Novel', *Eighteenth-Century Fiction*, 9: 249–66.

—— (1997*b*), 'Defoe, Imperialism, and the Travel Books Reconsidered' (1st pub. 1983), in Roger D. Lund (ed.), *Critical Essays on Daniel Defoe* (New York: G. K. Hall), 78–96.

Dupré, Louis (1993), *Passage to Modernity: An Essay in the Hermeneutics of Nature and Culture* (New Haven: Yale University Press).

Durán Luzio, Juan (1970), 'Sobre Tomás Moro en el Inca Garcilaso', *Revista Iberoamericana*, 42: 349–62.

Durán, Manuel (1974), 'Cervantes and Ariosto', in Josep M. Sola-Solé, Alessandro Crisafulli, and Bruno Damiani (eds.), *Estudios literarios de hispanistas norteamericanos dedicados a Helmut Hatzfeld con motivo de su 80 aniversario* (Barcelona: Ediciones Hispam), 87–101.

—— (1992), 'Bernal Díaz del Castillo: crónica, historia, mito', *Hispania*, 75: 795–804.

Durán, Manuel (1996), 'Closing Remarks', Cervantes, a Celebration: Symposium in Honor of Manuel Durán, Yale University, 2 Nov. 1996.

Durand, José (1948), 'La biblioteca del Inca', *Nueva Revista de Filología Hispánica*, 2/3: 239–64.

—— (1963), 'Garcilaso: Between the World of the Incas and that of Renaissance Concepts', *Diogenes*, 43: 14–29.

—— (1966), 'Los silencios del Inca Garcilaso', *Mundo Nuevo*, 4: 66–72.

—— (1976), *El Inca Garcilaso, clásico de América* (Mexico: Sep Setentas).

—— (1988), 'En Torno a la Prosa del Inca Garcilaso', *Nuevo Texto Crítico*, 1/2: 209–27.

Eisenberg, Daniel (1982), *Romances of Chivalry and the Spanish Golden Age* (Newark, Del.: Juan de la Cuesta Press).

—— (1987), *A Study of 'Don Quixote'* (Newark, Del.: Juan de la Cuesta Press).

—— (1991), '¿Tenía Cervantes una biblioteca?', in *Estudios Cervantinos* (Barcelona: Sirmio), 11–36.

Elliott, J. H. (1970), *The Old World and the New: 1492–1650* (Cambridge: Cambridge University Press).

—— (1977), 'Self-Perception and Decline in Early Seventeenth-Century Spain', *Past and Present*, 74: 41–61.

—— (1989), *Spain and its World: 1500–1700* (New Haven: Yale University Press).

—— (1995), 'The Old World and the New Revisited', in Karen Ordahl Kupperman (ed.), *America in European Consciousness, 1493–1750* (Chapel Hill, NC: University of North Carolina Press), 391–408.

Emerson, Caryl (1984) (ed. and trans.), 'Editor's Preface', in Mikhail Bakhtin (ed.), *Problems of Dostoevsky's Poetics* (Minneapolis: University of Minnesota Press), pp. xxix–xliii.

Entwistle, William (1969), 'Ocean of Story', in Lowry Nelson, Jr. (ed.), *Cervantes: A Collection of Critical Essays* (Englewood Cliffs, NJ: Prentice-Hall).

Erasmus, Desiderius (1971), *Praise of Folly and Letter to Martin Dorp*, trans. and ed. Betty Radice (Harmondsworth: Penguin).

—— (1989), *The Praise of Folly and Other Writings*, ed. and trans. Robert M. Adams (New York: W. W. Norton).

Ercilla y Zúñiga, Alonso de (1979 and 1987), *La Araucana*, ed. Marcos A. Morínigo and Isaías Lerner, 2 vols. (Madrid: Clásicos Castalia).

Escobar, Alberto (1965), 'Lenguaje e historia en los *Comentarios reales*', in *Patio de Letras* (Lima: Caballos de Troya), 18–20.

Febres Cordero, Tulio (1930), *Don Quijote en América, o sea la cuarta salida del ingenioso hidalgo de la Mancha* (3rd edn., Caracas: Editorial Sur América).

Fernández de Oviedo, Gonzalo (1851–5), *Historia general y natural de las Indias (1535)*, ed. José Amador de los Ríos, 4 vols. (Madrid: Real Academia de la Historia).

Fernández, James D. (1994), 'The Bonds of Patrimony: Cervantes and the New World', *PMLA* 109/5: 969–81.

Ferré, Rosario (1999), 'Writing In Between', *Hopscotch*, 1/1: 102–9.

Fielding, Henry (1987), *Joseph Andrews, With Shamela and Related Writings*, ed. Homer Goldberg (Norton Critical Edition; New York: W. W. Norton).

—— (1988), *The Covent-Garden Journal*, ed. Bertrand A. Goldgar (Oxford: Clarendon Press).

Flores, Robert M. (1982), 'The Role of Cide Hamete in *Don Quijote*', *Bulletin of Hispanic Studies*, 59: 3–14.

Forcione, Alban K. (1972), *Cervantes' Christian Romance: A Study of 'Persiles y Sigismunda'* (Princeton: Princeton University Press).

—— (1982), *Cervantes and the Humanist Vision: A Study of Four 'Exemplary Novels'* (Princeton: Princeton University Press).

Forsyth, Donald W. (1985), 'Three Cheers for Hans Staden: The Case for Brazilian Cannibalism', *Ethnohistory*, 32/1: 17–36.

Foucault, Michel (1973), *The Order of Things: An Archaeology of the Human Sciences*, trans. of *Les Mots et les choses* (New York: Vintage).

—— (1986), 'Of Other Spaces', trans. Jay Miskowiec, *Diacritics*, 16 (Spring): 22–7.

Fra-Molinero, Baltasar (1994), 'Sancho Panza y la esclavización de los negros', *Afro-Hispanic Review*, 13/2: 25–31.

Freud, Sigmund (1959), 'Psycho-Analytic Notes upon an Autobiographical Account of a case of Paranoia (Dementia Paranoides)', in vol. *Collected Papers* iii (New York: Basic Books), 387–470.

Freyer, Hans (1936), *Die politische Insel: Eine Geschicte der Utopien von Plato bis zur Gegenwart* (Leipzig: Bibliographisches institut ag).

Friedman, Edward (1994), 'Reading Redressed; or, The Media Circuits of Don Quijote', *Confluencia*, 9/2: 38–51.

Frye, Northrop (1976), *The Secular Scripture: A Study of the Structure of Romance* (Cambridge, Mass.: Harvard University Press).

Fuchs, Barbara (1996), 'Border Crossings: Transvestism and "Passing" in *Don Quixote*', *Cervantes*, 16/2: 4–28.

—— (1997), 'Conquering Islands: Contextualizing *The Tempest*', *Shakespeare Quarterly*, 48/1: 45–62.

—— (forthcoming), *Mimesis and Empire* (Cambridge: Cambridge University Press).

Fuentes, Carlos (1976), *Don Quixote, or the Critique of Reading* (Austin, Tex.: University of Texas Press).

—— (1992), *The Buried Mirror: Reflections on Spain and the New World* (Boston: Houghton Mifflin).

Galeano, Eduardo (1985), *Memory of Fire*, i. *Genesis*, pt i of a trilogy, trans. Cedric Belfrage (New York: Pantheon Books).

Garcés, María Antonia (1989), 'Zoraida's Veil: "The Other Scene" of *The Captive's Tale*', *Revista de Estudios Hispánicos*, 23/1: 65–98.

—— (1991), 'Lecciones del Nuevo Mundo: La estética de la palabra en el Inca Garcilaso de la Vega', *Texto y Contexto* (Bogotá), 17: 125–50.

—— (1992), 'Coaches, Litters, and Chariots of War: Montaigne and Atahualpa', *Journal of Hispanic Philology*, 16/2 (Winter): 155–83.

—— (1993), 'Berganza and the Abject: The Desecration of the Mother', in Ruth Anthony El Saffar and Diana de Armas Wilson (eds.), *Quixotic Desire: Psychoanalytic Perspectives on Cervantes* (Ithaca, NY: Cornell University Press), 292–314.

Garcilaso de la Vega, Inca (1949), *León Hebreo; Diálogos de Amor: Traducidos por Garcilaso Inga de la Vega* (1ˢᵗ pub. 1590), ed. Eduardo Juliá Martínez (Madrid: Victoriano Suárez).

—— (1960), *Historia general del Perú*, in *Obras completas del Inca Garcilaso de la Vega*, ed. P. Carmelo Saenz de Santa María, SI, vols. iii–iv (Madrid: Ediciones Atlas).

—— (1976), *Comentarios reales de los Incas*, ed. Aurelio Miró Quesada, 2 vols. (Caracas: Biblioteca Ayacucho).

—— (1984), *Comentarios reales* (Mexico City: Editorial Porrúa).

—— (1988), *La Florida*, ed. Carmen de Mora (Madrid: Alianza).

Garza de del Castillo, Ofelia (1986), 'Introducción', in Ercilla y Zuñiga, *La Araucana* (Mexico City: Editorial Porrúa).

Gaylord, Mary M. (1996), 'The True History of Early Modern Writing in Spanish: Some American Reflections', *Modern Language Quarterly*, 57/2: 213–35.

Gerbi, Antonello (1985), *Nature in the New World: From Christopher Columbus to González Fernández de Oviedo*, trans. Jeremy Moyle (Pittsburgh: University of Pittsburgh).

Gerli, E. Michael (1986), 'Elysium and the Cannibals: History and Humanism in Ercilla's *La Araucana*', in Bruno M. Damiani (ed.), *Renaissance and Golden Age Essays in Honor of D. W. McPheeters* (Potomac, Md.: Scripta Humanistica).

—— (1995), *Refiguring Authority: Reading, Writing, and Rewriting in Cervantes* (Lexington, Ky.: University Press of Kentucky).

Gibson, Charles (1971), Introduction to id. (ed.), *The Black Legend: Anti-Spanish Attitudes in the Old World and the New* (New York: Alfred A. Knopf).

Gil, Juan (1989), *Mitos y utopías del descubrimiento*, 3 vols. (Madrid: Alianza Editorial/Quinto Centenario).

Gildon, Charles (1923), *Robinson Crusoe Examin'd and Criticis'd or A New Edition of Charles Gildon's Famous Pamphlet Now Published with an Introduction and Explanatory Notes* (London and Paris: M. M. Dent).

—— (1970), From *An Epistle to Daniel Defoe . . .* (1ˢᵗ pub. 1719), in Ioan Williams (ed.), *Novel and Romance 1700–1800: A Documentary Record* (New York: Barnes & Noble), 57–63.

Gilman, Stephen (1961), 'Bernal Díaz del Castillo and *Amadís de Gaula*', in *Studia Philologicas: Homenaje Ofrecido a Dámaso Alonso*, vol. ii (Madrid: Gredos), 99–114.

—— (1989), *The Novel according to Cervantes* (Berkeley and Los Angeles: University of California Press).

Girard, René (1965), *Deceit, Desire, and the Novel: Self and Other in Literary Structure*, trans. Yvonne Freccero (Baltimore: Johns Hopkins Press).

Godzich, Wlad, and Spadaccini, Nicholas (1986), Introduction in eid (ed.), *Literature Among Discourses: The Spanish Golden Age* (Minneapolis: University of Minnesota Press).

—— with Spadaccini, Nicholas (1994), 'The Changing Face of History', in *The Culture of Literacy* (Cambridge, Mass.: Harvard University Press), 55–71.

González Echevarría, Roberto (1987), 'The Law of the Letter: Garcilaso's *Commentaries* and the Origins of the Latin American Narrative', *Yale Journal of Criticism*, 1/1 (Fall): 107–31.

—— (1990), *Myth and Archive: A Theory of Latin American Narrative* (Cambridge: Cambridge University Press).

González, Eduardo (1985), 'Érase una vez una isla obstinada', in *La persona y el relato: Proyecto de lectura psicoanalítica* (Madrid: José Porrúa Turanzas), 107–52.

—— (1992), *The Monstered Self: Narratives of Death and Performance in Latin American Fiction* (Durham, NC: Duke University Press).

Graf, E. C. (1999), 'Escritor/Excretor: Cervantes's "Humanism" on Philip II's Tomb', *Cervantes* 19/1 (Spring), 66–95.

Grafton, Anthony, with Shelford, April, and Siraisi, Nancy (1992), *New Worlds, Ancient Texts: The Power of Tradition and the Shock of Discovery* (Cambridge, Mass.: Belknap Press of Harvard University Press).

Greenblatt, Stephen (1991), *Marvelous Possessions: The Wonder of the New World* (Chicago: University of Chicago Press).

Greene, Roland (1992), ' "This Phrasis is Continuous": Love and Empire in 1590', *Journal of Hispanic Philology*, 16/2: 237–52.

Greene, Roland Arthur (1999), *Unrequited Conquests: Love and Empire in the Colonial Americas* (Chicago: University of Chicago Press).

Greene, Thomas M. (1968), 'The Flexibility of the Self in Renaissance Literature', in Peter Demetz, Thomas Greene, and Lowry Nelson, Jr. (eds.), *The Disciplines of Criticism* (New Haven: Yale University Press), 241–64.

—— (1982), *The Light in Troy: Imitation and Discovery in Renaissance Poetry* (New Haven: Yale University Press).

Grummond, Jane Lucas de (1961), *The Baratarians and the Battle of New Orleans* (Baton Rouge, La.: Louisiana State University Press).

Guevara, Antonio de (1945), *El Villano del Danubio y Otros Fragmentos* (Princeton: Princeton University Press).

Guillén, Claudio (1971), *Literature as System: Essays toward the Theory of Literary History* (Princeton: Princeton University Press).

Haedo, Fray Diego de (1929), *Topografía e historia general de Argel*, 3 vols. (Madrid: Sociedad de Bibliófilos Españoles).

Hakluyt, Richard (1935), *Discourse of the Western Planting: The Original Writings and the Correspondence of the Two Richard Hakluyts*, ed. D. M. Taylor, 2 vols. (London: The Hakluyt Society).

Haley, George (1965), 'The Narrator in *Don Quijote*: Maese Pedro's Puppet Show', *Modern Language Notes*, 80/2: 145–65.

Hammond, Brean S. (1998), 'Mid-Century Quixotism and the Defence of the Novel', *Eighteenth-Century Fiction*, 10/3: 1–20.

Hampton, Timothy (1990), *Writing from History: The Rhetoric of Exemplarity in Renaissance Literature* (Ithaca, NY: Cornell University Press).

Hanke, Lewis (1970), *Aristotle and the American Indians: A Study in Race Prejudice in the Modern World* (1st pub. 1959) (Bloomington, Ind.: Indiana University Press).

The Heath Anthology of American Literature (1990), gen. ed. Paul Lauter, ed. Juan Bruce-Novoa et al., 2 vols. (Lexington, Mass.: D. C. Heath & Co.).

Hegyi, Ottmar (1999), 'Algerian Babel Reflected in *Persiles*', in Ellen M. Anderson and Amy R. Williamsen (eds.), *'Ingeniosa Invención': Essays on Golden Age Spanish Literature for Geoffrey L. Stagg in Honor of His Eightieth Birthday* (Newark, Del.: Juan de la Cuesta Press), 225–39.

Hemming, John (1970), *The Conquest of the Incas* (New York: Harcourt Brace Jovanovich).

Hernández, Max (n.d.), *Memoria del bien perdido: Conflicto, identidad y nostalgia en el Inca Garcilaso de la Vega* (Sociedad Estatal Quinto Centenario; Spain: Ediciones Siruela).

Herrero, Javier (1983), 'More and Vives: Christian Radical Thought in the Renaissance', in *Spain: Church–State Relations* (Chicago: Loyola University Press).

Higuera, Henry (1995), *Eros and Empire: Politics and Christianity in 'Don Quixote'* (Lanham, Md.: Rowman & Littlefield).

Hulme, Peter (1986), *Colonial Encounters: Europe and the Native Caribbean, 1492–1797* (London: Methuen).

—— (1998), 'Introduction: The Cannibal Scene', in Francis Barker, Peter Hulme, and Margaret Iversen (eds.), *Cannibalism and the Colonial World* (Cambridge: Cambridge University Press), 1–38.

—— and Whitehead, Neil L. (1992), 'Introduction', in eid (eds.), *Wild Majesty: Encounters with Caribs from Columbus to the Present Day* (Oxford: Clarendon Press).

Hunter, J. Paul (1966), *The Reluctant Pilgrim* (Baltimore: Johns Hopkins University Press).

—— (1990), *Before Novels: The Cultural Contexts of Eighteenth-Century English Fiction* (New York: W. W. Norton).

Hutchinson, Steven (1987), 'Mapping Utopias', *Modern Philology*, 85/2 (Nov.), 170–85.

—— (1992), *Cervantine Journeys* (Madison: University of Wisconsin Press).

Ife, B. W. (1985), *Reading and Fiction in Golden-Age Spain: A Platonist Critique and Some Picaresque Replies* (Cambridge: Cambridge University Press).

—— (1994), 'The Literary Impact of the New World: Columbus to Carrizales', *Journal of the Institute of Romance Studies*, 3: 65–85.

Irving, Washington (1868), *The Life and Voyages of Christopher Columbus To Which Are Added Those of His Companions*, 3 vols. (New York: G. P. Putman's Sons).

James, Henry (1957), *The House of Fiction: Essays on the Novel by Henry James*, ed. Leon Edel (London: R. Hart-Davis).

Jameson, Fredric (1981), *The Political Unconscious: Narrative as a Socially Symbolic Act* (Ithaca, NY: Cornell University Press).

Javitch, Daniel (1980), 'Cantus Interruptus in the *Orlando Furioso*', *Modern Language Notes*, 95: 66–80.

Johnson, Barbara (1987), 'Les Fleurs du Mal Arme: Some Reflections on Intertextuality', in *A World of Difference* (Baltimore: Johns Hopkins University Press), 116–33.

Johnson, Carroll B. (1983), *Madness and Lust: A Psychoanalytical Approach to 'Don Quixote'* (Berkeley and Los Angeles: University of California Press).

—— (1990), *Don Quixote: The Quest for Modern Fiction* (Boston: Twayne).

—— (1993), 'Cervantes and the Unconscious', in Ruth El Saffar and Diana de Armas Wilson (eds.), *Quixotic Desire: Psychoanalytic Perspectives on Cervantes* (Ithaca, NY: Cornell University Press).

Jones, Ernest (1953), *The Life and Work of Sigmund Freud*, 3 vols. (New York: Basic Books).

Jones, Joseph R. (1999), 'The Baratarian Archipelago', in Ellen M. Anderson and Amy R. Williamsen (eds.), *'Ingeniosa Invención': Essays on Golden Age Spanish Literature for Geoffrey L. Stagg in Honor of His Eightieth Birthday* (Newark, Del.: Juan de la Cuesta Press), 137–47.

Joyce, James (1994), 'Daniel Defoe,' excerpt repr. in Defoe (1994*a*), 320–23.

Kagan, Richard L. (1996), 'Prescott's Paradigm: American Historical Scholarship and the Decline of Spain', *American Historical Review*, 101/2: 423–46.

Kagan, Richard L. and Parker, Geoffrey (1995) (eds.), *Spain, Europe and the Atlantic World: Essays in Honour of John H. Elliott* (Cambridge: Cambridge University Press).

Kamen, Henry (1997), *Philip of Spain* (New Haven and London: Yale University Press).

Keane, Patrick J. (1997), 'Slavery and the Slave Trade: Crusoe as Defoe's Representative', in Roger D. Lund (ed.), *Critical Essays on 'Daniel Defoe'* (New York: G. K. Hall), 97–117.

Kernan, Alvin (1990), *The Death of Literature* (New Haven: Yale University Press).

Kipling, Rudyard (n.d.), 'The Man Who Would Be King', in *The Works of Rudyard Kipling* (Roslyn, New York: Black's Readers Service).

Konstan, David (1994), *Sexual Symmetry: Love in the Ancient Novel and Related Genres* (Princeton: Princeton University Press).

Kristal, Efraín (1993), 'Fábulas clásicas y neoplatónicas en los *Comentarios reales de los Incas*', in Luis Cortest (ed.), *Homenaje a José Durand* (Madrid: Editorial Verbum, 1993), 47–59.

Kristeva, Julia (1986), *The Kristeva Reader*, ed. Toril Moi (New York: Columbia University Press).

Kundera, Milan (1981), *The Book of Laughter and Forgetting*, trans. Michael Henry Heim (New York: Penguin).

Kupperman, Karen Ordahl (1995), Introduction to ead. (ed.), *America in European Consciousness, 1493–1750* (Chapel Hill, NC: University of North Carolina Press).

Las Casas, Bartolomé de (1958), *Los tesoros del Perú*, ed. and trans. Ángel Losada, bilingual Latin/Spanish edn. (Madrid: Consejo Superior de Investigaciones Científicas).

—— (1966), *The Spanish Colonie, or Brief Chronicle of the Acts and gestes of the Spaniardes in the West Indies, called the newe World, for the space of xl. yeeres* (1ˢᵗ pub. 1583), trans. M. M. S. London, repr. in *March of America facsimile series, no. 8* (Ann Arbor: University Microfilms).

—— (1984), *Brevísima relación de la destruición de las Indias*, ed. André Saint-Lu (Madrid: Cátedra).

—— (1992), *Apologética Historia Sumaria III*, vol. viii of *Obras Completas*, ed. Vidal Abril Castelló, Jesús A. Barreda, Berta Ares Queija y Miguel J. Abril Stoffels (Madrid: Alianza Editorial).

Leonard, Irving A. (1992), *Books of the Brave* (1949), with a new introduction by Rolena Adorno (Berkeley and Los Angeles: University of California Press).

Levin, Harry (1972), *The Myth of the Golden Age in the Renaissance* (New York: Oxford University Press).

Leyda, Jay (1951), *The Melville Log: A Documentary Life of Herman Melville, 1819–1891*, 2 vols. (New York: Harcourt, Brace & Co.).

Lezra, Jacques (1997), *Unspeakable Subjects: The Genealogy of the Event in Early Modern Europe* (Stanford, Calif.: Stanford University Press).

Lienhard, Martín (1996), 'De mestizajes, heterogeneidades, hibridismos y otras quimeras', in José Antonio Mazzotti and U. Juan Zevallos Aguilar (eds.), *Asedios a la Heterogeneidad Cultural: Libro de homenaje a Antonio Cornejo Polar* (Philadelphia: International Association of Peruvianists), 57–80.

Loomba, Ania (1998), *Colonialism/Postcolonialism* (London and New York: Routledge).

López de Gómara, Francisco (1858), *Hispania victrix: Primera y Segunda Parte, in Historiadores primitivos de Indias* (Biblioteca de Autores Españoles, vol. 1), ed. Enrique de Vidia (Madrid: M. Rivadeneyra).

—— (1979), *Historia general de las Indias y Vida de Hernán Cortés: Historia de la conquista de México*, ed. Jorge Gurría Lacroix, 2 vols. (Caracas: Biblioteca Ayacucho).

Lukács, Georg (1971), *The Theory of the Novel* (1ˢᵗ pub. 1920), trans. Anna Bostock (Cambridge, Mass.: MIT Press).

McGaha, Michael (1996), 'Hacia la verdadera historia del cautivo Miguel de Cervantes', *Revista Canadiense de Estudios Hispánicos*, 20: 540–6.

McKeon, Michael (1987), *The Origins of the English Novel: 1600–1740* (Baltimore: Johns Hopkins University Press).

MacPhail, Eric (1994), 'The Uses of the Past: Prophecy and Genealogy in *Don Quijote*', *Cervantes*, 14/1 (Spring 1994), 61–74.

Madariaga, Salvador de (1942), *Spain* (London: Jonathan Cape).

Mañach, Jorge (1950), *Examen del quijotismo* (Buenos Aires: Editorial Sudamericana).

Mancing, Howard (1982), *The Chivalric World of 'Don Quijote'* (Columbia, Mo.: University of Missouri Press).

Mann, Thomas (1965), 'Voyage with Don Quixote' (1ˢᵗ pub. 1934), in *Essays of Three Decades*, trans. H. T. Lowe-Porter (New York: Alfred A. Knopf).

Maravall, José Antonio (1974), 'Utopía y primitivismo en Las Casas', *Revista de Occidente*, 141 (Dec.): 311–88.

—— (1976), *Utopía y contrautopía en el 'Quijote'* (Santiago de Compostela: Editorial Pico Sacro).

—— (1991), *Utopia and Counterutopia in the 'Quixote'*, trans. Robert W. Felkel (Detroit: Wayne State University Press).

Mariscal, George (1990), '*Persiles* and the Remaking of Spanish Culture', *Cervantes*, 10/1 (Spring): 93–102.

—— (1991), *Contradictory Subjects: Quevedo, Cervantes, and Seventeenth-Century Spanish Culture* (Ithaca, NY: Cornell University Press).

—— (1994), '*La gran sultana* and the Issue of Cervantes's Modernity', *Revista de Estudios Hispánicos*, 28/2: 185–211.

Mariscal, George (1998), 'The Crisis of Hispanism as Apocalyptic Myth,' in Cruz and Johnson (1998), 201–17.

Márquez Villanueva, Francisco (1995), *Trabajos y días cervantinos* (Alcalá de Henares: Centro de Estudios Cervantinos).

Martín, Adrienne Laskier (1991), *Cervantes and the Burlesque Sonnet* (Berkeley and Los Angeles: University of California Press).

Martínez, José Luis (1992), *El mundo privado de los emigrantes en Indias* (Mexico City: Fondo de Cultura Económica).

Martyr de Angleria, Petrus (1966), *De orbe novo decades octo*, in *Opera*, introd. Erich Woldan (Graz, Austria: Akademische Druck- und Verlagsanstalt), 40–1.

Martyr, Peter (1912), *De Orbe Novo: The Eight Decades of Peter Martyr D'Anghera* (1st pub. 1494–1526), trans. Francis Augustus MacNutt, 2 vols. (New York: G. P. Putnam's Sons).

Mather, Cotton (1990), *The Heath Anthology of American Literature*, vol. i (Toronto: D. C. Heath and Co.), 232.

Maura, Juan Francisco (1989), 'Introducción', in id. (ed.), *Naufragios* (Madrid: Ediciones Cátedra), 9–64.

Mayer, María E. (1994), 'El detalle de una "historia verdadera": Don Quijote y Bernal Díaz', *Cervantes*, 14/2: 93–118.

Melville, Herman (1987), *The Piazza Tales and Other Prose Pieces (1839–1860)*, ed. Harrison Hayford, Alma A. MacDougall, G. Thomas Tanselle, et al. (Evanston, Ill. and Chicago: Northwestern University Press and The Newberry Library).

Menéndez y Pelayo, Marcelino (1905–15). *Orígenes de la novela*, 4 vols. (Madrid: Bailly-Balliere e hijos).

Menocal, María Rosa (1994), *Shards of Love: Exile and the Origins of the Lyric* (Durham, NC: Duke University Press).

Mesa, Padre Carlos E. (1948), 'Divagaciones en torno al *Persiles*', in E. Caballero Calderón, *Cervantes en Colombia* (Madrid: Afrodisio Aguado), 421–50.

Mignolo, Walter D. (1981), 'El metatexto historiográfico y la historiografía indiana', *Modern Language Notes*, 96: 358–402.

—— (1982), 'Cartas, crónicas y relaciones del descubrimiento y la conquista', in Iñigo Madrigal (ed.), *Historia de la literatura hispanoamericana, i. Época colonial* (Madrid: Cátedra), 57–116.

—— (1995), *The Darker Side of the Renaissance: Literacy, Territoriality, and Colonization* (Ann Arbor: University of Michigan Press).

—— (1996), 'Linguistic Maps, Literary Geographies, and Cultural Landscapes: Languages, Languaging, and (Trans)nationalism', *Modern Language Quarterly*, 57/2: 181–96.

Milton, John (1957), *John Milton: Complete Poems and Major Prose*, ed. Merrit Y. Hughes (New York: Macmillan).

Miró Quesada, Aurelio (1976) (ed.), *Comentarios reales de los Incas*, 2 vols. (Venezuela: Biblioteca Ayacucho).

Momigliano, Arnaldo (1958), 'The Place of Herodotus in the History of Historiography', *History*, 43: 1–13.

—— (1981), 'The Rhetoric of History and the History of Rhetoric: On Hayden White's Tropes', in *Comparative Criticism: A Yearbook*, vol. iii (Cambridge: Cambridge University Press), 259–68.

Moner, Michel (1990), 'Cervantes y la traducción', *Nueva Revista de filología Hispánica*, 38/2: 513–24.

Montaigne, M. (1957), 'Of cannibals' (1ˢᵗ pub. 1580), in *The Complete Works of Montaigne*, trans. Donald M. Frame (Stanford, Calif.: Stanford University Press).

Montrose, Louis (1991), 'The Work of Gender in the Discourse of Discovery', *Representations*, 33 (Winter 1991): 1–41.

More, Sir Thomas (1992), *Utopia*, trans. and ed. Robert M. Adams (Norton Critical Edition; New York: W. W. Norton).

Morínigo, Marcos A. (1979), 'Introducción', in Ercilla y Zúñiga (1979), vol. i.

Morson, Gary Saul (1981), *The Boundaries of Genre: Dostoevsky's 'Diary of a Writer' and the Traditions of Literary Utopia* (Austin, Tex.: University of Texas Press).

—— and Emerson, Caryl (1990), *Mikhail Bakhtin: Creation of a Prosaics* (Stanford, Calif.: Stanford University Press).

Morton, Thomas (1990), *New English Canaan* (1ˢᵗ pub. 1637), in *The Heath Anthology of American Literature*, vol. i (Toronto: D. C. Heath and Co.), 186–7.

Mosquera, Daniel O. (1994), '*Don Quijote* and the *Quixotics* of Translation', in Jeanette Beer, Ben Lawton, and Patricia Hart (eds.), *Romance Languages Annual*, vol. vi (West Lafayette, Ind.), 546–50.

Muñiz-Huberman, Angelina (1992), *Dulcinea encantada* (Mexico City: Editorial Joaquín Mortiz).

Murillo, Luis Andrés (1981), 'El Ur-Quijote: Nueva hipótesis', *Cervantes*, 1/1–2: 43–50.

Myers, Kathleen A. (1992), 'Imitation, Authority, and Revision in Fernández de Oviedo's *Historia General y Natural de las Indias*', in Jeanette Beer, Ben Lawton, and Patricia Hart (eds.), *Romance Languages Annual*, vol. iii (West Lafayette, Ind.), 523–30.

Naipaul, V. S. (1969), *The Loss of El Dorado: A History* (Harmondsworth: Penguin).

Negley, Glenn, and Patrick, J. Max (1952) (eds.), *The Quest for Utopia: An Anthology of Imaginary Societies* (New York: H. Schuman).

Neikov, Todor (1994) (trans.), *Don Kijot* (Pegas: Slovo).

Nicolopulos, James (2000), *The Poetics of Empire in the Indies: Prophecy and Imitation in 'La Araucana' and 'Os Lusiadas'* (University Park, Pa.: Pennsylvania State University Press).

Nietzsche, Friedrich (1956), *The Birth of Tragedy* (1ˢᵗ pub. 1872), trans. Francis Golffing (New York: Doubleday-Anchor).

Nietzsche, Friedrich (1967), *On the Genealogy of Morals* (1ˢᵗ pub. 1887), trans. Walter Kaufmann and R. J. Hollingdale, and *Ecce homo* (1ˢᵗ pub. 1908), trans. and ed. Walter Kaufmann (New York: Vintage).

Novak, Maximillian E. (1962), *Economics and the Fiction of Daniel Defoe* (University of California English Studies, 24; Berkeley and Los Angeles: University of California).

—— (1964), 'Defoe's Theory of Fiction', *Studies In Philology*, 61/4 (Oct.), 650–8.

O'Gorman, Edmundo (1962), 'Prólogo', in El P. Joseph de Acosta, *Historia natural y moral de las Indias* ed. O'Gorman (Mexico City and Buenos Aires: Fondo de Cultura Económica).

Ortega y Gasset, José (1961), *Meditations on Quixote*, trans. Evelyn Rugg and Diego Marín (New York: W. W. Norton).

Ortega, Julio (1992*a*), 'Garcilaso y el modelo de la nueva cultura', *Nueva Revista de Filología Hispánica*, 40/1 (1992): 199–215.

Ortega, Julio (1992*b*) (ed.), *La Cervantiada* (Mexico City: UNAM).

Ortiz, Fernando (1995), *Cuban Counterpoint: Tobacco and Sugar*, trans. of *Contrapunteo cubano del tabaco y el azúcar* (1ˢᵗ pub. 1940), by Harriet de Onís (Durham, NC: Duke University Press).

Pagden, Anthony (1982), *The Fall of Natural Man: The American Indian and the Origins of Comparative Ethnology* (Cambridge: Cambridge University Press).

—— (1986) (ed. and trans.), *Hernán Cortés: Letters from Mexico* (New Haven and London: Yale University Press).

—— (1995), *Lords of All the World: Ideologies of Empire in Spain, Britain, and France, 1492–1830* (New Haven: Yale University Press).

Parker, Geoffrey (1995), 'David or Goliath? Philip II and his World in the 1580s', in Richard L. Kagan and Geoffrey Parker (ed.) *Spain, Europe and the Atlantic world: Essays in honour of John H. Elliott* (Cambridge: Cambridge University Press).

Parr, James A. (1988), '*Don Quixote': An Anatomy of Subversive Discourse* (Newark, Del.: Juan de la Cuesta).

Pastor, Beatriz (1989), 'Silence and Writing: The History of the Conquest', in René Jara and Nicholas Spadaccini (eds.), *1492–1992: Re/Discovering Colonial Writing* (Minneapolis: Prisma Institute).

Paulson, Ronald (1998), *Don Quixote in England: The Aesthetics of Laughter* (Baltimore: Johns Hopkins University Press).

Pedro, Valentín de (1954), *América en las letras españolas del Siglo de Oro* (Buenos Aires: Editorial Sudamericana).

Pelliot, Paul (1922–3), 'Les Mongols et la papauté', *Revue de l'Orient Chrétien*, 3/1–2: 4–28.

Percas de Ponseti, Helena (1981), 'The Cave of Montesinos: Cervantes' Art of Fiction', in Miguel de Cervantes, *Don Quixote* (the Ormsby Translation, revised), ed. Joseph R. Jones and Kenneth Douglas (New York: W. W. Norton).

—— (1991), 'Cervantes y su sentido de la lengua: Traducción', *Actas del Segundo Coloquio Internacional de la Asociación de Cervantistas, Alcalá de Henares 6–9 Nov. 1989* (Barcelona: Anthropos).

—— (1996), '¿Quién era Belerma?', *Revista Hispánica Moderna*, 49: 375–92.

—— (1999), 'Unas palabras más sobre Belerma (*Quijote* II, 23)', *Cervantes*, 19: 180–4.

Percy, Walker (1977), *Lancelot* (New York: Farrar, Straus and Giroux).

Pérez Beato, Dr Manuel (1929), *Cervantes en Cuba: Estudio Bibliográfico con la Reproducción del 'Quijote' en versos de D. Eugenio de Arriaza* (Havana: F. Verdugo).

Pérez Bustamante, Ciriaco (1952), 'El lascasismo en *La Araucana*', *Revista de Estudios Políticos*, 49: 157–68.

Pierce, Frank (1982), 'The Fame of the *Araucana*', *Bulletin of Hispanic Studies*, 59: 230–6.

Polar, J. M. (1927), *Don Quijote en Yanquilandia* (Cartagena, Spain: Editorial Juvenilia).

Porras Barrenechea, Raúl (1955), *El Inca Garcilaso en Montilla (1561–1614)* (Lima: Editorial San Marcos).

Pratt, Mary Louise (1992), *Imperial Eyes: Travel Writing and Transculturation* (London: Routledge).

—— (1993), ' "Yo Soy La Malinche": Chicana Writers and the Poetics of Ethnonationalism', *Callaloo*, 16: 859–73.

—— (1873), *History of the Conquest of Mexico*, ed. John Foster Kirk, 3 vols. (Philadelphia: Lippincott).

Puiggrós, Rodolfo (1989), *La España que conquistó el Nuevo Mundo* (Bogotá: El Áncora Editores).

Quevedo, Francisco de (1790), 'Noticia, juicio y recomendación de la *Utopía* de Tomás Moro', Prologue to the Spanish trans. of More's *Utopía* (2nd edn., Madrid: Aznar).

Quint, David (1983), *Origin and Originality in Renaissance Literature: Versions of the Source* (New Haven: Yale University Press).

—— (1993), *Epic and Empire: Politics and Generic Form from Virgil to Milton* (Princeton: Princeton University Press).

Rabasa, José (1989), 'Utopian Ethnology in Las Casas', in René Jara and Nicholas Spadaccini (eds.), *1492–1992: Re/Discovering Colonial Writing* (Minneapolis: Prisma Institute), 263–89.

Raleigh, Sir Walter (1820), *History of the World* (1st pub. 1600), vol. vi (Edinburgh: Archibald Constable & Co.).

Rama, Ángel (1985), *Transculturación narrativa en América Latina* (Mexico City: Siglo Veintiuno Editores).

Reed, Walter (1981), *An Exemplary History of the Novel: The Quixotic versus the Picaresque* (Chicago: University of Chicago Press).

—— (1994), '*Don Quixote*: The Birth, Rise and Death of the Novel', *Indiana Journal of Hispanic Literatures*, 5 (Fall): 263–78.

Reiss, Timothy J. (1997), 'Caribbean Knights: Quijote, Galahad, and the Telling of History', *Studies in the Novel*, 29/3: 297–322.

Revello, José Torre (1940), *El libro, la imprenta y el periodismo en América durante la dominación española* (Buenos Aires: Jacobo Peuser).

Riley, E. C. (1954), 'Don Quixote and the Imitation of Models', *Bulletin of Hispanic Studies*, 31: 3–16.

—— (1962), *Cervantes's Theory of the Novel* (Oxford: Clarendon Press).

—— (1980), 'Cervantes: Una Cuestión de Género', in George Haley (ed.), *El 'Quijote' de Cervantes* (Madrid: Taurus), 37–51.

—— (1981), ' "Romance" y novela en Cervantes', in Manuel Criado de Val (ed.), *Cervantes: Su obra y su mundo, Actas del Primer Congreso Internacional sobre Cervantes* (Madrid: EDI-6), 5–13.

—— (1986), *Don Quixote* (London: Allen & Unwin).

—— (1990), *Introducción al Quijote* (Barcelona: Editorial Crítica).

Riquer, Martín de (1973), 'Cervantes y la caballeresca', in Juan Bautista Avalle-Arce and E. C. Riley (eds.), *Suma Cervantina* (London: Támesis), 273–92.

Rivers, Elias L. (1974), *Garcilaso de la Vega: Obras completas con comentario* (Madrid: Editorial Castalia; Columbus, Ohio: Ohio State University Press, 1974).

—— (1976), 'Talking and Writing in *Don Quixote*', *Thought*, 51/202 (Sept.), 296–305.

—— (1983*a*), 'Cervantes y Garcilaso', in *Homenaje a José Manuel Blecua* (Madrid: Gredos), 565–70.

—— (1983*b*), *Quixotic Scriptures: Essays on the Textuality of Hispanic Literature* (Bloomington, Ind.: Indiana University Press).

Robert, Marthe (1980), *Origins of the Novel*, trans. Sacha Rabinovitch (Bloomington, Ind.: Indiana University Press).

Rodríguez de Montalvo, Garci (1525), 'Las sergas del virtuoso cavallero esplandián hijo de amadís de gaula', British Library MS: shelf-mark c.20.e.11.

—— (1950), *El ramo que de los cuatro libros de Amadis de Gaula sale; llamado Sergas del muy esforzado caballero Esplandian, hijo del excelente rey Amadis de Gaula*, (ed.). Pascual de Gayangos, *Libros de Caballerías* (Biblioteca de Autores Españoles, vol. 40; Madrid: Ediciones Atlas).

Rodríguez García, José María (1997), 'From the Communal "We" to the Individual "I": The Rhetoric of Self-Legitimation in Bernal Díaz's *Historia*', *Revista de Estudios Hispánicos*, 31: 475–503.

Rodríguez Garrido, José A. (1998), 'Introduction', in José Anadón (ed.), *Garcilaso de la Vega: An American Humanist* (Notre Dame, Ind.: Unviersity of Notre Dame), 1–7.

Rodríguez Marín, Francisco (1911), *El 'Quijote' y Don Quijote en América* (Madrid: Librería Hernando).

—— (1921) (ed.), *Don Quijote en América en 1607: Relación peruana* (Madrid: Tip. de la 'Revista de Archivos, Bibliotecas y museos').

—— (1947–9) (ed.), *El ingenioso hidalgo Don Quijote de la Mancha* de Miguel de Cervantes, New Critical edition, 10 vols. (Madrid: Atlas).

Rodríguez Prampolini, Ida (1948), *Amadises en América: La hazaña de Indias como empresa caballeresca* (Mexico City: Junta Mexicana de Investigaciones Históricas).

Romancero de Palacio (Siglo XVI) (1999), ed. José Labrador Herraiz, Ralph A. Difranco, and Lori A. Bernard (Cleveland: Cancioneros Castellanos).

Rogers, Pat (1980), 'The Making of Defoe's *A Tour thro' Great Britain,* Volumes II and III', *Prose Studies,* 3: 109–37.

Rose, Margaret A. (1979), *Parody//Meta-Fiction: An Analysis of Parody as a Critical Mirror to the Writing and Reception of Fiction* (London: Croom Helm).

Roubaud, Sylvia (1998), 'Los Libros de Caballerías', in Francisco Rico et al. (ed.), *Don Quixote de la Mancha,* 2 vols. (Barcelona: Instituto Cervantes), vol. i, pp. cv–cxxviii.

Round, Nicholas G. (1994), 'Towards a Typology of Quixotisms', in Edwin Williamson (ed.), *Cervantes and the Modernists: The Question of Influence* (London: Tamesis), 9–28.

Rouse, Irving (1987), 'Origin and Development of the Indians Discovered by Columbus', in *Columbus and his World* (Ft. Lauderdale, Fla.: CCFL), 293–312.

Rushdie, Salman (1991), *Imaginary Homelands: Essays and Criticism, 1981–1991* (London: Granta Books).

—— (1995), *The Moor's Last Sigh* (New York: Pantheon).

—— (1996), 'In Defense of the Novel, Yet Again', *New Yorker* (24 June & 1 July), 48–55.

Russell, Peter (1964), 'Arms versus Letters: Towards a Definition of Spanish Fifteenth-Century Humanism', in Archibald R. Lewis (ed.), *Aspects of the Renaissance: A Symposium* (Austin, Tex.: University of Texas).

—— (1985), *Cervantes* (Oxford: Oxford University Press).

Said, Edward W. (1993), *Culture and Imperialism* (New York: Alfred A. Knopf).

Saínz de Robles, Federico (1953), *Ensayo de un diccionario de la literatura,* vol. ii (2ⁿᵈ edn., Madrid: Aguilar).

Salingar, L. G. (1966), 'Don Quixote as a Prose Epic', *Forum for Modern Language Studies,* 2: 53–68.

Sánchez, Marta E. (1998), 'La Malinche at the Intersection: Race and Gender in *Down These Mean Streets*', *PMLA* 113/1 (Jan. 1998): 117–28.

Schama, Simon (1992), 'They All Laughed at Christopher Columbus', *New Republic,* 205: 30–40.

Schevill, Rodolfo, and Bonilla, Adolfo (1914), 'Introducción', in Cervantes, *Persiles y Sigismunda,* 2 vols. (Madrid: Imprenta de Bernardo Rodríguez).

Scholes, Robert, and Kellogg, Robert (1975), *The Nature of Narrative* (1ˢᵗ pub. 1966) (Oxford: Oxford University Press).

Schulman, Aline (1997) (trans.), *L'Ingénieux Hidalgo Don Quichotte de la Mancha* (Paris: Seuil).

Seed, Patricia (1995), *Ceremonies of Possession in Europe's Conquest of the New World, 1492–1640* (Cambridge: Cambridge University Press).

Sidney, Philip (1966), *A Defense of Poetry*, ed. J. A. Van Dorsten (Oxford: Oxford University Press).

Sieber, Diane E. (1998), 'Mapping Identity in the Captive's Tale: Cervantes and Ethnographic Narrative', *Cervantes*, 18/1: 115–33.

Sieber, Harry (1985), 'The Romance of Chivalry in Spain from Rodríguez de Montalvo to Cervantes', in Kevin Brownlee and Marina Scordilis Brownlee (eds.), *Romance: Generic Transformation from Chrétien de Troyes to Cervantes* (Hanover, NH: University Press of New England), 203–19.

Siebers, Tobin (1994), 'Introduction', in id. (ed.), *Heterotopia: Postmodern Utopia and the Body Politic* (Ann Arbor: University of Michigan Press).

Simerka, Barbara A. (1998), ' "That the rulers should sleep without bad dreams": Anti-Epic Discourse in *La Numancia* and *Arauco domado*', *Cervantes*, 18/1 (Spring): 46–70.

Skinner, John (1987), 'Don Quixote in 18th-Century England: A Study in Reader Response', *Cervantes* 7/1: 45–57.

Skroiski-Landau, Beatris, and Landau, Luis (1994) (trans.), *Don Kihoteh de lah Mantsah*, 2 vols. (Tel Aviv: Biblioteca Unida-Asociación Pública de Arte y Cultura).

Smith, Paul Julian (1988), *Writing in the Margin: Spanish Literature of the Golden Age* (Oxford: Clarendon Press).

—— (1993), ' "The Captive's Tale": Race, Text, Gender', in Ruth El Saffar and Diana de Armas Wilson (eds.), *Quixotic Desire: Psychoanalytic Perspectives on Cervantes* (Ithaca, NY: Cornell University Press), 227–35.

Sommer, Doris (1996), Introduction to 'The Places of History: Regionalism Revisited in Latin America' (special issue) *Modern Language Quarterly*, 57/2: 119–27.

Spectator (1871), Review of *The Novels and Novelists of the Eighteenth Century in Illustration of the Manners and Morals of the Age* by W. Forsyth, MA (22 Apr. 1871), 484–5.

Spadaccini, Nicholas, and Talens, Jenaro (1993), *Through the Shattering Glass: Cervantes and the Self-Made World* (Minneapolis: University of Minnesota Press).

Spitzer, Leo (1948), 'Linguistic Perspectivism in the *Don Quijote*', in *Linguistics and Literary History* (Princeton: Princeton University Press), 41–85.

Starr, G. A. (1965–6), 'Escape from Barbary: A Seventeenth-Century Genre', *Huntington Library Quarterly*, 29: 35–52.

Stephens, Susan A. (1994), 'Who Read Ancient Novels?', in James Tatum (ed.), *The Search for the Ancient Novel* (Baltimore: Johns Hopkins University Press), 405–18.

—— (1995), Introduction to Panel on 'Devising Social Fictions', American Philological Association, 29 Dec.

—— and Winkler, J. J. (1995) (eds.), *Ancient Greek Novels: The Fragments* (Princeton: Princeton University Press, 1995).

Sullivan, Henry W. (1996), *Grotesque Purgatory: A Study of Cervantes's 'Don Quixote', Part II* (University Park, Pa.: Pennsylvania State University Press).

Tatum, James (1994), 'Introduction', in id. (ed.), *The Search for the Ancient Novel* (Baltimore: Johns Hopkins University Press), 1–19.

Temple, Sir William (1690), *Miscellanea. The Second Part* (2nd edn., London: Printed by J. and R. for *Ri.* and *Ra. Simpson*, at the Sign of the *Harp* in St. *Paul's* Church-yard).

Ter Horst, Robert (1992), 'From Poem to Novel: The Syntax of the Baroque', *Indiana Journal of Hispanic Literatures*, 1/1 (Fall), 39–61.

—— (1995), 'Cervantes and the Paternity of the English Novel', in Marina S. Brownlee and Hans Ulrich Gumbrecht (eds.), *Cultural Authority in Golden Age Spain* (Baltimore: Johns Hopkins University Press), 165–77.

—— (forthcoming), *The Fortunes of the Novel: A Study in the Transposition of a Genre* (New York: Peter Lang).

Testa, Daniel P. (1986), 'Parodia y mitificación del Nuevo Mundo en el *Quijote*', *Cuadernos hispanoamericanos*, 430: 63–71.

Thiem, Jon (1995), 'The Translator as Hero in Postmodern Fiction', *Translation & Literature*, 4/2: 207–18.

Thomas, Henry (1952), *Las novelas de caballerías españolas y portuguesas*, trans. E. Pujales (Madrid: Consejo Superior de Investigaciones científicas).

Todorov, Tzvetan (1984), *The Conquest of America*, trans. Richard Howard (New York: Harper & Row).

—— (1990), *Genres in Discourse*, trans. Catherine Porter (Cambridge: Cambridge University Press).

Toribio Medina, José (1926), *Escritores americanos celebrados por Cervantes en el 'Canto de Calíope'* (Santiago, Chile: Nascimento).

—— (1958), 'Cervantes americanista: Lo que dijo de los hombres y cosas de América', *Estudios cervantinos* (Santiago de Chile: Fondo Histórico y Bibliográfico José Toribio Medina), 507–37.

Torres Lanzas, Pedro (1981), Miguel de Cervantes, [Transcripción de] *Información de Miguel de Cervantes de lo que ha servido a S. M. y de lo que ha hecho estando captivo en Argel, y por la certificación que aquí presenta del Duque de Sesa se verá como cuando le captivaron se le perdieron otras muchas informaciones, fees y recados que tenía de lo que había servido a S. M. (Documentos)* (Madrid: Ediciones El Arbol).

Trilling, Lionel (1950), *The Liberal Imagination* (New York: Viking).

Trumpener, Katie (1992), 'The Time of the Gypsies: A "People Without History" in the Narratives of the West', *Critical Inquiry*, 18/4: 843–84.

Urbina, Eduardo (1988), 'Chrétien de Troyes y Cervantes: Más allá de los libros de caballerías', *Anales cervantinos*, 24: 1–11.

Valbuena Prat, Ángel (1964), *Historia de la literatura española*, 4 vols. (7ᵗʰ edn., Barcelona: Editorial Gustavo Gili).

Varner, John Grier (1968), *El Inca: The Life and Times of Garcilaso de la Vega* (Austin, Tex.: University of Texas Press).

Vattimo, Gianni (1992), *The Transparent Society*, trans. David Webb (Baltimore: Johns Hopkins University Press).

Vespucci, Amerigo (1951), *El nuevo mundo: Cartas relativas a sus viajes y descubrimientos, Textos en italiano, español e inglés*, ed. Roberto Levillier (Buenos Aires: Editorial Nova).

Wachtel, Nathan (1977), *The Vision of the Vanquished: The Spanish Conquest of Peru Through Indian Eyes, 1530–1570*, trans. Ben Reynolds and Siân Reynolds (New York: Harper and Row).

Warner, William B. (1992), 'The Elevation of the Novel in England: Hegemony and Literary History', *English Literary History*, 59: 577–96.

Watt, Ian (1962), *The Rise of the Novel: Studies in Defoe, Richardson and Fielding* (1ˢᵗ pub. 1957) (Berkeley and Los Angeles: University of California Press).

—— (1968), 'Serious Reflections on *The Rise of the Novel*', *Novel: A Forum on Fiction*, 1/3: 205–18.

—— (1994), 'Robinson Crusoe as a Myth' (1ˢᵗ pub. 1951 in *Essays in Criticism: A Quarterly Journal of Literary Criticism:* 95–119), slightly revised and repr. in Defoe (1994*a*), 288–306.

—— (1996), *Myths of Modern Individualism* (Cambridge: Cambridge University Press).

Wey-Gómez, Nicolás (1998), ' "Nuestro Padre el Sol": Scholastic Cosmology and the Cult of the Sun in Inca Garcilaso's *Comentarios Reales*', *Latin American Literary Review*, 26/52: 19–26.

—— (forthcoming), *The Machine of the World*.

White, Hayden (1973), *Metahistory: The Historical Imagination in Nineteenth-Century Europe* (Baltimore: Johns Hopkins University Press).

Wicke, Jennifer, and Sprinker, Michael (1992), 'Interview with Edward Said', in Sprinker (ed.), *Edward Said: A Critical Reader* (Oxford: Blackwell), 221–64.

Williamson, Edwin (1984), *The Half-way House of Fiction: 'Don Quixote' and Arthurian Romance* (Oxford: Clarendon Press).

Wilson, Diana de Armas (1991), *Allegories of Love: Cervantes's 'Persiles and Sigismunda'* (Princeton: Princeton University Press).

—— (1992), '"Unreason's Reason": Cervantes at the Frontiers of Discourse', *Philosophy and Literature*, 16: 49–67.

—— (1993), 'Cervantes and the Night Visitors: Dream Work in the Cave of Montesinos', in Ruth Anthony El Saffar and Diana de Armas Wilson (eds.), *Quixotic Desire: Psychoanalytic Perspectives on Cervantes* (Ithaca, NY: Cornell University Press), 59–80.

—— (1994), 'Homage to Apuleius: Cervantes's Avenging Psyche', in James Tatum (ed.), *The Search for the Ancient Novel* (Baltimore: Johns Hopkins University Press).

Wolf, Elizabeth (forthcoming), '"The Cardinal Tenet of the Now Familiar Myth": A History of "White" Creolization in Kate Chopin's *The Awakening*'.

Woolf, Virginia (1994), 'Robinson Crusoe', repr. in Defoe (1994*a*), 283–7.

Yansheng, Dong (1995) (trans.), *Don Quijote de la Mancha* (Zheijang: Artes y Letras).

Zamora, Margarita (1988), *Language, Authority and Indigenous History in the 'Comentarios reales de los Incas'* (Cambridge: Cambridge University Press).

Zavala, Silvio (1965), *La utopía de Tomás Moro en la Nueva España: Recuerdo de Vasco de Quiroga* (Mexico City: Porrúa).

Index

Printed in the United States
941100001B

9 780198 160052